MW00613589

DESIRING A BETTER COUNTRY

for
Michael
with best wishes

Desiring a Better Country

Forays in Political Theology

DOUGLAS FARROW

McGill-Queen's University Press
Montreal & Kingston · London · Chicago

© McGill-Queen's University Press 2015

ISBN 978-0-7735-4584-7 (cloth)
ISBN 978-0-7735-4585-4 (paper)
ISBN 978-0-7735-9752-5 (ePDF)
ISBN 978-0-7735-9753-2 (ePUB)

Legal deposit third quarter 2015
Bibliothèque nationale du Québec

Printed in Canada on acid-free paper that is 100% ancient forest free
(100% post-consumer recycled), processed chlorine free

This book has been published with the help of a grant from the Canadian
Federation for the Humanities and Social Sciences, through the Awards
to Scholarly Publications Program, using funds provided by the Social
Sciences and Humanities Research Council of Canada.

McGill-Queen's University Press acknowledges the support of the
Canada Council for the Arts for our publishing program. We also
acknowledge the financial support of the Government of Canada
through the Canada Book Fund for our publishing activities.

Library and Archives Canada Cataloguing in Publication

Farrow, Douglas, 1953–, author
Desiring a better country: forays in political theology/Douglas Farrow.

Includes bibliographical references and index.
Issued in print and electronic formats.
ISBN 978-0-7735-4584-7 (cloth). – ISBN 978-0-7735-4585-4 (paper). –
ISBN 978-0-7735-9752-5 (PDF). – ISBN 978-0-7735-9753-2 (ePUB)

1. Political theology. I. Title.

BT83.59.F37 2015   261.7   C2015-903680-1

This book was typeset by Interscript in 10.5/13 Sabon.

For my father
CRESSWELL BRYCE MACKAY FARROW
(1919–2015)
and for his fathers,
pioneers from before Confederation

Contents

Preface

For people who speak thus make it clear that they are seeking a homeland.
If they had been thinking of that land from which they had gone out, they
would have had opportunity to return. But as it is, they desire a better
country, that is, a heavenly one. Therefore God is not ashamed to be called
their God, for he has prepared for them a city.

Hebrews 11:14–16[1]

Christianity is a very political religion. It aims at a polis, and not just
any polis, but one whose builder and maker is God. In a certain
sense, then, it is a politically subversive religion, for it has turned its
back on the city that is built by men and populated with gods, in
favour of the city that is built by God and populated with men. And
it encourages others to do likewise. Yet its subversion is not of the
kind that the rulers of men, or their court philosophers, commonly
suppose. While it has not hesitated to offer stinging critiques of man-
made cities, cultures, and empires, pointing out their more demonic
dimensions, it has also taken a deep interest in those same cities and
cultures. It can sound very like the prophet Jonah: "Yet forty days,
and this great city shall be overthrown!"[2] But, unlike Jonah, it does
not sit under a gourd on the hillside as a spectator to the destruction.
It seeks, rather, to inculturate its own hope for the coming city of
God within the city of man. That is what Christians have done for
almost two millennia in Mosul, for example, though (as I write)
members of the *soi disant* Islamic State have driven them out at
sword point, having first desecrated the tomb of Jonah.

Christians, wherever they live, seek a new homeland. They desire
a better country, a heavenly one. Yet they do not lose all interest in
the present earthly one. They do not abandon concern for its welfare, whether in this age or the age to come. They do not, if they are

faithful, refuse to suffer with and for it. They turn their backs on its false hopes and false gods, but they still expect to see "the glory and the honour of the nations"[3] brought into the city of God by the kings of the earth.[4] Hence they desire also a better country here and now.

There are good utilitarian reasons for that, of course, as Augustine observed, and even better sacramental reasons. For in and through the church the earthly is eucharistically related to the heavenly, the matter and history of the one – by a miracle of divine grace – to the shape and substance of the other. Or so Catholic Christians believe. To believe that, of course, is to put the earthly in a very different light, and to appreciate it accordingly. It is also, and necessarily, to subject it to a searching scrutiny: to question it not only about the coherence of its political ends, or about its understanding and ordering of authorities and sovereignties, of rights and freedoms, of laws and economies; but also, and at the same time, about its common loves, about its openness to divine purposes and possibilities and judgments, about its understanding of man himself as subject to God.

That is what political theology does, or ought to do.[5] And it does not merely question; it also instructs and experiments, bringing out of the ecclesial treasure-house things old and new. It has known failure as well as success, but it has been successful enough that it cannot easily be ignored even by those who regard it with distaste. Thus, for example, does Brian Tierney remark that "it is impossible really to understand the growth of Western constitutional thought unless we consider constantly, side by side, ecclesiology and political theory, ideas about the church and ideas about the state."[6] This side-by-side consideration, when it becomes both critically and constructively engaged in the process of reasoning on both sides, is what characterizes political theology, whatever the topic at hand. That its practitioners are likely to be better informed and more reliable on one side than the other goes without saying (though there are exceptions) and should not be held too much against it.[7]

I, alas, though much occupied with ideas of church and state, am not among the exceptions, nor have I dared attempt anything very systematic. (One may look to an exception, such as Oliver O'Donovan, for that.) Nevertheless, I do not see how any theologian can neglect political theology altogether. In my own case, work on the ascension made it unavoidable, for that doctrine is incomprehensible without its political dimension, as is "common era" thought and history without reference to the doctrine's many permutations.

The political theology of the present book, however, is of a different genre than what appears in my *Ascension Theology*. The stress here falls on the adjective rather than on the noun, and the engagement with law, politics, and culture is elaborated in contextually specific ways. Readers from other countries will forgive me, I hope, if the context is more often Canadian than American or European; the issues and challenges are not so very dissimilar, whatever may be said of the cultures and constitutional arrangements. They may perhaps find it more difficult, if approaching from the legal or political theory side, to forgive my naïvetés and solipsisms, or a rhetorical style that sometimes favours directness over subtlety and nuance. But I would point them, and every patient reader, to the extensive notes that to one degree or another should compensate for that.

Desiring a Better Country is a collection of individual essays rather than a single treatise. Though they are all new and otherwise unpublished, there is overlap between them that I have made no attempt to eliminate. Each was delivered originally to a different audience. Chapter 1 concerns a question I was asked to address at St. Thomas University in Fredericton. Chapter 2 was presented to a meeting of Evangelicals and Catholics Together in New York, provoking some controversy there. Chapter 3 derives from a symposium on Faith in the Public Square at the Munk Centre in Toronto, sponsored by St. Augustine's Seminary and the Archdiocese. Chapter 4 belonged to a conference at McGill on religious freedom in education, and chapter 5 was my inaugural lecture as Kennedy Smith Chair in Catholic Studies. The ordering is logical rather than chronological, but each was conceived, and can be read, independently.

My recent forays in political theology (for that, as I say, is all they are) also involve a couple of long essays published in the English edition of *Nova et Vetera*, such as "Baking Bricks for Babel?",[8] as well as shorter pieces in *First Things* and *Touchstone* and *Convivium*, such as "The Audacity of the State,"[9] but as they are already available there I have not included them here. What I have included, as an appendix, is my expert witness report in the *Loyola* case. While that court document has been available online, it has not appeared in print until now. It stands here in support of the third chapter in particular.

The present collection is admittedly critical to a fault. In it I am preoccupied with certain misconceptions about secularity, about pluralism, and about rights and freedoms, that threaten to undo much of what is admirable about our countries or even our civilization, and that also threaten the church,[10] both internally and externally. I nevertheless hope that in addressing these concerns I have managed to say a number of things of a constructive nature that readers will find stimulating, whether or not they share my understanding of Western history or of the issues in question. Catholic readers will not be surprised to find, by the time they reach the final chapters, a further attempt (pursuant to "Babel") to wrestle with the continuity and discontinuity of modern Catholic political theology; in this case, to wrestle with John Courtney Murray's alternative, so influential at the Second Vatican Council, to the Leonine tradition. I'm afraid I'm rather critical of Murray as well, but not, I hope, too critical.

Permit me here to express my appreciation, albeit collectively, to those who invited me to deliver these papers, to those who patiently listened or responded to them in the first instance, and to colleagues – especially Dan Cere, whom I would be remiss not to mention by name – who did so much to stimulate and to test my thoughts. The civility of our exchanges, even adversarial exchanges begun in court, has been a constant source of encouragement. I am very conscious of generosities extended to me across disciplines and across borders of various other kinds. That includes the 49th parallel, and the kindnesses of friends such as Rusty Reno and George Weigel, as well as philosophical and cultural and linguistic borders internal to both our countries.

Also, and most especially, I would like to thank my wife, Anna, who not only listened to garbled accounts of these conversations but did so much to enable me to take part in them. Our children, too, made many allowances, and I hope that what I offer here will serve them in some way, and their generation.

A word of gratitude, finally, for our late dean, Professor Ellen Aitken, whose friendship and support we at McGill, like so many others elsewhere, greatly miss. She has gone, very prematurely from our point of view, from this country, which she did make better, in prayerful hope of the Country that cannot be bettered. *Requiem aeternam dona ei, Domine.*

DESIRING A BETTER COUNTRY

I

Can We Have Human Rights without God?

They fashioned a tomb for thee, O holy and high one –
The Cretans, always liars, evil beasts, idle bellies!
But thou art not dead: thou livest and abidest forever,
For in thee we live and move and have our being.[1]

This verse from the sixth century before Christ, penned by the Greek
poet Epimenides and preserved in a medieval Syriac commentary on
Acts, pronounces scathingly on the Cretan heresy that Zeus was
mortal. We, who live in an age when the Cretan heresy has been
revived, are chided by our own poets and prophets – Nietzsche, for
example, or very differently, Solzhenitsyn – for failing to reckon with
the implications of that heresy.

The implications that concern us here are the implications for
human rights and freedoms. If God is dead – or at all events if metaphysics is dead, and first philosophy along with it; if theology of any
description has been banished from the sphere of public reason,
where matters such as rights and freedoms are negotiated – then a
number of very serious questions must be asked.

If we no longer think of ourselves as living and moving and having
our being in God, in what *do* we live and move and have our being?
In some play of inexorable cosmic forces? To say that would be to
revive the old pagan concept of fate, and with it the ancient gods in
all their arbitrary unjustness.

Do we exist, rather, in a play of merely political forces? – that is,
in some humanly constructed cosmos that may or may not manage
to insulate itself from these grim and capricious gods? But what governs politics? Can the merely political offer any guarantee of clearly
conceived rights and freedoms that will triumph over the fickleness
of the human will, in whose image the old gods were conceived, and
restrain for long the human propensity to evil?

Or do we live and move and have our being in ourselves alone? But then my right may be your wrong, my freedom your bondage. Who will negotiate between us, and to what higher principles will they appeal in this negotiation? Moreover, I too am fickle and unreliable, as are you. There is no solid ground here either for anything resembling inviolable rights and freedoms.

In 1990, as Eastern Europe emerged from its incarceration within the Soviet empire – an empire that had trampled into the dust the rights and freedoms of millions – the Polish poet, Czesław Miłosz, remarked on the enthusiasm with which so many appealed anew to the language of rights and freedoms: "What is surprising in the present moment," he said, "as the Cold War order collapses, are those beautiful and deeply moving words pronounced with veneration in Prague and Warsaw, words which pertain to the old repertory of honesty, the rights of man, and the dignity of the person." He had in mind, no doubt, the inspiring preamble to the *Universal Declaration of Human Rights*:

Whereas recognition of the inherent dignity and of the equal and inalienable rights of all members of the human family is the foundation of freedom, justice and peace in the world,

Whereas disregard and contempt for human rights have resulted in barbarous acts which have outraged the conscience of mankind, and the advent of a world in which human beings shall enjoy freedom of speech and belief and freedom from fear and want has been proclaimed as the highest aspiration of the common people,

Whereas it is essential, if man is not to be compelled to have recourse, as a last resort, to rebellion against tyranny and oppression, that human rights should be protected by the rule of law ...

Whereas the peoples of the United Nations have in the Charter reaffirmed their faith in fundamental human rights, in the dignity and worth of the human person ...

But Miłosz poignantly and somewhat wistfully added: "I wonder at this phenomenon because, maybe, underneath there is an abyss. After all, those ideas have had their foundation in religion, and I am not over-optimistic as to the survival of religion in a scientific-technological civilization. In Eastern Europe, notions that seemed buried forever by communism, like the value of the individual, have resurfaced. But how long can they stay afloat if the bottom is taken out?"[2]

In other words: Can we have human rights without God? Can we have human dignity – the dignity presupposed by rights talk – without God?

BASING RIGHTS TALK IN EMPATHY

Generally speaking, we are Cretans in practice rather than by profession.[3] So when we fashion tombs for God we tend to call them by other names – perhaps the Canadian Museum for Human Rights, or something like that. But does a tomb for God, by whatever name, require a tomb for human rights also? Is that what it necessarily becomes? Or can we have human rights without God?

Some seem to think so. Ten years after Miłosz's remarks, in a 50th-anniversary reflection on the Universal Declaration, Michael Ignatieff (he who later aspired to be Canada's prime minister before returning in defeat to Harvard) asserted that "it is not clear why human rights need the idea of the sacred at all."[4] Ignatieff noted that in the drafting of the Declaration "a cloak of silence" was cast over the question of God: "The Brazilian delegation proposed that Article One include the proposition that men are 'created in the image and likeness of God,' and 'endowed with reason and conscience.' Communist and non-Communist delegations joined in rejecting these totemic references on the grounds that they would detract from the Declaration's universal appeal." This debate is very much alive today, though some have shifted sides. (One wonders whether the Brazilians, for example, would now stand with the communists.) Ignatieff even speaks of "a philosophical crisis: a sense that the silences in the Universal Declaration need to be confronted."

The crisis, he suggests, is generated in part by people worried about the bottom falling out, to use Miłosz's expression. "In a world of resurgent religious conviction," says Ignatieff, the secularism of the Declaration's premises "is ever more open to doubt." The doubters, on his reading, are bothered by a suspicion that human rights, conceived in a non-theological fashion, "are just another form of arrogant make-believe, putting Man on a pedestal when he should be down in the mud where he deserves to be. If human rights exist to define and uphold limits to the abuse of human beings, then their underlying philosophy, religiously inclined thinkers imply, ought to define man as a beast in need of restraint. Instead human rights make Man the measure of all things, and from a religious point of view this is a form of idolatry."

The clear implication here – and we shall return to it – is that the very people who think that human rights discourse must ultimately be theological are people with a very *low* view of human dignity, not a high view. But why, he asks, "do we need an idea of God in order to believe that human beings should not be beaten, tortured, coerced, indoctrinated, or in any way sacrificed against their will? These intuitions derive from our own experience of pain and our capacity to imagine the pain of others. Believing that men are sacred does not necessarily strengthen these injunctions. The reverse is often true: acts of torture or persecution are frequently justified as serving some sacred purpose. Indeed the strength of a purely secular ethics is its insistence that there are no sacred purposes which can ever justify the inhuman use of human beings."

On Ignatieff's own view, a secular defence of human rights can be mounted simply by appealing to "the idea of moral reciprocity: that we cannot conceive of any circumstances in which we or anyone we know would wish to be abused in mind or body." This seems a sort of photo-negative, as it were, of the claim that all men want to be happy, though as a negative it lacks life. Ignatieff tries to inject some moral colour into it: "Being capable of such empathy we all possess a conscience, and because we do, we wish to be free to make up our own minds and express our own justifications for our views. The fact that there are many humans who remain indifferent to the pain of others does not imply they cannot imagine it or prove that they do not possess a conscience, only that this conscience is free to do both good and evil. Such natural facts about human beings provide the grounds for an entitlement to protection from physical and mental abuse and to the right to freedom of thought and speech."

Ignatieff admits that such a "minimalist anthropology will necessarily leave religious thinkers unsatisfied." He also recognizes that many of the latter regard secular humanism as unable to command universal assent; hence "a lot of effort has been expended" to reinterpret the Declaration as something derived from the world's religions – "as the summing up of the accumulated moral wisdom of the ages."[5] "This religious syncretism is innocuous as historical or inspirational rhetoric," he allows, but as a matter of fact "only Western culture turned widely shared propositions about human dignity and equality into a working doctrine of rights."

Ignatieff does not follow up on this last point, unfortunately, or ask where these presuppositions came from. For "the really interesting new development" that catches his eye "is how the moral unanimity of the West itself is beginning to fracture." What is needed, then, is indeed something minimalist – "not much more than the basic intuition that what is pain and humiliation for you is bound to be pain and humiliation for me." Human rights can then be seen "not as the universal credo of a global society, not [as] a secular religion, but [as] something much more limited and yet just as valuable: the common ground on which our arguments [about how to treat each other] can begin."

In *Human Rights as Politics and Idolatry*[6] Ignatieff goes on to argue that the lack of a global moral culture, and of any consensus on the foundations of human rights, combined with the irresolvable tensions between various rights claims, means that we cannot establish any non-controversial set of universal rights. We must therefore not act as if we could. That would indeed amount to an idolatry of human rights – an idolatry rooted in the dogma of the sacredness of human life – that in practice would serve to support cultural and even military imperialism. Rather, in the spirit of reciprocity, we ought simply to do our best to support human flourishing and the empowerment of individuals in their local contexts to lead the lives they wish, but that means balancing the rights of citizens with the rights of states, which provide a necessary bulwark against chaos. Human rights is not above politics; indeed it is nothing *but* politics.

TAKING RIGHT AND WRONG OUT OF RIGHTS ⚜

I think Ignatieff is right that the silence of the Universal Declaration must be confronted and give way to honest debate about the theological and anthropological presuppositions of human rights claims. I think he is right also to warn against a human rights idolatry. There are several difficulties, however, in what he has said here.

First, an historical difficulty: The Declaration does not rest on secularist presuppositions. Its silence about God was a silence imposed by communist veto. But the document did not arise either from a communist world view or from some other secularist world view. It arose chiefly from a Christian world view, with prominent Catholic and Protestant components. Though Ignatieff is correct in saying that the push for human rights was a mainly Western phenomenon, and that it did not come about as a kind of natural or spontaneous synthesis of the accumulated wisdom of the world's religions, he is wrong to suggest that the cloak over the God question covers up a foundation lacking theological cornerstones or theistic impulses. Shall we say the same thing about its silence with respect to nature – that it covers up a lack of commitment to what is natural? But the truth is that, once "God" was vetoed by the communist bloc, the use of "nature" was deliberately restricted for fear that it would be deployed in a pantheistic or atheistic fashion.[7] Only in article 16, where the theistic side thought it absolutely indispensable in order to defend the family from the state, does "nature" make an appearance.

Second, a logical difficulty, or rather several of them: Ignatieff rejects the charge that secularist human rights doctrines are idolatrous in making man the measure of all things. He counters by calling idolatrous any approach to human rights that is grounded in the dogma of the sanctity of life, and indeed by relativizing human rights to more pragmatic considerations. At the same time, he contends that religious thinkers who hold this dogma actually despise humans as creatures of mud who need human rights doctrines to restrain their natural nastiness. Apparently their view of man is at once too high and too low. But what is Ignatieff's alternative? His preferred ground for human rights lies in an ethics of reciprocity; in short, it lies in the so-called golden rule. Not the golden rule of Jesus, mind you, for "do unto others as you would have them do unto you" is an escalation, even a transformation, of what otherwise passes in human wisdom for the golden rule. Ignatieff seems, rather, to adopt the Confucian form of the rule, despite the irony that this is the very epitome of that kind of wisdom that he dismisses as religious syncretism.[8] "That which you hate to be done to you, do not do to another," pretty nicely summarizes what he is proffering. This, of course, shorn of particular religious imperatives, is simply good counsel, based on enlightened self-interest and perhaps, but only perhaps, on what Ignatieff refers to as empathy. At all events, there is nothing in it of rights. The tradition of the *Magna Carta Libertatum*, or the *Declaration of Independence*, or even of the (godless) *Déclaration des droits de l'Homme et du citoyen*, and the (not entirely godless) *Canadian Charter of Rights and Freedoms* can find no *terra firma* here. Is all that idolatry, then? Shall we dispense with it all? No. Ignatieff is in favour of using constitutional instruments. But on what grounds shall we retain them? What authority shall we accord them? And what does account for this tradition, this very Western tradition, if neither theology nor general religious wisdom?

Ignatieff's argument is not only muddled but self-defeating. By reducing the future foundations for human rights to "not much more than the basic intuition that what is pain and humiliation for you is bound to be pain and humiliation for me," he takes the right and wrong out of rights, and the justice or duty also. What is he left with? A very questionable assumption about the universality of human sentiments – the very thing he is at pains to deny when he gets to treating cultural differences – and a still more questionable assumption about the general efficacy of the counsel contained in the golden rule. Moreover, he avoids the question as to who qualifies as a proper object of empathy, and why. It has recently been argued, for example, not only by Peter Singer but by the likes of Giubilini and Minerva, that infants and young children do not necessarily qualify. Indeed, where empathy is lacking they have no rights at all and may be put to death.[9] And why not? Empathy cannot be commanded and may not be felt; nor must it be acted upon, if there is nothing sacred about human life. Human rights is politics, and no more than politics.

Third, then, an anthropological difficulty that is also, we may say, a soteriological difficulty: not only is Ignatieff's "minimalist anthropology" unable to ground rights talk at all, but it also cannot explain man to himself in any way that really matters. Ignatieff tries to throw his own cloak over this by complaining that traditional rights talk, building as it does on theological claims about the sanctity of human life, really regards man as no better than an unruly beast. The truth, of course – as he must know – is that the high view of man, as a creature having distinct rights lacking to the beasts, and the low view of man, as a creature prone to evil, are mediated by the doctrine of the fall and the hope of human salvation. This Judeo-Christian anthropology does indeed provide a basis for asserting and defending human rights, because it gives a consistent account both of human dignity and of the indignities that humans inflict on one another. Ignatieff's reliance on the politics of empathy seems impoverished and powerless by comparison. If conscience is simply a derivative of the capacity for empathy, what do "good" and "evil" mean anyway? And how are we to translate the capacity to imagine someone's pain, or expressions of empathy and failures of empathy, into social norms, binding laws, crime and punishment?

The problem with his minimalist anthropology is that it doesn't achieve what it is meant to: a lowest common denominator by reference to which human behaviour can be regulated.[10] In isolating the capacity for empathy from other dimensions of the human being and of the moral universe (if there is one), it leaves empathy without any real moral force. It may well be true "that we cannot conceive of any circumstances in which we or anyone we know would wish to be abused in mind or body" (if we are not sado-masochists, that is, though of course some people are). But that begs the question of what constitutes abuse, and of what personal wishes have to do with it when other people, particularly those foreign to us, are in view, and when other factors, which may seem quite compelling, are in play. Though he makes some stabs at treating this problem, his minimalist anthropology seems hopelessly naive. It lacks any sound analysis of human beings and of human behaviour, as well as any motivating soteriology other than a general desire to ameliorate the human condition.

This impression is confirmed when one turns to Ignatieff's Massey lectures in *The Rights Revolution*. There he takes up, in the context of the sexual revolution of the sixties, the deep conflict – much deeper, he says, than prior generations imagined – "between being faithful to others and being faithful to ourselves."[11] This very recent rights revolution – is it continuous or discontinuous with what came before it? – Ignatieff characterizes as an attempt to see that self-giving or self-sacrifice do not override self-fulfillment. Of course, he is not going to consider any theological reconciliation of these concepts. His advice, frankly, is typical of the irresponsible generation to which he and I belong: Be true to yourself, while doing your best to recognize that your neighbours and kin are best off being true to themselves also. This doesn't even rise to the (Confucian) golden rule. At bottom it is just the old Romantic trope, canonized by J.S. Mill, about spontaneous self-fulfillment. Not "the truth shall make you free," as Jesus said, but rather, "freedom will make you true."

It is not just religious thinkers who find all this unsatisfying. As Conor Gearty, a professor of law at the London School of Economics, puts it: "The holy grail of human rights is a universal theory ... [a] set of foundations that explains why it is right as well as morally pleasing to promote human rights across the world." According to Gearty, "advances in evolutionary biology and the neurological sciences" hold out hope that the grail can be found. The "recent addiction to uncertainty as the only possible truth" is fading, he says, "a victim of our intuition that good and evil have a meaning beyond our mere agreement to use these words in a certain way." Perhaps "a universal theory of human rights, rooted in truth, is emerging into view"? I am equally skeptical of Gearty's optimism, however, for the view of the human being to which he refers is itself highly reductionist, and its approach to good and evil likewise.[12] If we want something more satisfying than the sort of thing Ignatieff proffers, we need to turn, not to evolutionary biology, but to the theological and anthropological presuppositions that gave birth to robust rights claims.

What were those presuppositions and what has happened to them?

INVERTING RIGHTS TALK

The origins of the concept of human rights can be traced back to natural law claims found in Aristotle or Cicero, for example, and the assertion of a moral order inherent in man and operative among the nations is one of its main prerequisites. Particular rights are as ancient as contracts and treaties, of course – as ancient as civilization. What we are talking about is universal rights, rights that inhere in man as such, including slaves, women, children, non-citizens, and people with whom we share nothing but our common humanity.[13] The concept of rights in this sense begins to develop in earnest only with the advent of Christianity. There is a reason for that. Christianity, in obedience to Jesus, announced a universal evangel. At a stroke (delivered by the Jerusalem Council) it rendered race, class, and sex irrelevant at the most fundamental level. As St Paul put it, "There is neither Jew nor Greek, there is neither slave nor free, there is neither male nor female; for you are all one in Christ Jesus."[14] The development of the doctrine of the incarnation fortified this. Jesus was said (at the Council of Chalcedon) to be "at once complete in Godhead and complete in manhood, truly God and truly man, consisting also of a reasonable soul and body; of one substance with the Father as regards his Godhead, and at the same time of one substance with us as regards his manhood; like us in all respects, apart from sin."[15] This teaching levelled all humanity, *qua* humanity, as called to participation in God through Christ. It also fixed our attention on the very fact of our common humanity.

Of course the implications had to be worked out over time. Christianity did not see this fact as simply abolishing all existing social order – for example, as making slavery inconceivable. But it changed the way slavery was conceived, began a movement to change the way it was practised, rendered it almost non-existent in its own sphere of influence, fought hard but successful battles to recognize the humanity of those threatened by slavery in far-flung places, and ultimately achieved its delegitimization even as a concept – though it could not, of course, bring about on a universal scale an end to enslavement.

This was a messy process, naturally. So were parallel developments, such as those oriented to the protection of property-owning subjects against sovereigns, or to the rights of citizens as such (something to which the Reformation and the Enlightenment contributed substantially), which produced a new synthesis of Christian and Hellenic precedents that could be directed against abuses by prelates as well as by princes, by states as well as by corporations or other private interests.[16] Messier yet – indeed, covered in blood – was the *Déclaration des droits de l'homme et du citoyen* of 1789, which represents the first attempt to produce a human rights document in which no appeal to God can be discerned, even if there remain definite traces of nature, reason, and natural law. But the *Déclaration* was something of an aberration. The American *Declaration of Independence* had already embraced the spirit of the new synthesis without the reactionary atheism or neo-paganism of the French Revolution, and captured it in a famously succinct expression: "We hold these truths to be self-evident, that all men are created equal, that they are endowed by their Creator with certain unalienable Rights, that among these are Life, Liberty and the pursuit of Happiness."[17]

The spirit of the latter Declaration was still operative in Martin Luther King Jr's letter from a Birmingham jail, though it had taken two centuries to reach this particular point of fulfillment. It is noteworthy that King quotes Aquinas in support of what he calls "God-given civil rights" over inhumane positive law. "A just law," writes King, "is a man-made code that squares with the moral law or the law of God. An unjust law is a code that is out of harmony with the moral law. To put it in the terms of Saint Thomas Aquinas, an unjust law is a human law that is not rooted in eternal and natural law."[18]

That same spirit, and indeed the Holy Spirit, was operative also in *Dignitatis humanae*, which appeared two years later, in 1965, insisting (in the face of revolutionary and counter-revolutionary denials) on a reckoning with the dignity of man, and especially that "the highest of man's rights and duties – to live a religious life with freedom in society – must be respected" as the cornerstone of a just civil order.[19] The conciliar fathers, of course, had no trouble saying what the Universal Declaration was unable to say about the origin of human dignity; here the communists had no veto! Nor did they fail to point out that Jesus Christ had shown the path to life, liberty, and happiness. The eudaemonic vocation of man, on which the Greek and Latin and Christian philosophers all agreed – though Christians understood it very differently, in light of the two great commandments and the hope of the resurrection of the dead[20] – was not indefinable or unattainable, as some modern thinkers alleged.

But the aberrant spirit of the French Revolution also lived on, combining with the socialist and communist movements to produce a new kind of rights revolution in the mid-nineteenth century, by which inalienable rights – rights inherent in the person, not able to be given away or taken away with justice – began to morph into entitlement rights: rights to receive this or that from another, and especially from the government. This was not all bad, and the Church tried early on to shape it for the good, through Leo XIII's *Rerum novarum* (1891) and the subsequent encyclical tradition, while safeguarding the more fundamental freedoms to which we have already alluded. However, the notion of rights as entitlements, rather than as basic liberties, quickly became detached from any substantive notion of human dignity. It was annexed and deployed instead by proponents of the sexual revolution, on the one hand, and by the state – the nanny or "saviour state," as I call it – on the other. This led to a tremendous inflation of pseudo-rights at the expense of human obligations, and to a corresponding increase in the power of the state over the ordinary citizen, including that "great and pernicious error," against which Leo warned, by which that power extends even into "a man's own house" – indeed, into God's house too, that is, into places of worship and into the organs and instruments of the church. Witness the recent and notorious Health and Human Services mandate south of the border.

All of this has meant the breakdown of one kind of rights under pressure of another, leaving society defenceless, as Solzhenitsyn pointed out, against those who in fact do great harm to society and to basic human freedoms.[21] As for anyone who dares, however modestly, to emulate Martin Luther King, they are likely to be rebuked by the magistrate, as was Mary Wagner in Ontario not long ago, by Mr Justice S. Ford Clements, who purportedly observed to that indomitable pro-life counsellor: "You appear to be governed by a higher moral order than the laws of our country."[22] The price for that was another three months in jail.

As John Paul II foresaw, and in *Evangelium vitae* forewarned: "With tragic consequences, a long historical process is reaching a turning-point. The process which once led to discovering the idea of 'human rights' – rights inherent in every person and prior to any Constitution and State legislation – is today marked by a surprising contradiction. Precisely in an age when the inviolable rights of the person are solemnly proclaimed and the value of life is publicly affirmed, the very right to life is being denied or trampled upon, especially at the more significant moments of existence: the moment of birth and the moment of death."[23]

The eclipse of the sense of God, he contends, necessarily results in an eclipse of the sense of man as well, whose proper dignity is no longer seen or understood or promoted. Rights talk is then turned upside down and backwards. It becomes a cover for the destruction of human life rather than for its protection.

IS RIGHTS TALK NECESSARY?

In light of these developments, some are asking a more radical question than "Can we have human rights without God?" They are asking, rather: Do we really want or need rights talk at all? Is rights language the right language for asserting human dignity or for making laws that respect human dignity? Or have we been misled by it? As Tom Campbell puts it, "There is nothing inevitable about the current dominance of rights in political discourse."[24]

Joan Lockwood O'Donovan, for one, wants us to reconsider our allegiance to this discourse. She offers a very critical account of how modern rights language arose. She suggests that a Pelagian or legalist turn in Western Christendom associated with the development of the penitentials, together with a proprietary notion of the self that sprang from the controversy between the Franciscans and the papacy over the idea of absolute poverty, combined with Hobbesian individualism[25] (and with political principles, traceable to Marsilius of

Padua, that minimize the role of natural and divine law) to generate our modern subjectivist rights culture. That culture more or less reduces justice to rights, viewed as claims or entitlements belonging to persons and deriving from their self-ownership. Thus it atomizes the common good and effectively destroys the Western cultural tradition. While the notion of human rights is widely accepted by Christians as "adequately expressing the moral attributes of a theologically conceived humanity," its true history, she claims, casts doubt on this adequacy.[26]

O'Donovan questions the propriety of rights language, then, and argues that Christians should distance themselves from it. What is required instead is the language of created order, of goodness and grace, of obligation and obedience – the language of right and wrong rather than of human rights. "The liberal-democratic rights culture of today," she insists, has been propped up by what remains of these older notions, but because of its inherently impossible attempt "to combine radical spiritual and moral individualism with political and social egalitarianism [it] is in danger of collapsing into legal and political incoherence." The concept of human rights needs to go on the back burner, so to say, while the original recipe for our civilization is recovered. "If liberal democratic polities are to retain any semblance of legal coherence, they will have to ensure that the concept of rights is a secondary language of justice, subordinate to and continuous with that of law, in the sense of objective right and duty, as expressing a community of political judgement."[27]

Yale's Nicholas Wolterstorff, however, takes a very different line in his book, *Justice: Rights and Wrongs*. Wolterstorff does not think rights talk "inherently individualistic and possessive," but traces it back to notions about natural rights developed by the canon lawyers of the twelfth century and, even further, to the scriptures themselves.[28] He thinks that biblical religion opened up a space in the Western tradition for human rights, and that a grasp of human rights – grounded in the two great commandments and in the knowledge of human dignity that flows from revelation of the particular love of God for each and every human being – corrects and transcends our prior understanding of morality. Rights talk has a perfective function that Christians should respect and pursue, even if a good many secularists (for reasons quite different from Joan O'Donovan's) are also questioning the grounding and viability of rights talk.

This intramural argument is far from finished. Oliver O'Donovan has offered a rejoinder questioning, among other things, Wolterstorff's reading of the scriptures, in which the former finds much support for the idea of right and none for rights, subjectively understood. The point O'Donovan presses is that we do indeed have here "two fundamentally different ways of thinking about justice," one unitary, represented by the language of right (*ius*), and one plural, represented by the language of rights (*iura*). He quotes Wolterstorff against himself: "As Wolterstorff very lucidly declares, 'the debate at bottom is over the deep structure of the moral universe: what accounts for what?' Either 'rights' are 'foundational to human community', so that 'justice is ultimately grounded on inherent rights,' or 'right is foundational, and rights derive from it.'"[29]

Oliver O'Donovan draws a bright red line between these competing structures, between which he thinks we must choose. For "at the root of the disagreement over the language of rights is a question of moral ontology." The problem of the one and the many reasserts itself in the moral sphere: "Multiple rights express a plural ontology of difference, the difference between each right-bearer and every other, instead of a unitary ontology of human likeness. *Suum cuique*, to each his own, is [its] formula for justice, not *similia similibus*, like treatment for like cases. This has the effect of setting what is due to each above every idea of moral order. The classical doctrine repeated by Augustine, *ius de fonte iustitiae manat*, 'right flows from the source of rightness' (City of God XIX.21), is turned on its head to become what we find in Wolterstorff: 'justice is ultimately grounded on inherent rights.'"[30]

The recurrence of this debate today, O'Donovan claims, "was fated for us by the decision of sixty years ago to base post-war reconstruction, self-consciously critical of positive justice, on a *Universal Declaration of Human Rights*. The logical necessity of our present discussions springs from that moment of resolute new beginning," in which justice is refounded "independently of moral order." And this refounding "reveals a despair of how prevailing doctrines (Christianity among them, but also its sickly child Democracy) could ever summon up the intellectual and moral coherence to found a civilization free of brutality."[31]

On this side of the argument, then, one would not say, as Wolterstorff does, that in the absence of God we cannot have human rights. One would say, rather, that a false emphasis on human rights is what we get when God has gone missing, and human nature with him.[32] We ought to start from right, as a function of the divine order in creation, and derive rights from right, rather than seeing rights as themselves foundational to human being and deriving our sense of justice from our attention to rights.

The argument is not merely academic, I hasten to add. We can illustrate its practical impact by reference to abortion. Those who are against abortion often speak of the fetus's right to life, while those in favour of abortion deny that right or say that it is trumped by the mother's right to control her own body and anything in her body. But does a fetus really have such a right, and is that the basis of the wrongness of killing a fetus? Or is it wrong to kill a fetus – or an infant, for that matter, or an adult – simply because it is always wrong to take innocent human life? Theologically put, is it wrong because God, rather than man or woman, has jurisdiction over the fetus and its future? Likewise, does the mother have the right she is claiming, with or without consideration of a fetus, or is what is right or wrong for the mother or indeed the father to do, whether in the sexual relations that lead to pregnancy or in actions that may follow afterwards, determined rather by divine design, by the human voca- tion, by a moral order independent of the mother or father and recognizable by natural and/or divine law? If we take the "inherent rights" alternative, we risk either an over- or an under-determined claim, leaving ourselves open to a potentially irresolvable conflict of rights.[33]

Or take marriage as an example, and the controversy over same- sex marriage. If we start from the dignity of the individual *qua* indi- vidual, what prevents us from allowing the individual himself to tell us in what his own dignity lies? Who else can tell us? So, if he feels diminished by his exclusion from the honour attached to the insti- tution of marriage – not because he cannot marry, of course, but because he has chosen a same-sex partnership as the path to his self- fulfillment – he may demand that marriage be redefined to include same-sex partnerships. And we will grant his wish, because if we do not grant it we will be in denial of his dignity, and of the priority of exalting dignity as the very condition of doing justice.

These illustrations may serve to reinforce Oliver O'Donovan's point that rights discourse tempts us to prescind from the task of addressing human nature and creaturely order, and of seeking justice in conformity with that order. That is the act of despair that he wants us to avoid. But the question remains as to whether we can somehow find rights at the centre of that order, working outward from it in pursuit of justice, or whether we can find our way to rights discourse only subsequently and secondarily, starting from some other point. Wolterstorff thinks the first option viable. He moves from divine love, as the font of human worth or dignity, to a doctrine of natural rights – rights to certain goods, especially respect from other human beings, which rights are not bestowed by others but are inherent in human beings as the objects of God's love – to a more general theory of justice based on rights.[34] O'Donovan is skeptical. He prefers to work from God as the source of creaturely order to a doctrine of right that embraces both natural and divine law – via thankful participation in the created order – to a general theory of justice and, derivatively, to rights as legitimate claims arising from appropriate structures of authority and agreement among human beings.

Both sides agree, of course, that no non-theological account of natural human rights (such as Ignatieff's) can hope to be successful. Yet Wolterstorff finds fault with O'Donovan because he thinks that O'Donovan has bought into a false narrative that associates rights with possessive individualism, failing to see that the inspiration for rights talk actually comes from the Bible. O'Donovan, for his part, is sticking with that narrative: "The language of rights ... was promoted precisely to challenge our moral intuitions, intending to educate us out of them ... Creation was wholly coherent, its logic all encompassing and all reconciling. That is how Christians have always spoken, but the modern world is not minded to accept the claim, and what clearer sign of its rejection could there be than a resolution to found social relations anew, outside the realm of morality and metaphysics, on a purely juridical basis?"[35]

O'Donovan finds fault with Wolterstorff, not because the latter grounds rights in human worth and human worth in God, but because he does so in a way that isolates rather than connects human beings.[36] "If God loves, in the mode of attachment, each and every human being equally and permanently, then natural human rights inhere in the worth bestowed on human beings by that love," Wolterstorff claims.[37] But this, so to say, is too Kierkegaardian for O'Donovan's liking. It is one thing to insist that the individual be seen in his individuality before God; it is another to order human affairs wisely and justly. For that we need a sense of what is right and wrong in human relations, and this horizontal plane of justice cannot be derived directly or immediately from the vertical plane of each person's relation to God. O'Donovan worries that Wolterstorff thinks it can; that here, also, there is a form of despair with respect to the mandate to live justly, covered up by taking flight into the clouds – the glory-lined *shekinah* clouds – of individual dignity and individual rights.

THE MEDIATION OF RIGHT AND RIGHTS

This debate "over the deep structure of the moral universe," however fascinating, is somewhat puzzling to a Catholic. For the modern Leonine tradition of Catholic social thought suggests a both/and rather than an either/or approach. Certainly that tradition "notes with alarm the fragmentation of the human rights project since 1948" and recognizes (in Russell Hittinger's words) the grave problem "of liberty unseated from nature." It reckons with "a human rights movement that has gone awry, multiplying and changing the content of rights to such an extent that only an apophatic universal remains" – that is, a "negative anthropology" that does not allow us to say what man is, or how his dignity is grounded, prior to his self-determination.[38] Here it is very much on the same page as the O'Donovans. The Leonine tradition does not put human rights at the very centre of its thinking about justice. It knows that rights talk is not the proper starting point for anthropology, politics, justice, or law. At the dawn of the twentieth century – and a grim dawn it proved to be – Leo admonished his fellow bishops thus: "The world has heard enough of the so-called 'rights of man.' Let it hear something of the rights of God!"[39]

On the other hand, Catholic social thought has not recommended giving up rights talk altogether as a bad business, as if it were inherently individualistic or irredeemably subjective. An individual and subjective element there may well be, if (as John Paul II has said) "the person is a good towards which the only proper and adequate attitude is love."[40] Yet the love of God for human persons does endow these persons with rights simply by placing on their fellows a moral imperative of respect. To this extent the Catholic social tradition is on the same page with Wolterstorff. It has embraced the language of rights in a creative and indeed redemptive fashion, contributing to the formation of key articles of the Universal Declaration, for example – especially article 16 on marriage, which it expanded into the *Charter of the Rights of the Family* published by the Holy See in 1983 – as well as providing vigorous defences of various corporate and personal rights in a stream of papal encyclicals and other documents from Leo to Francis. No tradition and no institution, its flaws and failings notwithstanding, has done more to defend the weak and the vulnerable from the crushing grip of the violent and the strong, and the Church has not been reluctant to use the language of rights to that end.[41]

In Leo's *Jesus Christ the Redeemer* we find a prescription for the only possible mediation between these two positions. That they need mediation, that the difficulty is not an imaginary one or a category mistake of some kind, I think we must grant. An approach from the side of the one and an approach from the side of the many will always need mediation. And the mediation here must be real and concrete, not merely notional. Where do the one and the many meet, where do right and rights meet, where for that matter do justice and love meet, if not in Jesus Christ? The worth and the righteousness of God, like the rights of God, are grounded in God himself. But the worth and righteousness of man, and the rights of man, are grounded, neither in the race (that is, in human nature) nor in individual members thereof, but in this particular man, the man who is also God. To him "we must both feel and render with our whole hearts gratitude," says Leo, for in him we see, and from him we learn, the truth about ourselves as God has established it. This is the truth that makes us free.[42]

It is because of the mediator that we can confidently say that "the person is a good towards which the only proper and adequate attitude is love." It is because of the mediator that we can say that the person *is* a person by virtue of participation, at some level, in the love of the Father for the Son. The worth that attaches to their personhood, if inherent, is inherent in no other way. To ignore this is to ensure that the debate over the deep structure of the moral universe will find no resolution; that a pluralist ontology of difference and a unitary ontology of likeness will not cohere. Indeed, that we will not be able to offer to the likes of Ignatieff what we desire to offer, namely, a way of overcoming the impasse "between being faithful to others and being faithful to ourselves;" or to utilitarians such as Peter Singer (who once boasted that only he and John Paul really understood what was at stake in the abortion issue) a proper answer to their narrowing of personhood to a capacity for holding preferences and making plans.[43]

If considerations of justice must begin with created order and with human nature, with what is right in the objective sense, while consideration of rights begins with persons and the dignity of persons, these are not mutually exclusive proceedings when both are trinitarian and incarnational.[44] Rather, each is cross-referenced to the other.[45] Just as any consideration of God requires attention to the dialectic of being, which is indivisible, and of persons, who are distinct – indeed, just as the very meaning of "being" and of "person," where God is concerned, can be given only within this dialectic and not prior to it – so also the meaning of human nature and of human dignity can be given only dialectically. Hence we need not ask whether the deepest reason for the runaway subjectivism of the modern human rights tradition is that it evades the question of nature, or whether the deepest reason is that it has been made to rest on a concept of the dignity of the person to which the notions of gift and givenness are foreign.[46] These two factors are equally to blame. If we really mean to preserve the idea of human rights from its impending failure we must restore both concepts, nature and gift, to a central place in our discourse.

This, however, cannot be done without reaffirming the Christian insight that humans have a eucharistic vocation. *Vere dignum et iustus est* – "it is truly right and just, our duty and our salvation, always and everywhere to give you thanks, Father most holy, through your beloved Son, Jesus Christ."[47] Our proper starting point is just this thankful reckoning with the rightful claim of God on each and all of us.

To illustrate by putting the point in practical terms, if it is wrong to kill a human fetus, it is wrong because this interrupts the vocation of that fetus to praise God and enjoy him forever, a vocation given it by God himself in and with the gift of existence, a vocation we may not override for purposes of our own without offending against the rights of God. Note that on such a view we must be as critical of Singer's own dignity criterion (the ability to plan) as of the criterion he rejects (possession of human DNA); both root human dignity in something possessed by the other and recognized by me, but neither accounts for the eucharistic relation to God.[48]

INDICIUM LIBERTATIS

It is from this point that a proper theory of justice, as of rights, can be constructed. Here the notion of what is right, what is fitting, what is worthy, what is just, is not grounded in claims that we have or make on one another, even in view of God's love for us. Nor is it grounded in a natural order that operates by law alone. Rather, it is grounded in the meeting of divine rights and of human liberty, experienced corporately and ecclesially by participation in Christ. The Eucharist, in all its concreteness, is what Irenaeus called the *indicium libertatis*, the sign of liberty, in which we discover authentic freedom through the genuine subjection to God that love makes possible.[49] The Eucharist embodies the dialectic with which we ought to work, and with which we may work – in the work of the people, the liturgy – whether we grasp it intellectually or not.

O'Donovan comes close to a eucharistic way of seeing things, I think, when he states that "morality is man's participation in the created order" and then adds: "Christian morality is his glad response to the deed of God which has restored, proved and fulfilled that order, making man free to conform to it."[50] The complaint will be made, of course, that with such language we are speaking only to Christians; that the very concreteness of our starting point, the sectarian nature of our proposal, cuts us off from the world at large and so from any moral or human rights discourse capable of gaining a hearing outside the church.[51] Two things may be said in reply.

First, it is no less true in this sphere than in any other that concreteness is an advantage. No proposal that fails to be concrete can supply human rights discourse with the necessary resources with which to sustain itself. Moreover, it is an established fact, however disputable the particulars of this or that genealogy, that the discourse in question owes its origin and its life-blood to Christianity; in Ignatieff's rather vague expression, "only Western culture turned widely shared propositions about human dignity and equality into a working doctrine of rights." It is a fact, to be more precise, that the appearance of Jesus Christ had among its chief civilizational consequences the renewal or even the creation of specific rights and duties, and a frame of reference in which to understand them.[52] And it is also a fact that the God-question can no longer be evaded. As Solzhenitsyn insisted in his 1983 Templeton address, "all attempts to find a way out of the plight of today's world are fruitless unless we redirect our consciousness, in repentance, to the Creator of all: without this, no exit will be illumined, and we shall seek it in vain."[53]

Second, it should not be missed that Christian morality, so conceived, is not something discontinuous with a more general morality.

Rather, it is a penetration to the very heart of morality. Not everyone knows that thanks to God can and may be given through Jesus Christ, or that it cannot be given adequately, as the church believes, except through Jesus Christ. But everyone knows, or ought to know, that thanks is indeed to be given. For he who denies that, denies that the order on which justice and rights and other features of morality are founded is a *given* order, a good order, an order for which respect is obligatory. He thus becomes amoral, or at all events ceases to be morally coherent. Man's participation in the created order goes wrong from the moment he ceases to give thanks.[54]

In the present climate there is nothing more important to say. The human rights we get when we do not say this are either twisted beyond recognition (like the "right" to marry a same-sex partner or to choose death for one's baby or to commit medically assisted suicide) or else rendered ephemeral and altogether insecure (like the right, say, to freedom of conscience or of religion). The truth of the matter is that we cannot have human rights that are rightly or justly ordered without acknowledging God and rendering thanks to God. And this fact is just what Jesus Christ confronts us with.

"It may be clearly seen," warned Leo at the beginning of the last century, "what consequences are to be expected from that false pride which, rejecting our Saviour's Kingship, places man at the summit of all things and declares that human nature must rule supreme." These consequences, grimly rehearsed by Solzhenitsyn at the end of the century, are the demise of human nature and the destruction of human beings; indeed, of whole human societies. For the supreme rule of man, in defiant abstraction from Christ, "can neither be attained nor even defined." The true rule, the rule of Jesus Christ, "derives its form and its power from Divine Love: a holy and orderly charity is both its foundation and its crown. Its necessary consequences are the strict fulfilment of duty, respect of mutual rights, the estimation of the things of heaven above those of earth, the preference of the love of God to all things. But this supremacy of man, which openly rejects Christ, or at least ignores Him, is entirely founded upon selfishness, knowing neither charity nor self-devotion."[55]

Leo, however, concluded more hopefully – as perhaps we yet may do? – that "it is rather ignorance than ill-will which keeps multitudes away from Jesus Christ." And so he advised: "The first step, then, is to substitute knowledge for ignorance, so that He may no longer be despised or rejected because He is unknown. We conjure all

Christians throughout the world to strive all they can to know their Redeemer as He really is."[56]

Those who heed Leo's advice, even at this late hour, will be like Epimenides, reminding the Cretans that God is very much alive when they foolishly supposed him to be dead. They will also be like Paul on Mars Hill, proclaiming even to the Athenians something they know they ought to acknowledge, something they at least gesture toward, yet do not properly know: namely, what justice is and what rights are, when they appear together, in their truth, under the aegis of Love.

2

Same-Sex Marriage and the Sublation
of Civil Society

Rousseau remarks in a footnote to *The Social Contract* that "marriage, being a civil contract, has civil consequences; and without them it is impossible for society even to subsist." The first claim is tautologically true. The truth of the second we may soon discover, for civil marriage is not only in decline, but also in imminent danger of disappearing.

There are, of course, many factors in the decline of marriage as a vital social institution. The industrial revolution and urbanization, the fading of faith and the sexual revolution, the demographic curve, and the culture of death are among those that come to mind. The current determination to redefine marriage, however, requires us to attend to an additional factor – one already in play in the footnote in question. That factor is the struggle between church and state for the soul of civil society, a struggle that in late modernity takes place not through the mechanism of lay investiture, as once it did, but rather through legal control over marriage. Rousseau continues thus:

> If we assume that the clergy succeed in arrogating to themselves the sole right to perform the act of marriage, a right which, of necessity, they will usurp whenever they serve an intolerant religion, is it not obvious that, by establishing the authority of the Church in this matter, they will render that of the Prince null, and create a situation in which the Prince will have as subjects only such as the clergy shall see fit to give him? Being in a position to permit or to refuse marriage, according as whether those concerned do, or do not, hold certain doctrines, whether they admit or denounce the validity of this or that formula, whether

they be more or less devout, the Church, surely, if only it use a
little tact and refuse to yield ground, will be the sole controller
of inheritances, offices, citizens, and the State itself, which could
not continue were it composed only of bastards.[1]

As I observed in *Nation of Bastards*, the shoe is now on the other
foot: the state, taking Rousseau's advice, is assuming full control
over marriage. Not content, however, merely to insist on civil marriage as the only legally relevant form of marriage, it has decided
to modify the very substance of marriage, objections – in France,
remarkably vociferous objections – of the citizenry notwithstanding.
The effect can only be the end of marriage and the absorption of
civil society into the state itself.

AND GOD CREATED THEM
NEITHER MALE NOR FEMALE

In my own country this Rousseauvian move was accomplished by
judicial fiat and with judicial blessing. When the federal government
referred to the Supreme Court the question as to whether it had the
authority to redefine marriage, as a provincial court had demanded,
it was told that it did indeed have such authority, for civil purposes.
Religious marriage, on the other hand, was an altogether different
matter, of no particular concern to the state, said the court. So, since
2005, marriage in Canada has been the union of two persons rather
than the union of a man and a woman.

In British common law, of course, marriage had been defined as
"the voluntary union for life of one man and one woman to the
exclusion of all others,"[2] a definition owing much to that formulated
for Roman jurisprudence in the third century by Modestinus: "Marriage is the union of a man and a woman, a consortium for the whole
of life involving the communication of divine and human rights."[3]
The new definition, I suppose, could also claim an older precedent,
for Hugh of St Victor defined matrimony as "the lawful consent of
two apt persons to be joined together."[4] There was never any doubt,
however, as parallel definitions make plain, that "apt" was a specifi-
cation that included sexual difference and complementarity.

I hasten to agree with proponents of the new definition who point
out that the sky has not fallen. Indeed it hasn't. Life goes on under
the sky, as ever before. Only now there is another god in heaven,

exercising its authority over things human. There has been a change of regime on high, and of image-bearing below. What it means to be human, what the young will be taught about this, what public officials will say and do in recognition of the dignity of the person, what citizens may say or do without culpably besmirching that dignity – all this has changed.

Under the new regime there is a new anthropology, in which there is to be no privileging, in any form whatsoever, of male-female relations. Here in Quebec the government has launched a full-scale war against "heteronormism," declaring its intention to stamp out this sin from the private as well as the public sphere, and even funding a professorial chair (not to mention an anonymous tip line) to keep track of offences. Internationally, lists of human rights are being revised to secure the claims and interests of the new undifferentiated man.[5] Moreover, old and venerable distinctions between being and behaviour, between inherent and earned dignity, between sin and sinner are beginning to be suppressed. In a recent hate speech case the Supreme Court of Canada explicitly disallowed appeal to such distinctions (under particular conditions) as a defence in the matter of homosexuality.[6]

There is nothing surprising about any of this. The change in the definition of marriage is a change in the definition of man as such. Man is no longer male and female. Man is simply this person or that person: an individual bundle of desires who is the bearer of corresponding (if often conflicting) rights.[7] This change in anthropology goes all the way down. Formerly, it was said that man has an intelligible nature bestowed by God, a nature that reaches fulfillment in determinate actions proper to that nature and to the graces freely bestowed on that nature. Now it is said that human nature itself is nothing determinate, but rather something largely protean. Only if man is not constrained by an *a priori* "nature" is he truly free. Only if he is liberated from constructs imposed on him from above or from below, is he capable of fulfillment. The truly emancipated man is the man capable of making and remaking himself at will, right down to his sex or gender.[8]

This creates a linguistic problem, the problem of pronouns such as "he" and "she." It creates a substantive problem, the problem of nouns like "man" or "nature," which become conceptually confused if not objectionable.[9] It creates, or rather reflects, a theological problem; for, as the Serpent suggested, only the man who is neither for

God, nor trained and constrained by God, is like God. It also creates a problem for man himself, since it alienates him from his own body. All the talk about diversity and dignity, about rights and equality, about sensitivity and compassion – however necessary where people actually do feel alienated from their bodies – cannot disguise this fact. *The body itself is under attack.* Man is no longer a rational animal, comprising body and soul in harmony. Man is a sovereign will, using or manipulating a body (whether his own or another's) for comfort or pleasure or simply to display his autonomy. At the moment, marriage is the primary point of attack, though some of the shock troops, flying "trans" or some other flag of convenience, have surged beyond that target.[10]

GOODS GONE MISSING

Now this patently gnostic anthropology, in which man is neither male nor female, necessarily deracinates marriage, depriving it of its proper goods. What are those goods?

Traditionally, they are three: *proles, fides, et sacramentum.* Procreation is first, because the chief public good that the institution serves is the generation and rearing of children, and the perpetuation of kinship. Faithfulness ("observing the marriage compact") is next, because it serves and dignifies the marriage in respect of the other two goods.[11] The permanent bonding or inseparability of the couple is last, but not least. Indeed, it is the greatest of the three in the sense that, without it, there is no marriage: the other two goods, equally required in principle, may fail in practice without the marriage itself failing or being invalidated. It is greatest of the three also in the sense that it refers both to a natural and to a supernatural good; that is, to the sacrament of holy matrimony.[12] This requires a word of explanation, if we are to grasp what is happening today.

In Catholic Christianity, matrimony is said to have been instituted "both as an office of nature and as a sacrament of the Church."[13] Which means that it is capable, by grace, of becoming "a sanctifying remedy against sin" – such are sacraments generally – and a sign of the union between Christ and his ecclesial bride.[14] To be sure, that latter or mystical union is present only in *signum*, not in *res*; that is, as something signified but not (as in the Eucharist) actually contained. *Qua* remedy for sin, however, the sacrament of holy matrimony does contain what it signifies. Husband and wife are united in such a way that their baptismal bond in Christ is brought to bear on the entire relationship, including the weaknesses and sins of the partners. This has a transforming effect on all the natural goods of marriage, but in particular on the third good, which is here based on something more solid than a vow of life-long allegiance (*sacramentum* in the mundane legal sense). It is based more fundamentally on the grace of God in Jesus Christ received in baptism. And this renders it, not only in sign but also in reality, indissoluble. The breaking of the vow, even the disavowal of the vow, does not break the marriage.[15]

Already in Augustine, without benefit of a mature sacramental theology, the deepening and transforming character of sacramental marriage is evident. The goods native to marriage appear in sharp relief under a supernatural light. In holy matrimony, says Augustine,

> let these nuptial blessings be the objects of our love – offspring, fidelity, the sacramental bond. *Offspring*, not that it be born only, but born again; for it is born to punishment unless it be born again to life. *Fidelity*, not such as even unbelievers observe one towards the other, in their ardent love of the flesh ... but [as] a member of Christ [who] ought to be afraid of adultery, not on account of himself, but of his spouse; and ought to hope to receive from Christ the reward of that fidelity which he shows to his spouse. The *bond* [*sacramentum*] again, which is lost neither by divorce nor by adultery, should be guarded by husband and wife with concord and chastity. For it alone is that which even an unfruitful marriage retains by the law of piety, now that all that hope of fruitfulness is lost for the purpose of which the couple married. Let these nuptial blessings be praised in marriage by him who wishes to extol the nuptial institution.[16]

In decisive fashion, then, Christianity raised the stakes respecting marriage, both civilly and religiously, while at the same time relativizing it to the ecclesial mystery to which it points and to the eschatological reality at which it ultimately aims.[17] Greater attention was soon being paid to its legal accidents in light of its deepening theological substance, a process that continued into the modern period. As the Tridentine fathers attest, "Christ himself, the instituter and perfecter of the most holy sacraments, merited for us by his passion the grace that would perfect natural love, strengthen the unbreakable unity, and sanctify the spouses."[18] This grace "raises marriage in

the dispensation of the gospel above the unions of the old law" –
though not above celibacy, which is also put in a new light – and
hence requires that it become the object of greater canonical care.

The marital institution was thus reformed in such a way as to
secure all three of its goods as matters of public concern and clear
regulation. One aim of this reform was to deliver it from manipula-
tion by third parties, whether individuals or families or corrupt cler-
ics or civic officials: "As it is the height of wickedness to violate the
freedom of marriage, and for injustices to be meted out by those
from whom justice is expected, the holy council forbids all of whatever rank or dignity or state they may be, under pain of anathema
automatically incurred, to use any pressure on their subjects or anyone else to prevent them marrying freely."[19] Our own common law
tradition reflects many of these assumptions and developments, and
embodies in the *Hyde v. Hyde* definition, which prevailed until the
new millennium, the goods on which they are based. But, again,
what has happened to them?

Tellingly, the definition now in place in Canada does away with
two of the three goods – the two, in fact, that are most essential.
Marriage as "the lawful union of two persons to the exclusion of all
others" is an institution that tries to do without procreation (only
thus can it become inclusive of same-sex couples) and without the
intergenerational bonds of kinship. It is also an institution that tries
to do without permanence; the words "for life" have disappeared. It
is, in other words, an institution that focuses exclusively on *fides* or
exclusivity.[20] And, of course, it does away with any openness to the
sacramental grace of holy matrimony by removing the ordered complementarity that grounds marriage's signifying function with respect
to the union of Christ and his church.

Or perhaps that is not quite right. Perhaps we should say, rather,
that this newly minted institution perverts the sacramental dimension by de-sacralizing marriage and re-sacralizing the state, which,
by taking up the power of definition and exercising it in this way,
lays claim to an authority it does not have: an authority over nature
itself, and even over the church.

Certainly the state that thus defines marriage lays claim – let no
one be in doubt about this –to authority over the natural family. For,
absent *proles* as the first good of marriage, the natural family no
longer has in marriage an institutional home or guardian. It is no
longer recognized at law as a pre-political entity bearing natural

rights that the state is obliged to respect. Even the child-parent relation has perforce been politicized. It has, as Canadian law explicitly
recognizes, become a purely legal relation even when it is a blood
relation. The as-yet-unanswered question of the new marriage regime
is: "Who owns the children?"[21]

BIOPOLITICAL TYRANNY?

F.C. DeCoste, writing in the *Alberta Law Review* just as Canada was
capitulating to the anti-marriage forces, warned of the leviathan that
was now appearing. "Through the state's coercive power," he pre-
dicted, "social relationships will be, not just re-defined at law, but
changed root and branch by law."[22] And so they will, since human
nature at its most fundamental level has, by a kind of alchemy,
become but a legal construct.

It is to John Milbank's credit that he has come round to recognizing this. In *Nova et Vetera* I criticized his naive proposal that churches
bless same-sex partnerships but distinguish them from marriage, cel-
ebrating the latter in grand fashion so as to make the gentiles jeal-
ous.[23] But Milbank's latest article on the subject, "The Impossibility
of Gay Marriage and the Threat of Biopolitical Control," is more
astute. In it he puts the alternatives thus:

> Can we not live with differing definitions of marriage? Perhaps,
> in order to safeguard the churches from pressures to conform to
> the [new] norm, we should now welcome a withdrawal from
> the churches of their rights as a civil marriage broker. This
> would leave the churches free, in their turn, to claim that only
> natural and sacramental marriage are genuinely "marriage,"
> while state marriage is mere civil union. They could trump secu-
> larisation by declaring that the era of civil marriage had been
> a failed experiment.
>
> This may, indeed, be the direction that the churches now need
> to take. However, the graver fear surrounding the new legislation
> is that secular thought will not so readily let go of the demand
> for absolutely equal rights based on identical definitions. In that
> case, we face an altogether more drastic prospect. Not only
> would "marriage" have been redefined so as to include gay mar-
> riage, it would inevitably be redefined even for heterosexual peo-
> ple in *homosexual terms*. Thus "consummation" and "adultery"

would cease to be seen as having any relevance to the binding
and loosing of straight unions.

Many may welcome such a development as yet a further
removal of state intrusion into our private lives, but that would
be to fail to consider all the implications. In the first place, it
would end public recognition of the importance of marriage as
a union of sexual difference. But the joining together and har-
monisation of the asymmetrical perspectives of the two sexes are
crucial both to kinship relations over time and to social peace.
Where the reality of sexual difference is denied, then it gets
reinvented in perverse ways – just as the over-sexualisation of
women and the confinement of men to a marginalised machismo.

Secondly, it would end the public legal recognition of a social
reality defined in terms of the natural link between sex and procreation. In direct consequence, the natural children of heterosexual couples would then be only legally their children if the
state decided that they might be legally "adopted" by them.

And this, I argue, reveals what is really at issue here. There was
no *demand* for "gay marriage" and this has nothing to do with
gay rights. Instead, it is a strategic move in the modern state's
drive to assume direct control over the reproduction of the population, bypassing our interpersonal encounters. This is not about
natural justice, but the desire on the part of biopolitical tyranny
to destroy marriage and the family as the most fundamental
mediating social institution.

Heterosexual exchange and reproduction has always been the
very "grammar" of social relating as such. The abandonment of
this grammar would thus imply a society no longer primarily
constituted by extended kinship, but rather by state control and
merely monetary exchange and reproduction.[24]

Is the case overstated? I don't think so, even if it may be doubted
that the move in question is the product of some grand conspiracy.[25]
From the gradual advances of the monastic era through to the sud-
den shocks of the industrial revolution and the accelerated pace of
change since then, events themselves have conspired to put marriage
and the family in peril – weakening in turn the church, which is
heavily invested in the *ecclesia domestica* as its primary constitu-
ency, while undermining religious communities generally. And now
the advance of the bureaucratic state, combined with the growing

sexualization of our culture (much aided by a new facility in contraception and in the distribution of pornographic images), is at last bringing marriage to its knees, and civil society with it. A biopolitical tyranny, backed by enormous technological prowess, is no longer the stuff of fiction only.

A FAUSTIAN BARGAIN

By "sexualization" I refer to our collective preoccupation with sexual interests and activities altogether detached from the goods of marriage. What began as a search for a sexual autonomy (with this, too, Rousseau had something to do) analogous to the intellectual autonomy of the Enlightenment, degenerated eventually into a fixation on sexual self-expression. In a parody of Trent, it has now become the height of violence, and a fundamental affront to human dignity, to interfere with anyone's sexual "identity." Which is what marriage does, in a systemic fashion. The problem with marriage is that it privileges a certain kind of identity. As we know it, marriage is irreducibly heteronormative. Therefore, a political and legal strategy for dealing with marriage must be devised. Marriage must be attacked as discriminatory.[26]

That the strategy chosen is quite transparently dishonest does not seem to trouble anyone. Of course, marriage is not actually discriminatory. If everyone is either a man or a woman, and if (fortune permitting) every man or woman may choose to marry and found a family, as the *Universal Declaration* affirms, no one is excluded in principle. Everyone is, at least potentially, an "apt" or marriageable person.[27] Whence arises discrimination then? Discrimination arises only if we play around unfairly with the accidents of marriage – as was done for a time with miscegenation laws, for example – *or* if we change the very definition of marriage, turning it into a close personal relationship without reference to sexual difference. That opens the door to new acts of discrimination by denying the right of a man to marry a man, or a woman a woman, as once was denied the right of a black man to marry a white woman.

Change the definition, in other words, and discrimination becomes possible; leave the definition alone and there is no discrimination. Hence, arguments for same-sex marriage are in fact arguments for creating the *possibility* of discrimination, and only then for repudiating the possibility thus created.[28]

The decision to deploy this sleight of hand entails a Faustian bargain. Sexual autonomy, thus conceived and pursued, is purchased at the price of political liberty. The devil to be paid is the state, which, absent the natural family unit as something legally recognized and protected by the institution of marriage, now gains custody of every child, becoming the sole proprietor of those rights and responsibilities that once were regarded as pre-political and (under normal circumstances) beyond its reach. As procreation is removed from the purview of marriage, blood relations are exchanged for mere legal constructs. The natural family as the fundamental school of personhood is set aside, together with the right of a child to its own father and mother. The family no longer stands over against the state as a buffering or mediating institution that provides refuge for the individual citizen. Vast tracts of social life are thus conceded to the state over which it has no proper authority.

A FOOLISH PROPOSAL

Thinking to break up this bargain somehow, some are calling for the state to withdraw from marriage altogether. If the state will drop its claim to civil marriage, contenting itself with various forms of contract law to deal with the diversity of our social and sexual arrangements, then the church can also abandon its own claims. Religious marriage will still exist, but not as a matter of civil or legal significance. This proposal, however, is not so much a compromise as a capitulation.

Why? First, because getting the state out of marriage is one of the main objectives of the proponents of redefinition. The immediate goal, to be sure, is to force marriage, against its nature, to further the process of normalizing same-sex relations and a no-holds-barred view of sex. But beyond that lies a further goal – the end of marriage itself as a public institution. And what better way to bring that about than to make marriage, *pro tempore*, do something it cannot: accommodate unions that are not conjugal unions and, just so, abandon its own traditional goods? Masha Gessen is oddly candid, as Robert George notes, about the requisite dissembling in the short term: "Fighting for gay marriage generally involves lying about what we are going to do with marriage when we get there – because we [claim] that the institution of marriage is not going to change, and that is a lie. The institution of marriage is going to change, and it should change … I don't think it should exist."[29]

Second, because the state itself must expand exponentially (as I have already said) in order to occupy all the territory that once was dealt with by way of the institution of marriage. Parallel arrangements for the handling of human affairs, one civil and the other religious, means reduplication at all levels. It entails far greater state supervision of our lives, not less. It still leaves us all as wards of the state, and sublates civil society into the state.

If the battle over the definition of marriage is indeed a battle over the limits of the state, this proposal can have no traction at all. It is necessary instead to defend marriage as a public good, a *necessary* good, while showing the public what marriage is.[30]

ON NOT BRACKETING HOMOSEXUALITY

The case for marriage as a public good has long required, but not received, a robust and convincing reformulation in the modern urban setting. Still, apart from some Marxists and feminists, few doubted that case until images of the new god, worshiped commercially as Sex and politically as Tolerance, were erected in the public square. In the presence of the latter it has become much more difficult to make, and those who attempt to make it often do so in a manner calculated not to offend the new god or gods.

Take, for example, the worthy attempt of Girgis, Anderson, and George in *What is Marriage?* They not only note the abandonment of a grammar – "redefining civil marriage would change its meaning for everyone"[31] – but spell out some of the inevitable consequences. On the other hand, they pay less attention than they might to the political implications of this abandonment. Moreover, they are very careful to insist that their book is precisely about marriage and not about homosexuality. That is a strategy easy to appreciate, and one I have been inclined to follow myself. But it must be asked whether marriage *can* be discussed or defended today without addressing the problem of homosexuality.

It was Bentham who first proposed that rejection of homosexuality is no more than a groundless prejudice. If that is right, and if homosexuality really is something to appreciate or celebrate – whether in the fashion of *Blue is the Warmest Colour* or in some less pornographic way – surely the defence of marriage becomes vastly more difficult. For the goods of marriage, and the institution as such, are predicated on the dimorphic and complementary nature of human sexuality; which is just what the celebration of homosexuality denies.

Truth be told, the trajectory from Bentham to *Blue* is one that is inimical to marriage and to civil society, which requires for its health the flourishing of the natural family. On that trajectory it is insisted that any law or policy that privileges conjugal marriage "codifies an animus towards gays and lesbians" and is therefore unacceptable. It is not enough to deny this animus. It is necessary to show, without animus, that the promotion of homosexuality is incompatible with a healthy society.

Inimical and incompatible? Yes. Girgis and company record the glee of some redefinition advocates that "conferring the legitimacy of marriage on homosexual relations will introduce an implicit revolt against the institution into its very heart."[32] Of course, there are others who do not admit any such revolt and find in every argument for refusing to recognize same-sex relationships a demeaning rationale; or, to be more precise, a lack (as Michael Perry puts it) of any "non-demeaning" rationale.[33] This seems strained, to say the least, but is the right response to steer clear of anything that might be deemed demeaning? The alternative is to have a frank and open discussion of homosexuality, something that is missing from many otherwise fine volumes on marriage.[34]

The task of addressing homosexuality is in part the task of querying the claims made on its behalf. What exactly is homosexuality, anyway? Is it a fixed feature of certain individuals, belonging to their biology, as the determinists claim? (This has the obvious advantage of making "homophobia" and "heterosexism" akin to racism.) Or is it a malleable feature, as the social constructivists claim? (This has the advantage of incorporating a wider spectrum of sexual identities into civil rights claims, so long as it is not much noticed that the two lines of argument, as popularly pursued, are incompatible.) What, moreover, is a homosexual union and how does it differ from the conjugal union? In what relation does it stand to the traditional goods of marriage? Is it, or can it be, the kind of thing that invites or conforms to the type of regulation that marriage law has traditionally entailed? What effects does same-sex behaviour have on the brain and on physical health? With what social or psychological or spiritual conditions is it associated? In what ways does it serve human flourishing or inhibit human flourishing?

Christians, out of concern for the truth, and for the well-being of others, ought to take a lead in the questioning process, and often have done so (with more than a little help from Mormons, I might add.) But Christians have something more to contribute, *viz.*, their insight into the anthropological and theological dimensions of the problem of homosexuality, and into the possibility of authentic sexual freedom. That is the greater task. For, when grace perfects nature, the questions posed to us by nature are posed more sharply and must be answered more decisively. Alas, it is also the more problematic task, because it quickly reveals glaring inconsistencies in the Christian community itself.

THE BEAM IN OUR OWN EYE

Christians claim that there is a God in heaven who is not of our fashioning. They also claim that this God has made us male and female, not heterosexual and homosexual, and that the former, complementary, categories are the ones that must prevail.[35] These are not private but public claims; those who have not been dhimmitized by (early) Rawlsian dogma do not hesitate to press them. As Sirach says: "All things are twofold, one opposite the other, and he has made nothing incomplete. One confirms the good things of the other, and who can have enough of beholding his glory?"[36]

Yet many of the very same Christians refuse to contemplate the way in which contraception, a practice in which they freely participate, contradicts all of this, rendering Christian strictures against same-sex behaviour either incoherent or hypocritical. That is the first inconsistency. Sterile sex is sterile sex, no matter who the partners are. A sex act in which the procreative and unitive aspects have been put asunder by man is a sex act that departs from the course of nature and from the will of nature's Designer. Marriage sanctifies sex, a natural good that in humans requires a sanctification not necessary in the case of other animals. But marriage is not a licence for lust or for acts contrary to nature. It does not render contraceptive sex right, nor does it produce a right to sex whenever sex is desired. Chastity, or virtue in sex, belongs to the discipline of marriage.

Professor Perry, for one, capitalizes on this inconsistency to call for greater acceptance of homosexuality. Those unwilling to accept that call must show that they are not in fact being inconsistent. They must give answer to *Humanae vitae* and to *Donum vitae*. They must also show how their appeal to a new "principle of totality" in marriage – not the principle of total self-giving that is present in Catholic teaching but rather the principle that the procreative good can be detached from particular sex acts for the sake of the unitive good – is not special pleading.[37] They must address Elizabeth Anscombe's claim in "Contraception and Chastity" (which reprises her 1968 essay in support of *Humanae vitae*, "You can have sex without children: Christianity and the New Offer") that "if contraceptive intercourse is all right then so are all forms of sexual activity" – just what our youth are being taught in sex education classes today![38]

Anscombe and Perry offer opposite counsel, but both link dissent from Catholic teaching about contraception to rejection of strictures against same-sex unions. Are they wrong? Or does contraceptive sex undo the whole logic of marriage by isolating the unitive from the procreative?[39] But perhaps we are being too generous to speak so much of the unitive, when by "unitive" we may mean no more than "pleasurable." In common arguments for contraceptive sex, even those that attempt (however inconsistently) to restrict the practice to marriage, it is an unstated premise that sexual pleasure is a good at least the equal of the traditional marital goods, or that the unhindered pursuit of pleasure is somehow essential to the unitive good. One does not have to agree entirely with Augustine about the nature and confines of sexual pleasure to see that this is both false and base.

The second inconsistency flows from the first, both logically and chronologically. It is the widespread acceptance of divorce, which represents a return not only to the Mosaic situation prior to Jesus but also to pagan practices that lie outside the covenantal context altogether.[40] The sexual autonomy principle underlies both these inconsistencies, just as it does the bloody violence of abortion that is a still further outcome. Which helps to explain why so many Christians do not see in same-sex marriage what is actually there to be seen: a bold affirmation that man is not essentially male and female, perhaps not even essentially embodied; that the love of Christ for the church is not the perfection of humanity, which has no need of it; and that there is no such God in heaven as Christians fancy. Instead, they see only an extension of the autonomy principle to the neighbour – an act of charity.

We should not overlook the fact that the first link in this chain is not the affirmation of homosexuality, but the misconstrual of sexual freedom. And the misconstrual of sexual freedom itself is a function, if St Paul is to be trusted (Bentham thought not), of a theological decision; that is, of a denial of the existence and manifest nature of

God, and of the obligation to render thanks to God.[41] That is the context in which sexual freedom is misunderstood, in which human nature itself is misunderstood, in which disordered desires and actions are said to be well-ordered, and in which homosexuality thrives as one manifestation of a more general phenomenon: the contraceptive mentality.

The church, which has been enabled evangelically and sacramentally to see into the heart of marriage – to recognize its covenantal as well as its contractual features, its eschatological as well as its civil consequences – has an obligation to nurture and protect marriage, not only for itself but for its neighbours. It has an obligation to defend the family and civil society from the threat of absorption into the state. It cannot do this, however, if it brackets the problem of homosexuality or fails to address the gnostic temptation inherent in the same-sex movement. Still less can it do so if it insists on bracketing its own problem: the complicity of its members in the culture of sterile sex. For it is only in that culture that same-sex marriage is thinkable.

A NOT ENTIRELY COMFORTING CONCLUSION

Following his election as bishop of Rome in 1959, John XXIII issued a prescient call to Christians to strengthen and defend the family. "We earnestly pray God," wrote the new pope, "to prevent any damage to this valuable, beneficial, and necessary union. The Christian family is a sacred institution. If it totters, if the norms which the divine Redeemer laid down for it are rejected or ignored, then the very foundations of the state tremble. Civil society stands betrayed and in peril. Everyone suffers."[42] But in the intervening half-century, St John's prayer and plea notwithstanding, the institution of marriage itself, on which the family is built, has plainly begun to totter. Even the diligent labours of his successors in the See of Rome have not been able to steady it. That is because the foundations have been eroding for some time; certainly from long before radical feminist or homosexualist movements emerged into view.

That learned and astute observer of marriage, John Witte Jr, describes the process of erosion thus: "The early Enlightenment ideals of marriage as a permanent contractual union designed for the sake of mutual love, procreation, and protection is slowly giving way to a new reality of marriage as a 'terminal sexual contract' designed for the gratification of the individual parties."[43] Quite so.

And, as this happens, the law (if I read him correctly) is striving to become ever more therapeutic, competing with, even usurping, the church's pastoral function, as the state wrestles with the church for full control of marriage.

Witte reminds us of Harold Berman's observation that "great legal revolutions always pass through radical phases before they reach an accommodation with the tradition that they had set out to destroy" or to supplant. Yet he himself thinks that today's "elementary deconstructions and dismissals of a millennium-long tradition of marriage and family law and life" are much too lean, and far too glib, to support the revolution that is now under way, or to justify its mounting costs. "The wild oats sown in the course of the American sexual revolution," he says, "have brought forth such a great forest of tangled structural, moral, and intellectual thorns that we seem almost powerless to cut it down. We seem to be living out the grim prophecy that Friedrich Nietzsche offered a century ago: that in the course of the twentieth century, 'the family will be slowly ground into a random collection of individuals,' haphazardly bound together 'in the common pursuit of selfish ends' – and in the common rejection of the structures and strictures of family, church, state, and civil society."[44]

If the situation is anything like that serious, and if in fact, as I have suggested, there looms behind the visage of Sex and Tolerance the more fearsome aspect of a resacralized and all-powerful state, then the response of Christians can no longer be half-hearted or ill disciplined. There are promising signs, such as the new statement from Evangelicals and Catholics Together,[45] that some are beginning to realize that. But Witte is entirely right that any statement on marriage we can make, if it is to be an effective statement, will have to be made with deeds and not merely with words. And though there is a certain irony here – John XXIII's prayer was uttered, after all, in the context of a plea for human as well as ecclesial unity – perhaps it will soon have to be made, in the spirit if not the fashion of Daniel and friends, with acts of civil disobedience. John himself, were he still here, might well say so; and, on the other side, Rousseau at least would not be surprised.[46]

3

Pluralism, the New Catholicism

Fifty years ago the world applauded as the Catholic Church announced its new political pluralism in *Dignitatis humanae*. That pluralism was grounded partly in practical considerations (the end of Catholic hegemony in many places) and partly in philosophical ones: "A sense of the dignity of the human person has been impressing itself more and more deeply on the consciousness of contemporary man, and the demand is increasingly made that men should act on their own judgment, enjoying and making use of a responsible freedom, not driven by coercion but motivated by a sense of duty. The demand is likewise made that constitutional limits should be set to the powers of government, in order that there may be no encroachment on the rightful freedom of the person and of associations. This demand for freedom in human society chiefly regards the quest for the values proper to the human spirit."[1]

On this line of thought the dignity of man entails responsible judgment; responsible judgment entails both duty and freedom; freedom requires constitutional limits on governmental power. While the word "pluralism" does not appear in the Declaration, its affirmation of religious freedom constitutes recognition in principle of the political legitimacy of competing world views and diverse communities with their respective modes of life. It expects only a common commitment to the dignity of man, and an acknowledgement that freedom is not merely freedom from constraint but rather freedom for the proper development of the human spirit.

Today, however, this Catholic pluralism is *passé*, if it were not already so at the time of its promulgation. Another kind of pluralism is in the ascendancy. Some call it normative pluralism, but we may (with a certain irony) call it the new catholicism. For though it seems at first glance to involve a much more radical affirmation of diversity – set out in conscious opposition to the Catholic affirmation, which it dismisses as belated and begrudging – it turns out to be even more restrictive and politically repressive than the pre-conciliar Catholicism to which it so objects.

THE PROBLEM WITH NORMATIVE PLURALISM

The character of this pluralism stands out clearly in the Loyola case, on which the Supreme Court of Canada has now ruled.[2] Professor Georges Leroux, the Ministry of Education's expert witness and a leading apologist for the Ethics and Religious Culture (ERC) program, sees that program as a "revolutionary" development in Quebec. And normative pluralism, he says, is its very *raison d'être*. Professor Leroux is quoted as saying: "The first reason that we, the Government and all those who have supported it, judged that it is necessary, even essential, to draw up the course of ethics and religious culture, is normative pluralism. It is essential that diversified experience, both on the moral and the religious level, be valued in its diversity."[3]

Now a Catholic ought to understand this and, more than anyone else perhaps, receive it sympathetically. Otherness is no threat, but in principle a joy, to one who holds the Nicene faith, which posits not only the otherness *of* God but also otherness *in* God. No xenophobic culture can claim, in that respect, to be Catholic. Diversity, as J.S. Mill says – well, actually, as Genesis 1 says – is not an evil but a good. But there is a problem here, as I argued before the lower court.[4] The problem is with the kind of pluralism in view and, more particularly, with its tendency to suppress, rather than to appreciate, genuine otherness.

Let it be said straight away that the expression "normative pluralism" does not, as some suppose, signify a fact on the ground; *viz.*, the sometimes fraught coexistence (needing a little encouragement or even management) of culturally and religiously diverse communities, living side by side within a larger social and legal framework. What would be new or revolutionary about that? Rather, it signifies a determination that valuing diverse moral and religious practices or perspectives should *become* the norm, such that "no one principle, ideal, or way of life can dominate."[5] None, that is, save pluralism itself, which is to serve society as the *norma normans non normata*.

Alas, wherever this norming norm appears, whether in Europe or in the Americas, it immediately generates conflicts with the right to religious freedom and to freedom of conscience. In the case at hand, the conflict was not in the entirely reasonable demand from the Ministry of Education that respect be shown to others in the process of exploring religious or ethical topics and cultures, but rather in the demand that Loyola High School abandon its own Catholic posture and pedagogy in favour of the putatively neutral posture and pedagogy of the Ministry. This demand Loyola rightly rejected. How can a Catholic person, whether a natural or (in the case of the school) a legal person, be asked *not* to be Catholic for a specified period or task? Could that person agree to do so without denying catholicity *tout court*? Does catholicity not entail the claim that all of life, that the cosmos itself in all its richness and diversity, belongs comprehensively to God in Christ? Would the Catholic faith not lapse into complete incoherence were it allowed that there is even some tiny interstice which does not belong to God? To act deliberately as if one did not oneself, in this matter or that, belong to God in Jesus Christ – is that not the very essence of sin, from a Catholic perspective?

Catholics propose this faith to others, but they do not *impose* it on others. Their own pluralism is a pluralism open to the other *as* other. But they expect the same openness in return.[6] The trial judge grasped the nub of the problem. "In short," he observed, "the Minister wants that subject, ERC, to be taught in a lay manner [*de façon laïque*], whereas Loyola agrees to teach it but must teach it in a denominational manner [*de façon confessionnelle*] so that the school complies with the precepts of the Catholic religion that governs it and that it has applied since it was founded in 1848."[7] The Minister's posture he found surprising "in this era of respect for fundamental rights, tolerance, reasonable accommodation and multiculturalism."[8] It left Loyola in an untenable position, because the latter could not be true to its own mandate or identity without violating the law; and, for that, there could be no Charter justification, absent any dispute about the basic objectives of the program. Justice Dugré did not mince his words: "The obligation imposed on Loyola to teach the ERC course in a secular [*laïque*] manner is totalitarian in nature and essentially tantamount to the command given to Galileo by the Inquisition to abjure the cosmology of Copernicus."[9]

That might have been the end of it, though the case immediately attracted international attention. Unfortunately – such is the hold of normative pluralism and the consequent attentuation of respect for religious freedom – the justices of the Court of Appeal saw no problem at all, opining without explanation that the Minister's demand infringed only trivially on any claim to religious freedom. Catholics, after all, can think and teach like Catholics *part* of the day; why should they demand to do so *all* day? The Supreme Court, in its final disposition of *Loyola*, adopted a view much closer to that of the trial judge, but not without some hesitation, which deserves our scrutiny.

Chief Justice McLachlin and Justice Moldaver, writing the minority's concurring reasons for a unanimous decision in favour of Loyola, argue that the school's Catholic identity must be respected, not only in its teaching about Catholicism but in all its teaching.[10] Otherwise, "faced with a position that is fundamentally at odds with the Catholic faith, Loyola's teachers would be coerced into adopting a false and facile posture of neutrality" or indeed be rendered mute.[11] Moreover, they are critical of the fact that ERC "compels teachers to adopt a professional posture of strict neutrality, such that all points of view and all religious perspectives are presented as equally valid." They challenge the assumption that "if a religious perspective is offered, then all other viewpoints that do not conform to it will necessarily be derogated and disrespected." They recognize "subtle but important distinctions ... between the respectful treatment of differing viewpoints that Loyola proposes, and the strict neutrality required under the generic ERC Program."[12]

These distinctions are too subtle for the majority, however.[13] Justice Abella (writing for the latter) employs the adjectives "respectful" and "objective" and "neutral" almost as if they were synonyms, and sometimes seems to share the Minister's assumption that all three may serve as antonyms for "religious."[14] She is not unaware that (normative) pluralism can be overly authoritarian, but she is concerned lest religious claims trump "core national values" or escape "the context of a secular, multicultural and democratic society with a strong interest in protecting dignity and diversity, promoting equality, and ensuring the vitality of a common belief in human rights." For it is pluralism, not religion, that protects these values and fosters social peace.[15]

While Justice Abella acknowledges that it is both impractical and unjust to demand that Loyola teach about Catholicism or ethics from a neutral point of view, she does not think it either impractical or unjust that it be asked to teach about other religions neutrally.[16] Taking a page from Richard Moon, she even worries that "the alternative program that Loyola submitted to the Minister would teach other ethical frameworks primarily through the lens of Catholic ethics and morality," such that "other religions would necessarily be seen not as differently legitimate belief systems, but as worthy of respect only to the extent that they aligned with the tenets of Catholicism."[17] In Professor Moon's own words: "If religion is an aspect of the individual's identity, then when the state treats his or her religious practices or beliefs as *less important or less true* than the practices of others, or when it marginalizes her or his religious community in some way, it is not simply rejecting the individual's views and values, it is denying her or his equal worth."[18]

Justices McLachlin and Moldaver notice the difficulty here, which goes beyond the tendency to sublate Loyola's interests within those of the state. Their words are trenchant and worth quoting in full:

This position presents a false dichotomy ... Requiring a religious school to present the viewpoints of other religions as equally legitimate and equally credible is incompatible with religious freedom. *Indeed, presenting fundamentally incompatible religious doctrines as equally legitimate and equally credible could imply that they are both equally false.* Surely this cannot be a perspective that a religious school can be compelled to adopt. Loyola's teachers cannot be expected to teach ethics or religious doctrines that are contrary to the Catholic faith in a way that portrays them as equally credible or worthy of belief. Respect, tolerance, and understanding are all properly required, and the highlighting of differences must not give rise to denigration or derision. However, ensuring that all viewpoints are regarded as equally credible or worthy of belief would require a degree of disconnect from, and suppression of, Loyola's own religious perspective that is incompatible with freedom of religion.[19]

It needs only to be added that requiring *anyone* to adopt such a posture is to require of them an absurdity. The very suggestion that incompatible beliefs can be equally valuable and equally true is an absurdity. So is the notion that to deny the truth or value of what someone claims, whether about others or about themselves, is to deny their equal worth as a person. But it is to just such absurdities that normative pluralism leads – unless perchance it is from them that it comes.

Normative pluralism, as *Loyola* illustrates, leaves us in a quandary. We mean to be tolerant of diversity, if not to celebrate it. But how can tolerance tolerate, much less celebrate, intolerance? How and where shall a line be drawn, limiting diversity for the sake of diversity, limiting tolerance without appearing intolerant? That is our dilemma, or at all events the court's dilemma, and it is not fully resolved in *Loyola*. Boundaries there must be, but who can say where? Trump cards are necessary, but who will choose them? And if these questions cannot be answered, or if we cannot say exactly what our "core national values" are, or whence they arise, or what they imply about the world we live in, who will prevent our pluralism from degenerating into what Richard John Neuhaus once called "the monism of indifference"?[20]

Recall a much earlier case, *Ross v. New Brunswick School District No. 15*. In deciding that the School District was justified in removing Ross from the classroom for his anti-Semitism, the court remarks as follows: "Ours is a free society built upon a foundation of diversity of views; it is also a society that seeks to accommodate this diversity to the greatest extent possible. Such accommodation reflects an adherence to the principle of equality, valuing all divergent views equally and recognizing the contribution that a wide range of beliefs may make in the search for truth. However, to give protection to views that attack and condemn the views, beliefs and practices of others is to undermine the principle that all views deserve equal protection and muzzles the voice of truth."[21]

A closer look at this passage reveals the same underlying confusion. Indeed, it reveals a confusion of pluralisms. On the one hand, there is insistence upon a free society, with the understanding that listening to "a wide range of voices" is characteristic of a free society. There is also a recognition that such a society is engaged in "the search for truth" and that it is open to "the voice of truth." It seeks "the values proper to the human spirit," to import the conciliar expression. On the other hand, the court makes the very odd claim that our society is "built upon a foundation of diversity of views" – what sort of foundation could that be? – and the still odder claim that it values "all divergent views equally." Surely to value all divergent views equally is to value no view in particular.[22] To build on a foundation of diversity of views is to build on no foundation at all. It is, in Jesus' famous saying, to build on sand. The search for truth is abandoned. Tolerance becomes, or tries to become, all encompassing.[23]

So what is left with which to censure Mr Ross? Not so much his anti-*Semitism* as his *anti*-Semitism. Ross, we are told, has "attacked and condemned the views, beliefs and practices of others." There is therefore no place for him in a public classroom. But on this logic there would be no place either for Cicero, say, or for Moses for that matter. Ross's anti-Semitism is trumped by nothing more than the court's anti-anti-ism. This is not the kind of thinking that preserves the foundations on which the country is built. It is not a resolution to the dilemma. It is the self-defeating logic of infinite regress.

COMPETING VISIONS OF HUMAN DIGNITY

I do not mean to make too much of *Ross*, of which I have not offered a full account.[24] Or too little of *Loyola*, which legal scholars have yet to digest. I only mean to say that in both cases the court appears to be halting between two opinions of pluralism, or rather between two different types of pluralism: the one making the truth about human dignity the basis for generating the political conditions under which responsible freedom can flourish; the other making freedom and diversity (or, as Mill has it, freedom and "a variety of situations") the basis for generating the conditions under which human dignity can flourish.

Let me unpack that a little. For the former, human dignity is a divine gift, consisting in the love of God that enables man, as a uniquely rational and volitional animal, to pursue a vocation to happiness through participation in God. Proper recognition of human dignity requires a polis in which man is aided rather than impeded in this pursuit. And he is not aided, but rather impeded, where attempts are made either to compel his pursuit or to discourage it. The polis is properly pluralistic where the pursuit is encouraged but not regimented or (*per impossible*) enforced. Hence the distancing at Vatican II from some political or legal practices once common in Christendom. Hence also, of course, the resistance to political systems or religious communities in which compulsion is prominent.

For the latter, however, human dignity is self-grounded, and the human vocation also. It is not denied that all men seek happiness, but happiness (being strictly individual) remains indeterminate.

Likewise dignity, which is detached from objective reference points and rendered largely subjective, is a matter of feeling. As the court itself puts it in *Carter*, "an individual's *response* ... is a matter critical to their dignity and autonomy."[25] The concept of rights has followed a similar trajectory, as it must, if rights are grounded in dignity. So has the philosophy of education, which comes to the fore in *Loyola*, and much else that concerns the law.

Here the relation between dignity and freedom is reversed. Instead of freedom deriving (as Anselm taught) from our simultaneous ordering to happiness and to justice,[26] which ordering is our dignity, freedom becomes (as Mill taught) a precondition for our self-directed pursuit of happiness. Freedom means as little restraint to the spontaneous exercise of free choice as possible, and requires only opportunity or a variety of situations – in a word, pluralism – as its positive counterpart. And from freedom flows the possibility of self-realization, hence of dignity.[27]

This reversal began, not in the eighteenth century, but in the tenth or eleventh; that is, with the advent of nominalism.[28] It gained much ground in the thirteenth and fourteenth, when Ockham taught us to think of free will in terms of the freedom of indifference: that is, to think that the will is free even before it engages the intellect, free before it stands at the intersection created by the pursuit of happiness (which is man's highest end) and the pressing question of justice *in* that pursuit; to think that the will is free absolutely, simply as the power of choice and without reference to what is being chosen or even to what the will is for.[29]

In this way of thinking, liberty, like free will, is essentially a negative concept. Whether individual or corporate, it is freedom *from* rather than freedom *for*. Liberty is simply the absence of constraint. As such it is detached from any positive claim respecting happiness, which itself is reduced to a feeling – an elusive and indefinable and, in any case, incommunicable feeling. As for justice, it is reconceived as an attempt to protect liberty, so understood. It is merely the weighing against each other of the constraints on individual freedom of choice that life (more specifically, life in society) inevitably produces.

This is the line of thought extended recently by Rawls, with his reduction of justice to fairness and his eschewal, for public purposes, of any comprehensive doctrine, even that of liberalism. Rawls makes a virtue out of necessity, we might say, for not surprisingly we have experienced a loss of common vision, of shared hope, of rational consensus on matters of substance. The crumbling of the foundations has created deep fissures in the life of the polis. And what have we done in response? Nothing more than some political bootstrapping. We have tried to make plurality itself the very basis of unity. Which cannot be done.

The outcome, in fact, can only be a political monism averse both to the voice of truth and to the voice of those who dissent for the sake of truth; averse indeed to authentic cultural diversity. The guiding mantra, to be sure, is "diversity not an evil, but a good."[30] Yet those who adopt this mantra are working to Mill's equation: freedom plus diversity equals spontaneous development, or individual and social progress. And their faith in that equation is such that they are quite ready to force dissenters to embrace diversity, just as Rousseau would force them to be free. What normative pluralism comes to mean in practice, then, is that those of Catholic faith, or those who for some other reason do not admit the new norming norm, are subject to economic, political, and even legal disenfranchisement.

Thus, for example, does Professor Leroux speak happily of the state becoming the *seul acteur* and indeed the "sole owner" in education.[31] Thus does the ERC program forbid the use of local priests, rabbis, imams, etc., in its classrooms. Thus are statutes set in place requiring GSAS (gay-straight alliances) in every school, or policies requiring instruction of children, even very young children, in forms of sexual activity their parents (whose resistance is often crushed by collusion between radical activists and state authorities) deem dangerously disordered. Meanwhile, pro-life clubs are prohibited. And it does not stop there; that is, with hegemony over the formation of the next generation. Medical staff are trained in procedures that violate their beliefs and convictions, and disciplined or fired for refusing to be complicit in processes they regard as immoral, even in practices they deem murderous.[32] Of doctors it is demanded that they either abort or refer for abortion, euthanize, or refer for euthanasia,[33] and of pharmacists that they dispense drugs injurious or fatal to life. Civil servants fare little better, as freedom of conscience comes under attack along with freedom of religion.[34] Even clergy are no longer exempt from pressure to yield up to state authorities that which cannot be yielded, the sanctity of the confessional or the integrity of holy matrimony.[35] The pluralism that tries to make diversity the ground of unity, the normative pluralism that insists that all views be valued equally, produces in the end only a false and oppressive unity – conformity by compulsion.

THE DOCTRINE OF DOUBLE TRUTH

How does this happen? First, the relation between dignity and freedom is reversed, as we have seen. But, second, truth is divided. It is not just that entirely discrete moral or religious claims are set alongside each other, without need of adjudication or hope of reconciliation. More than that, or rather because of that, a barrier is set up between private and public truth – not unlike the barrier set up long ago, in thirteenth-century Paris, between theological and philosophical truth – as if truth itself had no unity!

The Paris episode is worth recalling. Aristotle, that intrepid architect of one discipline after another, was at the centre of it. Much of his work, which had gone missing during the collapse of the Western empire, had now been recovered.[36] It was being enthusiastically devoured in the new universities of Latin Christendom, where he was widely admired as *the* philosopher, together with the work of Averroes, who was regarded as his greatest commentator. In Paris, the Faculty of Arts had begun establishing its independence from the Faculty of Theology, and by AD 1260 was teaching Aristotle as the basis of its curriculum. But Aristotle, not surprisingly, had ideas about the world that didn't fit with Christian ideas. So, of course, did the eccentrically Islamic Averroes. Some philosophy professors followed an Averroean line of thought into several positions contrary to Christian faith. For example, they taught the eternity of the world and the notion that there was a single world soul (the doctrine of monopsychism); they effectively denied free will and the Christian doctrine of divine providence. These teachings, along with a good many others emanating from both faculties, were condemned by the bishop of Paris in 1277.

Bishop Etienne Tempier was undoubtedly heavy-handed. He was concerned, however, not only with the particular points in dispute, but also with the epistemological implications of trying to hold both to Christian faith and to Aristotle on points where they were incompatible. These professors seemed to be advocating a doctrine of double truth; that is, to be saying that some things "are true according to philosophy but not according to the Catholic faith, 'as if there were two contrary truths.'"[37] To take such an approach was to put the whole notion of a *universitas* in jeopardy; it was neither Aristotelian nor Christian to deny the unity of truth and of knowledge. A university was a society of scholars united in the pursuit of truth, and commitment to the unity of truth was as essential to the university as to the Church herself.

Perhaps no one at the time really held this "doctrine of double truth" to which the bishop objected. What, after all, could be less Aristotelian than to defy the law of non-contradiction, or even to skirt it by pretending that truth could be divided neatly into hermetically sealed spheres? What could be less Catholic than to assert that truth itself is not *kata holon* – that there is no unity or wholeness to truth? But whatever the case then, today it seems that some people do hold such a doctrine, that they really do think that truth can be divided.

Justin Trudeau, for one, recently declared that the truth taught him by the Catholic Church via his father is one thing and the truth to which he and his caucus colleagues must adhere is another. Here is Trudeau *fils*, as reported in various interviews, brandishing the Liberal Party flag at the barricade between public and private truth in defence of abortion: "I had an extraordinary example in a father who had deeply, deeply held personal views that were informed by the fact that he went to church every Sunday, read the Bible regularly to us, and raised us very religious, very Catholic ... He held his personal views very, very strongly. But he understood that as leaders, as political figures, as representatives of a larger community, our utmost responsibility is to stand up for people's rights."[38] "The policy going forward is that every single Liberal MP will be expected to stand up for women's rights to choose."[39] "That doesn't impact or prevent someone from holding personal views – religious views – but it does mean that with our votes the Liberal party protects women's rights."[40]

And here is Trudeau *père*, commenting on the same issue some forty years earlier: "You know, at some point you are killing life in the foetus in self-defence – of what? Of the mother's health or her happiness or of her social rights or her privilege as a human being? I think she should have to answer for it and explain. Now, whether it should be to three doctors or one doctor or to a priest or a bishop or to her mother-in-law is a question you might want to argue ...

You do have a right over your own body – it is your body. But the foetus is not your body; it's someone else's body. And if you kill it, you'll have to explain."[41]

It will not do, of course, to mistake Pierre Trudeau's view for that of the Church. One does not explain that which is intrinsically evil; rather, one repents of it. And where the evil in question is killing the innocent, civil law, like natural and divine law, must forbid it. But what are we to make of Justin's notion that something can be fundamentally wrong according to sound religion and fundamentally right according to sound politics? We can draw but one of two conclusions. Either truth is indeed a house divided against itself, or else the realm of religion – of "deeply held personal views"[42] – is not really the realm of truth or rationality at all.[43]

The result again is repression. A more sensible man, Rex Murphy, put his finger on the problem that immediately arises for those who neither subscribe to a two-truths theory nor accept the bracketing of religion with the irrational: they are excluded from public life.

> What kind of politics are they which require an MP to renounce his deepest moral commitments; indeed, to go beyond renunciation and declare himself positively in favour of ideas and actions that his faith condemns, his Church forbids, and his conscience cannot abide? Religion, under these conditions, cannot survive political engagement. An understanding of politics based on an exclusion of thoughtful and engaged religious people – on the rejection of ideas and understandings offered by the great religious teachers and the massive legacy of thought our churches have to offer – is radically incomplete. As things now are, a truly religious person must actually stay out of politics – must forgo an active role in democratic government – because in our brazen and new age, he or she will be faced with irreconcilable moral choices. If elected, he or she will be required to betray their faith and themselves, and on those very issues that matter most: issues of life, family, autonomy and the dignity of persons.[44]

That is the effect of the doctrine of double truth as we encounter it today.

I will grant Justin Trudeau this, however: that he does not seem to be proposing that truth be divided within the sphere of politics, such that contraries are affirmed and a vain attempt made to value all views equally. He knows, or thinks he knows, what is right and what qualifies as a right. He knows, or thinks he knows, that there is a moral as well as a legal right to kill one's baby – a right it would be wrong for the state not to defend. He is confident enough of that, that he is not prepared to tolerate any diversity on the subject within his own party. Nor is he prepared to allow that people who say otherwise might be right. He is not for "a variety of truths" in the public sphere. But whether one says that all views must be valued equally (except, of course, the view that all views should *not* be valued equally) or whether one simply brackets out religious and moral teaching whenever it contradicts one's preferred view, the consequence is the same. Truth is divided; falsehood prevails. And not only falsehood, but oppression. Why oppression? Because people are indeed required to betray the truth, and to betray it at the very points where it matters most.[45]

THE EMACIATION OF PUBLIC REASON

So truth is divided and conquered: there is one kind of truth for the private sphere and another for the public sphere. That is the second step on the path by which pluralism becomes a form of oppression. But there is a further step, which is the misconstrual of the public sphere as such. The public sphere is viewed as a realm detached, not merely from religious and moral tradition, but from tradition generally. It becomes the realm of common process, but not of common good. It wastes away under a progressively thinner form of public reason.

This happens wherever reason is regarded as "public" only insofar as it can be detached from the traditions that define the particular communities that actually constitute civil society.[46] For this suppresses awareness of the plurality of perspectives that contribute to the search for a common good, and also sets the public sphere, as something primarily procedural or bureaucratic, at odds with the traditional – at odds, that is, with the practice of reverence for the established results of that search and for the authorities that have guided it.[47]

In reality, of course, this procedural republic (to use Sandel's label[48]), which is meant to be neutral and to "value all divergent views equally," regularly takes sides when disputes arise, as indeed it must. And the side it takes is usually that of liberal modernity, which imagines the individual in Romantic terms as someone needing the state to liberate him or her from other individuals and especially from traditional communities and their habits. Recall Mill's own advice:

> As it is useful that while mankind are imperfect there should be different opinions, so is it that there should be different experiments of living; that free scope should be given to varieties of character, short of injury to others; and that the worth of different modes of life should be proved practically, when any one thinks fit to try them. It is desirable, in short, that in things which do not primarily concern others, individuality should assert itself. Where, not the person's own character, but the traditions or customs of other people are the rule of conduct, there is wanting one of the principal ingredients of human happiness, and quite the chief ingredient of individual and social progress ... [S]ociety has now fairly got the better of individuality; and the danger which threatens human nature is not the excess, but the deficiency, of personal impulses and preferences.[49]

Working with this conception of the individual and with this prejudice against society, the state steadily accrues to itself functions that once belonged to social institutions. It adopts, at the urging of its "liberal" elite, a subjectivist approach to rights, in which the dignity of the person and "the values proper to the human spirit" are understood along nominalist and Romantic rather than Judeo-Christian lines. It then deploys the legal and political means at its disposal to refashion us in just that image. Ironically, liberty itself is the main casualty. "Responsible freedom ... motivated by a sense of duty" loses its meaning, or comes to mean only that one is obliged (a) not to interfere with one's neighbour and (b) to be subject to the state and to the state alone. No greater vision, and no greater good, informs either freedom or duty. The traditional communities whose beliefs and whose labours actually did build the country are marginalized, if not deliberately deconstructed.

Whether this is done in the name of liberalism or of secularism or of normative pluralism or even of multiculturalism hardly matters. What we are witnessing, as I said, is the emergence of a kind of inverse catholicism on the political level: not a common hope or a commonwealth of which local communities are particular and unique

expressions, but merely a common abstraction, a collective empti-
ness, that sucks the life out of local communities, which increasingly
are constrained to act on judgments about human flourishing that
are not their own.[50]

Meanwhile, some hardier souls seek a deeper and more authentic
pluralism, one that faces up to the fact that the citizen of any state
knows multiple allegiances and acknowledges diverse sources of
authority. They ask a certain modesty of the state so that actual communities and their traditions may flourish. Some (such as my law
colleague, Victor Muñiz-Fraticelli) try valiantly to mount "a defence
of the autonomy of associations and of the institutions necessary for
that autonomy to flourish" and to flesh out a theory of private law
that can function within a broader constitutional frame of reference.[51] This counter-movement may be welcomed, since it is pluralism of the (quite traditional) type "that 'refuses to limit the domain
of law to the law of the state' and that refuses to regard non-state
'authority' as existing and exercised only by state concession."[52] It is
unclear, however, just what authority and autonomy are, and how
they are related.[53] It is unclear how the state itself derives its own
authority, and how far it can or will cede authority to associations.[54]
Moreover, the moral or value pluralism that is presupposed here
remains problematic, as does the tendency to legal positivism. What,
if any, is the role of natural law in deep pluralism? Can the real problems it seeks to address actually be addressed where the question of
natural law and of moral validity is bracketed?[55]

This movement should not be mistaken for Catholic pluralism,
though it overlaps it at certain points. What it serves to highlight
is the unresolved dispute in the Rawlsian camp between comprehensive liberalism and political liberalism. Deep pluralism certainly
inclines to the latter, or rather it extends and seeks to entrench the
latter, but at the expense of the commitment to the unity of truth still
(defectively) at work in the former. It must also be observed that
ever-expanding webs of dependency, generated by urbanization and
technological advances, are overwhelming us economically, politically, culturally, and even biologically, and that all this works both for
and against autonomy, whether individual or institutional. Private
law will work only where private economies also function. For this
reason, too, I am not at all confident that deep pluralism is viable, or
that it is capable of being given a Christian baptism.

❧ RECOVERING CATHOLIC PLURALISM

The relation between dignity and freedom reversed; truth divided and indeed multiplied; public reason truncated to exclude tradition and traditional truth-claims: all of this leads to oppression because it refuses to allow for the truth of truth. We seek a unity based on diversity, a foundation of diversity of views. We call it pluralism, and we make of it a kind of civil religion, a comprehensive piety for everyone, to overcome the (putative) divisiveness of all other pieties. But this normative pluralism is no proper substitute for Catholic pluralism, and it affords – so we are beginning to discover – no real freedom.

Is it possible, then, to recover the vision of *Dignitatis*? Only if we are prepared to go back behind that document, rediscovering the tradition to which it belongs, as we have tried to do here with the tradition to which normative pluralism belongs. For, contrary to popular opinion, *Dignitatis* is not a brand-new departure. It represents only an adjustment to the trajectory of Catholic political thought.[56] It belongs to a series of responses that the magisterium has felt itself compelled to make to the changing conditions of modernity.

One of those responses came in 1888, when, some thirty years after Mill's famous work on the subject, Leo XIII issued his encyclical, *Libertas praestantissimum*. Its opening gambit was to identify liberty as "the highest of natural endowments" belonging to rational creatures, hence as the one that requires the most care. Leo went on to challenge the *faux* liberalism rooted in nominalism and rationalism, and especially that "worst kind of liberalism" in which is "cast off all obedience to [God] in public matters, or even in private and domestic affairs."[57] Authentic liberty, he insisted, "stands in need of light and strength to direct its actions to good and to restrain them from evil. Without this, the freedom of our will would be our ruin."[58] It requires the light of revelation as well, so that it may aspire to its highest end; that is, to God. Otherwise the human will, in its fallen condition, detaches itself from reason and corrupts the very essence of freedom. Good and evil, honour and dishonour, soon differ "not in their nature, but in the opinion and judgment of each one." Pleasure now becomes "the measure of what is lawful."[59] Truth and goodness become subject to majority vote. An unnatural chasm opens up between reason and religion, then between private and public reason. "And as to tolerance," observes Leo, "it is surprising how far removed from the equity and prudence of the Church are those who profess what is called liberalism. For, in allowing that boundless license of which We have spoken, they exceed all limits, and end at last by making no apparent distinction between truth and error, honesty and dishonesty."[60]

This analysis is accurate and describes all too well our situation today. Leo, like other modern popes, read well the trajectory that leads to normative pluralism and its relativist bedfellows. Though he was not familiar with such labels, he grasped the principles and forces in play. Likewise, he understood the trajectory that leads to the kind of freedom that we (ought to) desire, the freedom *Dignitatis* speaks of, that "responsible freedom, not driven by coercion but motivated by a sense of duty" and by "the values proper to the human spirit." These alternatives are starkly summarized by Leo at the outset: "Man, indeed, is free to obey his reason, to seek moral good, and to strive unswervingly after his last end. Yet he is free also to turn aside to all other things; and, in pursuing the empty semblance of good, to disturb rightful order and to fall headlong into the destruction which he has voluntarily chosen."

But what about us? Do we even grasp the fact that there are two trajectories to trace, rather than just one? The opening paragraph of *Dignitatis* falls, we might say, at the point on the graph where these two trajectories intersect. And this is confusing to some, particularly to those who remain unfamiliar with the exposition to be found in *Gaudium et spes*, or who fail to recognize there also – for that whole document shines a spotlight at precisely the same point – the convergence and divergence of trajectories.[61] That there *is* such a convergence and divergence is the message of the cross and resurrection of Jesus Christ, the very source of our joy and hope. To deny that there are two trajectories is to set the cross at nought and to rob the resurrection and ascension of their meaning. In *Gaudium*'s own words, "earthly progress must be carefully distinguished from the growth of Christ's kingdom," for the kingdom is present only in a mystery.[62]

If we really mean to recover the trajectory on which lies that other and very different kind of pluralism proffered in *Dignitatis*,[63] we will have to identify, then, not only what can be affirmed in the aspirations and self-perception of modern man but also what must be rejected. In the present context this means at least three things. First, we must offer a potent and relentless critique of our society's habitual evasion of truth. What we need to point out to our fellow citizens, taking a page from Leo, is that man is not and cannot be philosophically or theologically neutral. Neither then can politics, if politics means to be human. There is no presuppositionless political sphere, no sphere in which nothing is directly implied about the nature of God or of man. There is no polis that has no determinate loves, that makes no commitments, that renders no firm judgment of good and evil, that has no God or gods.

We can speak with Rawls of a public reason based on reciprocation and tolerance and respect for basic rights, but we cannot speak of it as a self-standing form, that from itself and by itself serves as the very criterion of reasonableness. We cannot speak of shared public reasons that can be given strictly "in terms of political conceptions of justice," as if the latter were quite detachable from other and higher conceptions of justice.[64] Nor can we speak of an overlapping consensus, one that eliminates certain comprehensive doctrines but not others, without pressing the question as to how this consensus has arisen and how it is to be maintained, and whether its core principles suffice for handling the difficult disagreements that must in fact be handled.

Rawls recognized that abortion is among these, but his comments on that subject betray the fact that he never really faced up to the limits of his theory, and indeed to its inadequacy. The abortion issue forces us to say who is included in our reciprocity, and who is not. It also forces us to reckon with the fact that we cannot order political values without ordering our ends, which is the very business of comprehensive world views. It forces us, as well, to consider the problem of complicity that necessarily arises with our reciprocal obligations. Rawls hints that justice in the matter means leaving some free to say they will abort so long as others are free to say they won't. But abortion requires public organization and approval. It requires medical training and facilities and money. It involves both the willing and the unwilling – the fetus, of course, is unwilling, but so are many others who perforce are involved. Abortion is a bloody token of our collective evasion of truth.[65]

Second, we must offer a reminder that it is impossible to love freedom without loving truth. The task today, as all the recent popes have emphasized, is to reconnect truth and freedom. And to reconnect both with happiness. For happiness is a, nay, *the* political subject. To cultivate a new conversation about human happiness is our task, our public and not merely our private task.

This means that we must aim to break the nominalist/secularist/ pluralist stranglehold on public discourse and political reason. We can only do that by speaking boldly of things our interlocutors may not be used to hearing: that is, by deliberately transgressing what Charles Taylor calls the immanent frame. It is altogether a mistake, on my view, to concede that frame or to be restricted by its false premises.[66] We do not concede it if we insist on talking about freedom only in the context of truth and of happiness.

Who will deny that all men seek happiness? What need have we of liberty, if not to pursue happiness? Yet in the nominalist era the pursuit of happiness has become problematic for political reason, making political reason itself problematic. Only the individual, we suppose, can say what happiness is or what its pursuit entails; hence the organization of society must be such as to allow, as far as possible, for personal experimentation with happiness. But the very notion of happiness, since it is now empty of content and tethered to nothing in particular, ceases to do any positive work.[67] It cannot order in any coherent fashion the particular goods that people band together in society to seek. This it could do only if it were itself a comprehensive good, or if it were allied to a comprehensive good. But to appeal to a comprehensive good is forbidden to political reason, as an assault on individual freedom and on the political order that exists chiefly to protect that freedom.[68]

Mill claims (and Rawls does not demur) that the only freedom that deserves the name is that of pursuing our own good in our own way, so long as we do not harm others. This is false. Why should we not say, rather, that the only freedom worthy of the name is that of pursuing our own good, and the other's good, in a way worthy of God – for who is free if not God? Why should we not say that liberty not in its right relation to happiness is not liberty, and that there is no other source of happiness than God himself?[69] These things are true, and we must not be afraid to say them, whether to the government, the guilds, the media, or even the courts.

But of course we must say something else as well – something I sometimes wonder whether we still know how to say. *Anyone* ought to be able to say, and should say, what has just been said. One need not be a Christian to say such things, though Christians may have said them better than anyone else.[70] But if we are Christians then we must say, in addition to all of this, that God has clarified the path to happiness and so clarified politics itself. We must say what we know in light of the resurrection and ascension of Jesus. We must say that Jesus is Lord, and that his dominion extends from sea to sea. His kingdom, to be sure, is not of this world, but his rule extends over this world. By divine justice he has acceded to power. He has been given true *auctoritas* and all judgment has been delivered into his hands.

This only Christians can say with conviction. They are not Christians if they do not say it and believe it, hoping that others will come to believe it as well. It is not only over Christians that Christ rules. It is not only on Christians that Christ shall pass judgment. We are only playing at politics, or for that matter at political philosophy – worse, we are only playing at being Christians – if we do not, with prudence and fortitude in equal measure, make this clear. "You are the light of the world. A city set on a hill cannot be hidden."[71]

Am I now repudiating Catholic pluralism along with normative pluralism? By no means. Catholic pluralism does not teach that secular politics and secular government have no obligation to Christ, any more than it teaches that citizens at large have no obligation to Christ. It only teaches that secular government, whether Christian in inspiration or not, has an obligation to aid, and not to impede or to force, its citizens in their pursuit of their proper vocation, and in particular not to impede the Church in its attempt to instruct them on that subject. It teaches the kind of modesty congruent with liberty, and the kind of liberty congruent with truth. It asks for opportunity to make its own message heard and for room for its own communities to thrive, and therefore it leaves room for others to be heard and to thrive as well. It is not, however, so foolish as to propose that all messages or manners of life or forms of religion are to be valued equally, and it does not deny the lordship of Christ.[72]

Now it will be said that this kind of pluralism was ruled out thirty years ago in *R. v. Big M Drug Mart*, which effectively forbade laws favouring any particular religion or religious aim.[73] *Big M* opened the door to the advance of normative pluralism through Charter jurisprudence, while also setting us on the path toward one of the most ridiculous and most dangerous of all putative rights – the right not to be offended.[74] It did so on the basis of faulty reasoning respecting both the *Lord's Day Act* and section 2 of the Charter, amply exposed by analysts such as Professor Waldron.[75] The court's confusion of a provision for religious practice with actual religious compulsion, hence with a violation of religious freedom, served to give freedom from religion – particularly from Christianity as the majority religion – the upper hand on freedom of and for religion.

Catholic pluralism cannot prevail over normative pluralism without correction of the *Big M* trajectory.[76] It cannot prevail without overcoming the notion that a law is invalidated by reason of a religious purpose. It cannot prevail without rediscovery of an *analogia iuris* that keeps positive law in touch with natural law. It cannot prevail without recovering the essential connection between the supremacy of God and the rule of law.[77] Arguably, it cannot prevail without making clear that the "Confederation compromise," which permits religious schools their place in public education, is not the exception that proves the secularist rule, but fundamental to the fabric of Canadian life.[78] Toward all of that – yes, toward a very different understanding of the separation of church and state, and of the relation between religious freedom and the state's own religious commitments – Christian jurists and philosophers and educators must labour, however difficult the circumstances in which they labour.[79] But resistance to normative pluralism requires a still more dedicated effort.

Truth be told, what Loyola did, in resisting the Ministry all the way to the Supreme Court, is anything but typical of Catholic schools and their constituencies. Loyola took seriously, not a thirty-year legal tradition in Charter jurisprudence, but something Leo said a hundred and thirty years ago in *Affari vos*, in response to the Manitoba schools controversy. It took seriously the right and responsibility to provide children with a genuinely Catholic education. That is the third thing we must do; and we must do it, insists Leo, as a matter of the utmost importance:

> For our children cannot go for instruction to schools which either ignore or of set purpose combat the Catholic religion, or in which its teachings are despised and its fundamental principles repudiated. Wherever the Church has allowed this to be done, it has only been with pain and through necessity, at the same time surrounding her children with many safeguards which, nevertheless … have been insufficient to cope successfully with the danger attending it. Similarly it is necessary to avoid at all costs, as most dangerous, those schools in which all beliefs are welcomed and treated as equal, as if, in what regards God and divine

things, it makes no difference whether one believes rightly
or wrongly, and takes up with truth or error. You know well,
Venerable Brethren, that every school of this kind has been condemned by the Church, because nothing can be more harmful
or better calculated to ruin the integrity of the faith and to turn
aside the tender minds of the young from the way of truth.[80]

Canadian Catholics, if I dare say so, have been rather careless
about all this in the intervening century. We have not properly protected children from predators within our own schools – I mean
both the physically and the ideologically abusive – and much of our
leadership remains supine in the face of ever-bolder subversion of
Catholic mores.[81] We have developed a habit of compliance with the
government, the courts, the guilds, and the wider culture in the general shape and character of the education we offer, even where that
habit threatens our own communal identity. On the whole, we are
no longer producing a distinctive result, to judge by the 2012 Cardus
Education Survey.[82] Meanwhile, the very education rights of which
Leo speaks are in grave danger; family and parental rights likewise,
as the Drummondville case showed.[83] Thankfully, the Supreme
Court restored some of those rights in *Loyola*, insisting (in the words
of its minority) that "suppression of Loyola's own religious perspective ... is incompatible with freedom of religion."[84] But the future of
freedom for Catholics, and for our non-Catholic neighbours too,
will depend more on whether we are prepared – *at all costs!* – to
provide the next generation with a properly Catholic education than
on anything decided in Ottawa.[85]

4

Does It Still Make Sense to Speak of Religious Freedom?

Few of the real problems today are susceptible of solution, or even of statement, in legal language.

John Courtney Murray

The late Robert Bellah, writing in *First Things* just before his death, indicated his belief that all the freedoms required by civil society are "extrapolations from that one central freedom, the freedom of reli-. gion."[1] This belief, despite its honourable pedigree, is not universal. Great turmoil surrounds the subject today. Some express doubts about the transparency of the term "religious freedom" and its suitability for anything other than a sort of neocolonial secularist project. Others contend that there is no good reason "to single out religion for anything like the special treatment it is accorded in existing Western legal systems."[2] They deny that religion is "a constitutional anomaly" or even "a category of human experience" warranting privileged or peculiar attention.[3]

Stephen Douglas Smith, taking the long view, argues that "the Western tradition of discourse about church-state separation and freedom of conscience, which began a millennium ago, has reached a point of exhaustion." Neither freedom of religion nor freedom of conscience has any very obvious place in an era that has abandoned any framing of itself in terms of the transcendent or the eschatological and opted instead for a secularist approach. Smith thinks that "the much noted incoherence in the modern jurisprudence of religious freedom is a product of this drastically altered situation."[4] The language of religious freedom is fading into the twilight as a political and jurisprudential reference point.[5]

Already in 1960, in *We hold these truths*, John Courtney Murray, the prominent American Jesuit who became one of the main architects of Vatican II's declaration on religious freedom, *Dignitatis humanae*, expressed doubts about the future of religious freedom. To understand his doubts, it is necessary to peer back into the era that Smith says is fading from view. For the roots of religious freedom run very deep into that era – far deeper than Bellah, who seems to think the discourse a product of the eighteenth century, lets on.[6]

Herewith, then, a potted history, for which I will doubtless be accused in certain quarters of anachronism, perhaps even of "neo-medievalism" or "misplaced nostalgia" for a time when pluralism was not. That worries me not at all. Such charges, as far as I can tell, serve only to distinguish between those who suppose the church, which is at the centre of this history, to be something truly unique and those who suppose it to be nothing very remarkable.[7]

THE RISE AND FALL OF RELIGIOUS FREEDOM

Freedom of religion or, less robustly, tolerance of minority practices with respect to religion is always a matter of degree. It is not, nor can it be, an absolute freedom – what merely human freedom ever is? – but is always subject to what *Dignitatis humanae* refers to as "the limits set by due public order."[8] Thus, for example, did Roman imperial authority distinguish between acceptable religion (*religio*) and unacceptable religion (*superstitio*). These categories delineated what was considered compatible with the common good, meaning the imperial good, from what was not.

Christianity, for three centuries, was regarded as a *superstitio* and at times cruelly suppressed. But Christians were taught by their religion to regard their sufferings with disdain. Listen to Athanasius in *De incarnatione*:

> For that death is destroyed, and that the Cross is become the victory over it, and that it has no more power but is verily dead, this is no small proof, or rather an evident warrant, that it is despised by all Christ's disciples ... [N]ow that the Saviour has raised His body, death is no longer terrible; for all who believe in Christ tread it under as nought, and choose rather to die than to deny their faith in Christ ... For as when a tyrant has been defeated by a real king, and bound hand and foot, then all that

pass by laugh him to scorn, buffeting and reviling him, no longer
fearing his fury and barbarity, because of the king who has
conquered him; so also, death having been conquered and
exposed by the Saviour on the Cross, and bound hand and foot,
all they who are in Christ, as they pass by, trample on him, and
witnessing to Christ scoff at death, jesting at him, and saying
what has been written against him of old: "O death, where is thy
victory? O grave, where is thy sting?"[9]

Of course there are rhetorical liberties here. But how shall we describe
the concession of Galerius, who in A D 3 1 1 granted Christians a certain freedom of religion, if not as the victory of the martyrs? "Finally
when our law had been promulgated to the effect that they should
conform to the institutes of antiquity, many were subdued by the
fear of danger, many even suffered death. And yet since most of them
persevered in their determination ... we thought that we ought to
grant our most prompt indulgence also to these, so that they may
again be Christians and may hold their conventicles, provided they
do nothing contrary to good order."[10]
This was followed two years later by the so-called edict of
Constantine and Licinius, who, "after considering everything that
pertained to the public welfare and security," decided (they tell us) to
"grant to the Christians and others full authority to observe that
religion which each preferred; whence any Divinity whatsoever in the
seat of the heavens may be propitious and kindly disposed to us and
all who are placed under our rule." They continue: "By this whole-
some counsel and most upright provision, we thought to arrange that
no one whatsoever should be denied the opportunity to give his heart
to the observance of the Christian religion, [or] of that religion which
he should think best for himself, so that the Supreme Deity (to whose
worship we freely yield our hearts) may show in all things His usual
favor and benevolence. Therefore ... it has pleased us to remove all
conditions whatsoever ... concerning the Christians and now any one
of these who wishes to observe Christian religion may do so freely
and openly, without molestation."[11] Thus was freedom of religion, in
a more principled sense, introduced into Western civilization.
We need not deny that the advent of Christendom brought renewed restrictions to religion, some quite draconian, nor conduct
here an argument as to which of them were justified. We do need to
recall that the next millennium and a half witnessed a prolonged and

profoundly important struggle between church and state over the question of the freedom of the former, a struggle centred on (but not confined to) the lay investiture question. It was, in fact, through the struggle of the church to be free *in Christendom* that the delicate flower, freedom of religion, came to bloom.[12]

Separation of church and state – preventing the church from becoming just another imperial or, later, national cult – was the centuries-long task that brought freedom of religion into play, not as a pragmatic political strategy, *per* Galerius or Constantine, but as a matter of theological principle and, only so, as a hard-won (but never secure) political principle. From Ambrose's struggle with Gratian in the fourth century through to the days of Leo XIII, the *libertas ecclesiae* had to be asserted and defended in high places, against Christianity's friends as well as its enemies. So did the *auctoritas ecclesiae*, pithily expressed in Pope Gelasius' admonition (AD 494) to Anastasius I: "*Two* there are, august Emperor, by which this world is ruled on title of original and sovereign right – the consecrated authority of the priesthood and the royal power."[13]

"On any showing, even merely historical," writes Murray, "we are here in the presence of a Great Idea, whose entrance into history marked the beginning of a new civilizational era." The liberty of the church, "though not a freedom of the political order, was Christianity's basic contribution to freedom in the political order."[14] As Murray notes, the positive freedom of the church, as a spiritual authority entrusted by God with the *cura animarum* during the present age, "has a negative aspect: the immunity of the Church, as the suprapolitical sacredness (*res sacra*), from all manner of politicization, through subordination to the state or enclosure within the state as *instrumentum regni*."[15]

Not only that, but the life of man, as ordered through the church to a higher, eternal reality, is itself invested with a new sacredness and a corresponding immunity from politicization.[16] "The chief example is the institution of the family," in which context freedom of education may also be mentioned, as it is in *Dignitatis humanae:*

> The family, since it is a society in its own original right, has the right freely to live its own domestic religious life under the guidance of parents. Parents, moreover, have the right to determine, in accordance with their own religious beliefs, the kind of religious education that their children are to receive. Government,

in consequence, must acknowledge the right of parents to make a genuinely free choice of schools and of other means of education, and the use of this freedom of choice is not to be made a reason for imposing unjust burdens on parents, whether directly or indirectly. Besides, the rights of parents are violated, if their children are forced to attend lessons or instructions which are not in agreement with their religious beliefs, or if a single system of education, from which all religious formation is excluded, is imposed upon all.[17]

What is more, the freedom of the church "furnished the ultimate directive principle of government." For the church stood "between the body politic and the public power, not only limiting the reach of the power over the people, but also mobilizing the moral consensus of the people and bringing it to bear upon the power, thus to insure that the king, in the fine phrase of John of Salisbury, would 'fight for justice and for the freedom of the people.'"[18]

Now, according to Murray, "the whole equilibrium of social forces which under the guidance of this theory made (however imperfectly) for freedom and justice within society was destroyed by the rise of the national monarchies and by the course of their political evolution in the era of royal absolutism." It fell to subsequent political theorists to provide an alternative, to re-establish the equilibrium.[19] "The process was simple. The early Christian dualism of Church and state ... was in a sense retained. That is, it endured in a secular political form, namely, in the distinction between state and society which had been the secular political outgrowth of the Christian distinction between Church and state. However, the freedom of the Church, again in its pregnant sense, was discarded as the mediating principle between society and state, between the people and the public power. Instead, a secular substitute was adopted in the form of free political institutions. Through these secular institutions the people would limit the power of government. They would also direct the power of government to its proper ends, which are perennially those of John of Salisbury – the fight for justice and for the freedom of the people."[20]

The new political edifice, continues Murray, was built around freedom of the conscience, on which was placed a weight such as it had never before been asked to bear. "Here precisely lies the newness of the modern experiment. A great act of trust was made. The trust was that the free individual conscience would effectively mediate the moral imperatives of the transcendental order of justice (whose existence was not doubted in the earlier phases of the modern experiment). Then, through the workings of free political institutions these imperatives would be transmitted to the public power as binding norms upon its action. The only sovereign spiritual authority would be the conscience of the free man. The freedom of the individual conscience, constitutionally guaranteed, would supply the armature of immunity to the sacred order, which now became, by modern definition, precisely the order of the private conscience."[21]

It should be interjected that the new edifice emerged out of the violent collapse of the old one, a collapse that was brought on in part by political philosophers of a nominalist stripe such as Marsilius of Padua, who steadily undermined it. These philosophers found congenial a line of thought extending back to the so-called Norman Anonymous – that is, to court theologians quite happy to serve up even christological heresy in a belated monarchist rebuff to Gelasius.[22] The viciousness with which the dismemberment of Christendom was finally achieved after the Protestant Reformation, a viciousness that drew alike from ethnic tensions, fanatical religious impulses, and the insatiable appetites of the powerful for more power, culminated in the Wars of Religion – the label being a convenient bit of metonymical misdirection – and in the *cuius regio* settlement of the religious problem. That settlement, of course, was a very serious setback for the whole idea of separation of church and state, which is why it was immediately repudiated by Innocent X in famously intemperate terms.[23] Far worse, the hyper-nationalism of this era (fuelled by new imperial ambitions) spilled over into the wars of irreligion that have dominated the last two centuries, covering the world with still more copious amounts of blood, including a good deal of martyrial blood.

But back to Murray, who finds in the indictment of Christianity by Hobbes and Rousseau for its doctrine of the Two, for its having made men "see double," the governing spirit of modern political thought. He traces modernity's "monist concept of the indivisibility of sovereignty" through various movements, from royal absolutism to revolutionary Jacobinism to communism to "the totalitarianizing tendency inherent in the contemporary idolatry of the democratic process" – in which is urged "a monism, not so much of the political order itself, as of a political technique." The message of democracy is clear: "*One* there is whereby this world is ruled – the power in the people, expressing itself in the preference of a majority, and beyond or beside or above this power there is no other."[24]

Christianity has always regarded the state as a limited order of action for limited purposes, to be chosen and pursued under the direction and correction of the organized moral conscience of society, whose judgments are formed and mobilized by the Church, an independent and autonomous community, qualified to be the interpreter of man's nature and destiny. [But] it has been specific of modernity to regard the state as a moral end in itself, a self-justifying entity with its own self-determined spiritual substance. It is within the secular state, and by appeal to secular sources, that man is to find the interpretation of his own nature and the means to his own destiny. The state itself creates the ethos of society, embodies it, imparts it to its citizens, and sanctions its observance with rewards and punishments. Outside the tradition of Jacobin or Communist dogmatism, the modern democratic secular state does not indeed pretend to be the Universe or to speak infallibly. But it does assert itself to be the embodiment of whatever fallible human wisdom may be available to man, because it is the highest school of human experience, beyond which man can find no other School and no other Teacher.[25]

What we encounter in modernity is an "ultimately monist" structure, then, "whatever may be its constituent and subordinate pluralisms." Its significance "lies in the fact that it confronts us with an experiment in human freedom which has consciously or unconsciously been based on a denial or a disregard of the essential Christian contribution to human freedom, which is the theorem of the freedom of the Church."[26] Perhaps modernity is congenitally incapable of grasping that theorem because it cannot grasp the Church itself, but stumbles over its otherness:

This "one ruler," the modern man, does not object to religion, provided that religion be regarded as a private matter which concerns only the conscience and feelings of the individual. In his more expansive moments he will not object even to organized religion – the "churches" – provided they accept the status of

voluntary associations for limited purposes which do not
impinge upon the public order. But he will not tolerate any mar-
ring of his image ... of democratic society as the universal community whose ends are coextensive with the ends of man himself.
It is the One Society, with One Law, and with One Sovereign, the
politically equal people. Modernity has declared the Gelasian
doctrine to be heretical and has outlawed it, in the name of
modern orthodoxy, which is a naturalist rationalism.[27]

The individual conscience is the key to this experiment, however.
For there would be no reason to repose any trust in democracy if
the individual himself were not to be trusted. Unfortunately, in
post-modernity the basis for that trust has eroded. It is no longer
clear to us that the individual has epistemic access, through his conscience, to an objective moral order. It is not even clear that he
shares a common aspiration for freedom. The optimism of Locke,
Rousseau, Mill, or Rawls about the individual seems less and less
grounded. But, asks Murray, "If there be no consensus with regard
to what freedom is, and whence it comes, and what it means within
the very soul of man, how shall freedom hope to live within society
and in its institutions?"[28]

We have abandoned "two there are" for "one there is."[29] All that
is left to us, then, is the hoary love of justice. But what is to prevent
justice from becoming a whore? What meaning can be given to
justice absent any consensus about an objective moral order? Why
should justice itself not become the plaything of power, as Nietzsche
proposed and Foucault believed to be the case? John Courtney
Murray is right: "a new work of thought"[30] is required if chaos and
violence are not to prevail.

AN APPEAL TO DIGNITATIS HUMANAE

Might the second Vatican council's declaration on religious freedom,
which is just turning fifty, be the new work of thought that is needed? Not according to those of Bellah's persuasion. On their view,
Dignitatis is but a tardy and somewhat reluctant concession of the
Church to a principle already established on non-religious grounds.
The real fathers of religious freedom are Locke and Jefferson and the
like. It may be that the martyrs made some limited contribution
centuries ago, and the bishops too. But it required exposure of the

destructive fanaticism of martyrial religion, through the Wars of Religion, for a more generous and robust sense of religious freedom to take hold – a sense rooted in a deliberately non-theological theory that emphasized the freedom of the state from the church rather than the freedom of the church from the state.

To respond properly to this line of thinking would require, among other things, a lengthy appeal to those who have rightly criticized "the myth of religious violence"[31] as a convenient shield for a tendentious and truncated account of Western intellectual history. I will not try your patience by attempting that here. I will say that those of Bellah's persuasion often misread what was happening at Vatican II.

Context, of course, is crucial. Westphalia had sounded the bell for a new round of conflict over separation of church and state, a round in which the Catholic Church was again forced onto the defensive, and into a predicament – much exacerbated by the French Revolution and the Gallican/ultramontanist struggle – that led ultimately to the first Vatican council. That council sought to consolidate the unity and independence of the Church through a deeper investment in the papacy.[32] Only after this was achieved was it possible to embrace, as a matter of theological principle rather than mere political pragmatism, the more generous understanding of freedom of religion that was accomplished at Vatican II in the form of *Dignitatis humanae*.

Now *Dignitatis* affirms that freedom of religion belongs in principle to every person, and understands it, minimally, as the right to immunity from coercion in matters of religion or conscience, within due limits. It expounds this freedom and this right as based on the dignity of the person, who (under normal circumstances) is equipped with reason, free will, and responsibility, especially responsibility to seek religious truth.[33] Freedom of religion is a correlate of this inherent dignity. That is, it is linked to the natural capacity to discern moral truth – including the truth, declared at Vatican I, that God is, and that God ought to be sought above all things – and so it appertains whether or not this capacity is properly exercised and developed.

Wrong is done to persons, and to the order established by God, if they are denied the free and corporate practice of their religion within the limits set by due public order. "The state is therefore obliged to give effective protection to the religious liberty of all citizens by just laws and other suitable means, and to ensure favourable conditions for fostering religious life."[34] From this society itself will benefit. The state indeed fails to do its duty if it does not recognize and promote the religious life of its citizens; on the other hand, it transgresses its own proper limits if it seeks either to direct or to prevent that life.

In all of this, *Dignitatis* does not take its bearings, as some fancy, from any non-theological political or anthropological principle. How could it? Rather, it takes its bearings from the evangel. First and foremost," says the declaration, "religious freedom in the social order fully corresponds with the freedom of the act of Christian faith."[35] That freedom is a pneumatological freedom; the act itself is enabled by divine grace. Yet the freedom of the act of Christian faith is something absolutely proper to the human being, whose nature and dignity is being restored and perfected by grace. It is therefore an *indicium libertatis* for society as such.

From this vantage point, the council is able to acknowledge past mistakes made in the matter of religious freedom by Christian societies and states, and even in the prudential judgment of the Church itself. Though it makes no attempt to specify these – that would be no small task! – it freely admits that there have been "ways of acting hardly in tune with the spirit of the Gospel or even opposed to it."[36] From this same vantage, albeit with a spirit of humility induced by awareness of past mistakes, the council can offer a definite point of reference for freedom of religion, a positive and not merely a negative criterion: "*The Church should enjoy all the freedom of action it needs in order to care for the salvation of humanity.*"[37] Any restriction of the type that inhibits the Church in fulfilling its primary vocation is an improper restriction.[38]

This criterion, if we take it seriously, goes a long way toward determining what "within the limits of due public order" means. It cannot mean, for example, what it appears to mean when a court orders a priest to violate the seal of the confessional, or a Catholic hospital to perform abortions, or even a Church adoption agency to place children in homes it deems unsuitable.[39] But neither can it mean that the Church has a right to eliminate the competition, so to speak, where that competition is external to its own society and not subject to its own discipline.[40] More broadly: The city of God has no authority to determine the social or political or religious order of the city of man, against the wishes of the latter.[41]

So, what conversion did the council undergo? If not to some independent principle of religious freedom, then to a fuller grasp of the political implications of the gospel? Yes. And what prompted this conversion? The confluence, I would say, of two quite different factors: on the one hand, the persecution of the Church in many places and a new sense of solidarity with the early Christians and with minorities generally; on the other hand, an optimism about the general yearning of man for freedom, expressions of which – even where, as in the French Revolution, they ran contrary to the truth about man and to the gospel itself – were indicators of a residual openness to the gospel, an openness that it was incumbent upon the Church to cultivate as far as possible. Whereas at Vatican I the task (largely defensive) had been to distinguish between a misconceived and self-defeating notion of human freedom, grounded in error, and the true freedom grounded both in reason and in revelation, the task of Vatican II (largely offensive) was to reach out in a more affirmative fashion to a world that itself desired freedom.

That is not to deny that there was considerable controversy over *Dignitatis humanae*. At the council there were men of an authoritarian bent who feared too much emphasis on freedom. And there were romantic conservatives, who perhaps misunderstood the battle that had been fought at the previous council or at all events were unready to take up the new challenge. There were those, too, who wondered whether the powerful note of optimism about the direction of modern man, sounded by John XXIII at the opening of the council, was fully justified. Some of the resistance can be accounted for in this way. But, at the deepest level, the controversy over *Dignitatis* was driven by concern for the relation between freedom and truth.

"You shall know the truth," said Jesus, "and the truth shall make you free."[42] Did *Dignitatis* threaten to reverse this maxim? Would freedom of religion displace freedom through religion? Did *Dignitatis* imply that error had the same rights as truth? Could error have rights at all? What would be the consequences of such ideas for civil society? Was the political order to be entirely independent of the spiritual order? Was the eternal to be subordinated to the temporal in human affairs? What could this be but a complete reversal of Christendom? What but a denial of the unity of truth and of the lordship of Christ?

These questions are all legitimate and indeed of the utmost importance. Yet, in its final draft, *Dignitatis* ultimately prevailed with only 70 *non placet* votes (against 2308 *placet*). The reason for that is that there are good answers to them, answers that maintain the priority of truth over freedom; or to put it another way, answers that maintain freedom *through* religion, the Catholic religion, without losing sight of the fact that freedom *of* religion is its proper corollary.[43]

REAFFIRMING THE LIBERTAS ECCLESIAE
AS THE TOUCHSTONE OF RELIGIOUS FREEDOM

It is my own view that *Dignitatis* points us to the only really viable
ground for coherently affirming religious freedom as the *sine qua
non* for authentic civil freedom: namely, a firm belief in the dignity
of man as something derived from God. But I did not conduct you
down this long and winding path just to say that. Something more
must be said, if I am reading *Dignitatis* aright. Commitment to the
libertas ecclesiae is the true touchstone of religious freedom.

When the subject of liberty arises, the *libertas ecclesiae* is the first
or most important question. It is a question that has had to be
answered over and over again down through the centuries, and in
being answered affirmatively has always given succour in one way
or another to civil liberties; witness England's *Magna Carta*,[44] for
example, or Poland's liberation from communism. And listen again
to *Dignitatis*, at section 13:

> Among the things that concern the good of the Church and
> indeed the welfare of society here on earth – things therefore
> that are always and everywhere to be kept secure and defended
> against all injury – this certainly is preeminent, namely, that the
> Church should enjoy that full measure of freedom which her
> care for the salvation of men requires. This is a sacred freedom,
> because the only-begotten Son endowed with it the Church
> which He purchased with His blood. Indeed it is so much the
> property of the Church that to act against it is to act against the
> will of God. The freedom of the Church is the fundamental
> principle in what concerns the relations between the Church
> and governments and the whole civil order.
>
> In human society and in the face of government the Church
> claims freedom for herself in her character as a spiritual author-
> ity, established by Christ the Lord, upon which there rests, by
> divine mandate, the duty of going out into the whole world and
> preaching the Gospel to every creature. The Church also claims
> freedom for herself in her character as a society of men who have
> the right to live in society in accordance with the precepts of the
> Christian faith.[45]

It is precisely the Church's conviction respecting its sacred freedom,
bestowed by divine mandate through Jesus Christ, that supplies it

with the courage to speak up also for its own and others' mundane freedoms and rightful civil liberties, which are rooted not in the *libertas ecclesiae*, nor yet in the generosity of the state, but rather in the human dignity granted to all people by their Creator.[46]

The *libertas ecclesiae*, the sacred freedom of the Church in and over against the state, is something distinct from freedom of religion in the more general sense.[47] Now the latter is already something both individual and communal, for "the freedom or immunity from coercion in matters religious which is the endowment of persons as individuals is also to be recognized as their right when they act in community." It extends not only to freedom of worship, but also to freedom for self-governance, for belief and the public proclamation of belief, and to the right "to establish educational, cultural, charitable and social organizations, under the impulse of their own religious sense."[48] But the *libertas ecclesiae* is something more than that. It is predicated on the basis of the Church's unique status as a *societas perfecta*, a society complete in itself. It belongs to the Church *qua* Church, or rather to the Church as *civitas dei*. It belongs to the Church's ambassadorial mission and standing. Hence it is not subject to curtailment by the state's prudential judgments in the way that ordinary religious freedom and mundane civil liberties are – though even these, insists *Dignitatis*, are subject to the state's prudential judgments only in so far as those judgments conform to human dignity and to the objective moral order.[49]

This of course calls for much negotiation, of the kind laid out in section 7.[50] But the *libertas ecclesiae* itself is a *principium fundamentale* that is not subject to negotiation. From the side of the Church, it must govern all negotiations. It is a manifestation of the divine freedom as it appears within the political sphere in the form of the Church, which is, so to say, a sovereign territory. The *libertas ecclesiae* is not transferable to other religions or religious bodies and does not take the place of freedom of religion in the more general sense, even for Christians or Christian institutions.[51]

Here I find myself in disagreement with Fr Murray, a disagreement I will develop properly in chapter 5. Murray claims, in an article written after the council, that the *libertas ecclesiae* is something that belongs to a transcendent order inaccessible to the state, and as such is incapable of being "urged in political society" as something more than ordinary corporate religious freedom.[52] Well, certainly it belongs to a transcendent order – the order of the resurrection and of the kingdom of God – but it is accessible in and to the secular order just so far as the presence of the Church within that order makes it accessible. And to that very same extent it is something to which the secular powers must respond.[53]

What does that mean in practice, if the response is positive? That other religions are to be the beneficiaries of freedom of religion, while the Church is to be the beneficiary of establishment, as it was under Theodosius and throughout the middle ages? The council makes no such demand, though (as Russell Hittinger points out) it expressly declares that "it leaves untouched traditional Catholic doctrine on the moral duty of men and societies toward the true religion and toward the one Church of Christ."[54] And in point of fact the Church in modern times – ever since the *cuius regio* doctrine appeared – has shied away from establishment, though it has not closed the door permanently on that arrangement.

So it does not mean that. It means, rather, that in the Church the state is confronted with a singular obligation, *viz.*, "that the Church should enjoy all the freedom of action it needs to care for the salvation of humanity." This is something that only the Church can know and communicate to it. Which is to say: the *libertas ecclesiae*, unlike religious freedom in general, generates a positive and not merely a negative obligation on the part of the state. It also means that in the Church the state comes up against a limit that is not abstract but concrete. For the Church confronts the state as having a still higher authority than the state, though not as having authority to run the state.[55]

CONCLUSION

What am I saying, then?

I am saying, first, that we should not underestimate the peril that the idea of religious freedom faces in our time. Perhaps Nietzsche is right that we have killed "God" without fully realizing what we have done. Certainly we are trying hard now to rid ourselves of the last remnants of the doctrine of the Two, and I have agreed with Fr Murray and with Stephen Smith that the discourse of religious freedom is on very shaky ground without that doctrine. "In sum," says Smith, "the commitment to special legal treatment for religion derives from a two-realm world view in which religion – meaning the church, and later the conscience – was understood to inhabit a separate jurisdiction that was in some respects outside the governance of the state." It derives, in other words, from recognition of a dyarchy. "But once that world view with its 'separate jurisdictions' component is abandoned or forgotten, what sense does it make to continue treating religion as a special legal category?"[56]

I am saying, further, that it will not be enough to reassert the dignity of the person, as a dignity grounded in God, in order to rescue religious freedom. That will go a very long way, perhaps. But religious freedom did not appear in history as a function of the dignity of the person. It appeared as a function of the *libertas ecclesiae*. And the denial of that liberty, or even (*pace* Fr Murray) of the political and juridical relevance of that liberty, leaves the liberty of the person, and indeed the liberty of associations of persons, exposed to assaults on both flanks. Without the doctrine of the Two there is nothing to restrain the state except its image of the person. And without the exercise of the *libertas ecclesiae* in its defence, the image of the person, whether in the mind of the state or in the mind of the citizen, is subject to the dissolving acids of rank individualism, on the one hand, and of pure political calculation on the other.

In short, if all the freedoms required by civil society are "extrapolations from that one central freedom, freedom of religion," as Bellah says, it behooves us to discover again that from which freedom of religion itself is an extrapolation.

5

Catholics and the Neutral State

An Augustinian Disquisition on the Doctrine of the Two in Dialogue with John Courtney Murray

There is deep confusion today about the role of religion in public life, a confusion shared by Catholics, who often do not know how to contest or even to criticize what Richard John Neuhaus called the naked public square.[1] The confusion is linguistically entrenched in our common misuse of the adjective "secular." Ours is a secular age, we are told, with a secular society and a secular state. What can that redundancy signify? Secular is derived from *saeculum*, which simply means "age" or "era."

When Oliver O'Donovan describes Christendom, historically, as the era "in which the truth of Christianity was taken to be a truth of secular politics" – that is, as the era of "a professedly Christian secular political order"[2] – this sounds oxymoronic to us, but in fact it is spot on. That is what Christendom was: the era in which human affairs were arranged with one eye on eternity, on a kingdom that, unlike the kingdoms of this world, is not merely provisional and temporary. Unless we are talking about priests, the antonym of "secular" is not "religious," but "eternal."[3]

Catholic secularism is, if you please, the earliest form of secularism. It is based on a belief that the *saeculum*, the present age, is bracketed by the first and second comings of Christ. Since the powers of this age, unlike Christ, can neither save nor damn, and will ultimately come to nothing, their proper vocation is to exercise with appropriate modesty a provisional form of justice, intended *pro tempore* for the good order and flourishing of the people, until the true justice of God, already revealed in Christ, intervenes to bring about the end of the age and establish an eternal kingdom of perfect and true happiness.[4]

Well, if by "secularism" these days we mean to signify that we no longer believe in such a kingdom, that we see ourselves as living in an age *not* bracketed by the appearance of the true King in Bethlehem or by his parousia yet to come – that we live not in the present "year of our Lord" but only, and rather vaguely, in some "common" era with no real beginning and no anticipated end – then Catholics can only dissent. And if we draw from this blinkered secularity, in which people no longer hope for the *saecula saeculorum* of Christ's kingdom, the conclusion that, in this age of ours which refuses to be bracketed, religion should have no place in the ordering of our collective affairs – indeed, that we must have a "neutral" state disinterested or even uninterested in matters religious, and that the public square must therefore be stripped of all its religious signs and symbols – then once again the Catholic must dissent. For to be Catholic is to believe in such a bracketing, and to hold up signs of that bracketing: the crib and the cross. For a Catholic, it is the bracketing that defines the secular, keeping it humble and modest, curbing its native tendencies to expand out of all control and to smother rather than support human flourishing.

Now of course you will tell me that I am overlooking something. Catholics may not be secularists in that sense, but they may still understand that in this so-called secular age their own position is no longer the consensus. The era of Christendom has passed. A new social contract is required that better incorporates agnostics and people of other faiths. Perhaps the new era should be called something other than "secular" or "common," but whatever it is called it must be capable of respecting a plurality of perspectives and of faith communities. The state that monitors and applies its social contract must therefore be disinterested – neutral, in that sense – though not altogether uninterested in affairs of religion. And if you tell me this, you will doubtless want to point out that the fathers of Vatican II, especially in the documents that fifty years ago completed the council's work – *Dignitatis humanae* and *Gaudium et spes* especially – took just such a line, turning their backs on a policy of the previous century that sought to revive Christendom.

Or did they? Our first task is to clear up some confusion on this point. I shall then try to identify the underlying weakness in certain Catholic attempts to wrestle with the problem of religious freedom, with the nature of the Church's own liberty, and with the relation between church and state, concentrating in particular on John

Courtney Murray. Afterward, I will propose another way of approaching these subjects, a way more in keeping with Catholic secularism.

HARD TIMES FOR THE DOCTRINE OF THE TWO

Basic to Christendom's "professedly Christian secular political order" was the doctrine of the Two, the Gelasian dyarchy: "Two there are," insisted the pope to the emperor, "by which this world is chiefly ruled: the sacred authority of priests and the royal power. Of these, that of the priests is the weightier, since they have to render an account in the divine judgment even for the kings of men."[5] Two, not one; and the first, by virtue of its higher responsibility – a responsibility for things eternal, not merely things temporal or secular – is the greater.

In modernity this doctrine, never entirely secure, was attacked with renewed vigour, especially in France and Italy, with a view to eliminating the Church as far as possible from political calculation by assigning its rule strictly to the private sphere, the realm of the soul, leaving the public sphere, the realm of the body, entirely in the hands of the state.[6] In 1864, when in his Syllabus of Errors Pius IX condemned proposition 55 – "The Church is to be separated from the state, and the state from the Church" – he was not rejecting the doctrine of the Two, or for that matter the proper autonomy of the state, but rather the new and militant secularism that masqueraded as political neutrality, the real aim of which (as Gregory XVI had already observed) was to dissolve "the concord between the secular and ecclesiastical authority."[7]

Pius objected, like Gregory before him and Leo after, to draconian laws that effectively deprived the Church of its liberty to engage in large-scale works of mercy, educational enterprises, and so forth, and of its role as counsellor to the state on things that mattered to the family and to the economic and social fabric; that is, to civil society. He objected to the attempt – broadly Rousseauvian, though of course there were many other influences, including by now that of Mill and Comte – to completely isolate *homo politicus* from *homo religiosus*, or alternatively to conflate the two under the banner of civil religion, as pre-Christian emperors had tried to do. He objected, that is, to a doctrine of the One, a doctrine that removed the Church altogether from the political picture.

There was no doubt at all that this new doctrine was anti-Catholic to its core. Rousseau himself was astute enough to realize that faithful

Catholics could never abide this sundering of body and soul, much less a re-sacralizing of the state. They must therefore be disciplined, if need be, by exile or even death. For their part, Gregory and Pius and Leo lived in an interlude in which things were not so bad as all that, but they knew what they were dealing with. They fought back with reassertions of the Church's political rights and privileges, by energetic diplomacy, by creating the modern tradition of social encyclicals, by laying the groundwork for what was later called Catholic Action, and by resisting Gallicanism in all its forms. This counter-revolutionary response was a straightforward reaffirmation of the doctrine of the Two, as Leo made plain in *Immortale dei*:

> The Almighty, therefore, has given the charge of the human race to two powers, the ecclesiastical and the civil, the one being set over divine, and the other over human, things. Each in its kind is supreme, each has fixed limits within which it is contained, limits which are defined by the nature and special object of the prov-ince of each, so that there is, we may say, an orbit traced out within which the action of each is brought into play by its own native right. But, inasmuch as each of these two powers has authority over the same subjects, and as it might come to pass that one and the same thing – related differently, but still remain-ing one and the same thing – might belong to the jurisdiction and determination of both, therefore God, who foresees all things, and who is the author of these two powers, has marked out the course of each in right correlation to the other.[8]

In his 1953 essay, "Leo XIII on Church and State: The General Structure of the Controversy," Fr John Courtney Murray probed this response both sympathetically and critically. The Church was cer-tainly faced with a real enemy, whether that enemy was (as Leo sup-posed) a vast Masonic conspiracy or not. A flood tide "threatened to wreck the traditional structure of politics" based on the doctrine of the Two, and indeed to "wash out the traditional substance of West-ern society." It would no longer be acknowledged that man lived in two orders, one eternal and the other temporal, between which there should be harmony. "[T]his differentiation of orders" was to be obliterated "by reducing the whole of man's social life to sheerly political life, and then subjecting it to the single direction of the power that is political." There was a disagreement here, as Leo knew, "over the very nature and destiny of man."[9]

At the heart of this disagreement Leo identified a false concept of autonomy and freedom, which he confronted by insisting that the whole man is wholly in the power of God. He wanted to reconnect "the power that is in man to the power of God, from which it had been cut loose."[10] Unfortunately, suggests Murray, Leo focused too narrowly on power (*potestas*) at the expense of law (*lex*). His polemical concerns caused him to overlook the importance of human consent in the political process, tainting his proposals with the absolutism of the post-mediaeval era.[11] Leo's alternative to the false concept of autonomy and freedom did not, therefore, stand out as clearly as his denunciation of it. Nor was he able to address the aspirations of the new era that was dawning. His approach was largely retrospective, not prospective. Faced with a situation in which the Church was no longer coextensive with society, and no longer in an agreeable dyarchy with the state in the ordering of society, he sought a return to what had been – but could no longer be.

Hence it fell ultimately to the fathers of the Second Vatican Council to revamp the doctrine of the Two in a way that actually connected with the modern era. This was accomplished by thinking in terms of church and *society* rather than church and state (an *aggiornamento* or "bringing up to date"), and so of thinking afresh about the relation between the city of God and the city of man (a *ressourcement*, or return to tradition).[12]

Especially in *Dignitatis humanae* and *Gaudium et spes*, there appeared an openness to and an optimism about modern man that was missing in Leonine literature, together with a cosmopolitanism lacking in Leo's Eurocentric perspective. The earthly Church and global society, both on a form of pilgrimage – perhaps in convergence? – these were the twin *foci* of the council fathers. "New theological insights into the concrete reality of the pilgrim Church, and other new insights made available by secular experience (notably the experience of the relation between religious freedom as a human right and the freedom of the Church), have resulted in genuine and fruitful development of doctrine," concludes Murray.[13]

RELIGIOUS FREEDOM AND THE NEUTRAL STATE

During the council Murray himself worked hard to achieve the result just described. It was indeed the question of religious freedom (exacerbated by the advance of communism) that brought into focus the need for a new understanding of both the church-state and the church-society relationship. In the context of the council's deliberations about religious freedom, Fr Murray encouraged abandonment of the old model of a church-state dyarchy and of Leonine demands that the state should work with the Church to inhibit the spread of religious, moral, or political error. He promoted, rather, the ideal of a neutral state, along lines that owed much to the (early) American model of church-state separation.[14]

On Murray's view, the state requires no theological or religious formation, and ought not to make religious commitments, as the individuals and groups comprised by civil society do. Working with the rationale that Jacques Maritain had applied to the *Universal Declaration of Human Rights*, Murray argued that the recognition of rights and freedoms belongs to natural law. Consensus about the divine origins or theological ground of human dignity and human rights is not necessary for these rights to be asserted in the public sphere; nor is it necessary to proclaim, as a matter of political relevance, that the whole man is wholly under the power of God. To Murray, it even seemed proper to regard the state as incompetent (*ineptam*) in matters of theology and religion, and hence to encourage its neutrality as being in the best interests of freedom of religion. He did not see this as militating altogether against church-state cooperation, provided that cooperation did not repudiate or threaten, as it did under the Leonine approach, the principle of equal freedom for all.

In 1964, while the text of *Dignitatis* was still in flux, Murray made his case in a paper entitled "The Problem of Religious Freedom," which contrasted the view he wished the council fathers to abandon with the view he wished them to adopt. In treating these two views, he called for a clear decision respecting "the competence of the public power with regard to religion. Does it extend to public care of religious truth ... or is it limited to public care of religious freedom ... ? Does it extend to a care for the Church herself, her doctrine, authority, prestige ... or is it limited to a care for the freedom of the Church ... ? Does it extend to a care for the religious unity of the people as related to their political unity ... or is it limited to a care for the religious freedom of the people as related to their civil and political freedom ... ?"[15] A decision in favour of the second option, he knew, would mark a clear change in the tradition, but this, he suggested, could be regarded as a matter of evolving prudential judgment rather than of fundamental doctrine.

When the text of *Dignitatis* was finally fixed, however, it contained an addition – in its very first article – declaring that it "leaves untouched traditional Catholic doctrine on the moral duty of men and societies toward the true religion and toward the one Church of Christ."[16] The council, in other words, drew back from embracing without reservation what had once been strongly condemned as a form of indifferentism. If men and societies do indeed have an obligation toward Catholic truth and the Catholic Church, they cannot rightly construct states that recognize no such obligation, any more than they can rightly construct states that compel citizens to meet or even to accept that obligation.

As Russell Hittinger points out, the final text also dropped the phrase *ineptam esse*. To admit that the state was, in principle, altogether incompetent religiously and theologically might contradict the claim that it should recognize the divine freedom of the Church, the *libertas ecclesiae*; or that the state is accountable legislatively to "the objective moral order" divinely established;[17] or that it is responsible to "ensure favourable conditions for fostering religious life" as well as religious liberty for all; or indeed that it should recognize religion itself as a fundamental good.[18]

This setback did not prevent Fr Murray from spinning the final document in his own direction. In 1966 he contended in another paper ("The Issue of Church and State at Vatican Council II") that the Church herself must not claim religious liberty "on anything but secular grounds,"[19] and this for two reasons. First, because "the Church would abdicate her transcendence were she to present her theological title to freedom in society for judgment by any organs of secular government," since these are "not empowered to make judgments *de meritis* in matters of theological truth."[20] That is an odd way to put the matter, for the state is never invited to make such judgments on its own, but is rather invited to recognize the truth it is taught by the Church. It makes no more sense to say that the Church abdicates its transcendence by making this invitation to the state than to say that it does so by extending the gospel invitation to every citizen.

But Murray goes on to offer a second and correlative reason: "At the same time, the due autonomy of the secular order would be violated, since this autonomy requires that the powers which rule the secular order should make judgments on the secular grounds proper to that order – the truth which is its foundation, the justice which is

its goal, the love or civic friendship which is its motivating and unifying force, the freedom which is at once its goal and its method of
pursuing the goal of justice. Hence the autonomy of the secular
order requires that, within this order and in the face of its constituted organs of government, the Church should present her claim to
freedom on these secular grounds – in the name of the human person, who is the foundation, the end, and the bearer of the whole
social process." Thus, for Murray, the Church must claim freedom of
religion in the general sense and not in some specifically ecclesial
sense. It is not, in other words, to address the state as *civitas* to *civitas* in the Leonine fashion. Rather, it is to make its approach using
the human person as proxy.

For him the freedom of the Church seems to be of two kinds.
There is a theological freedom – a positive freedom, divinely
bestowed, to live and proclaim the gospel – that belongs to the
Church above and beyond the secular order but not within it. And
there is a secular freedom, a negative freedom that it enjoys along
with other religious communities, in the form of immunity from
state intervention in its internal affairs. The latter, to be sure, is a
more primordial freedom than the freedom that belongs to persons
individually considered, but it is not unique to the Church. And this
is the freedom with which *Dignitatis* is chiefly concerned.

Dignitatis, however, does not construe the *libertas ecclesiae* in
quite this way. The *libertas ecclesiae* is never merely political, but it
is never less than political. In proclaiming the gospel, and declaring
her own liberty to do so, the Church addresses the citizens of the city
of man and their institutions as well, including the institutions of
state. It is not a matter of their competence to judge. The gospel
brings with it its own criteria for judgment, without which no one
can judge it. Nor is it a matter of autonomy, for the secular order has
no truth and knows no justice, love, or freedom that is given it independently of the lordship of Christ, in whom all things are created
and hold together, "whether thrones or dominions or principalities
or authorities."[21]

In claiming that the autonomy of the secular order requires that
the Church must present her claim to freedom on secular grounds
and in a name other than her own – the name of the human person –
Murray puts forward a concept of state neutrality that disallows
recognition of the Church *qua* Church, something the council does
not do. Indeed, he seems to deny that the lordship of Christ, as

expressed in the *libertas ecclesiae*, has any purchase on the secular order.[22] He also contradicts, as Hittinger observes, what Pope Paul VI said at the close of the council in *Aux gouvernants*, which still appeals, in its basic logic, to the classical doctrine of the Two.

> We proclaim publicly: We do honor to your authority and your sovereignty, we respect your office, we recognize your just laws, we esteem those who make them and those who apply them. But we have a sacrosanct word to speak to you and it is this: Only God is great. God alone is the beginning and the end. God alone is the source of your authority and the foundation of your laws.

> Your task is to be in the world the promoters of order and peace among men. But never forget this: It is God, the living and true God, who is the Father of men. And it is Christ, His eternal Son, who came to make this known to us and to teach us that we are all brothers. He it is who is the great artisan of order and peace on earth, for He it is who guides human history and who alone can incline hearts to renounce those evil passions which beget war and misfortune. It is He who blesses the bread of the human race, who sanctifies its work and its suffering, who gives it those joys which you can never give it, and strengthens it in those sufferings which you cannot console.[23]

For all Fr Murray's undoubted influence on the council and on the text of *Dignitatis humanae*, it is far from evident that the council fathers embraced his view of freedom of religion as it bears on the neutrality of the state. Hittinger argues that they "were careful to frame the civil right of religious liberty in such a way that it did not imply either a theoretical or practical endorsement of neutralism"; that is, of the idea that a government "on principled grounds must remain neutral on religion as such."[24] Indeed, in his final address to the council, Paul VI observed that the Church's "theocentric and theological concept of man and the universe, almost in defiance of the charge of anachronism and irrelevance, has been given a new prominence by the council, through claims which the world will at first judge to be foolish, but which, we hope, it will later come to recognize as being truly human, wise and salutary."[25] Obviously, the pope did not share Murray's brand of *aggiornamento*, which here seems closer to the Rawlsian than to the Catholic tradition.[26]

Murray is mistaken when he speaks of a "traditional doctrine that religion is a social good, a fundamental element of the common temporal good of society." There is no such doctrine, not if "religion" remains in the abstract and might mean any sort of religion at all. Likewise, he is mistaken when he claims that "the sense of the Declaration [is] to say that governmental favor of religion formally means favor of the freedom of religion," and nothing more.[27] How could we agree to that without agreeing that the autonomy of the political sphere is the kind of autonomy to which religious truth is extraneous – apart, of course, from the one religious truth that religion itself is a basic good? Which is nonsense. At all events it makes nonsense of the most fundamental Christian confession, the confession Κύριος Ἰησοῦς (Jesus is Lord), with which the whole discourse about the Two began.[28]

IS RELIGIOUS NEUTRALITY POSSIBLE?

Now let's pause for a moment to ask whether religious neutrality is even possible. When the call goes out for a neutral state, what is the rationale and what is the objective? A neutral state means a state without religious convictions or allegiances. It is not a state guided by no principles, in search of no particular good. That would be absurd. A neutral state is, in theory, a state committed to justice and to other good things such as liberty, equality, and fraternity. But what is justice? What is liberty? What kind of equality are we talking about? What makes for real fraternity? Is virtue necessary to such ideals? Which virtues, and how shall we cultivate them? Are we certain that they can be cultivated without religious reference or support?

Make no mistake: as soon as one attempts to answer such questions one is on theological ground. Indeed, as soon as one asks whether the state can or should be neutral one is on theological ground. For if we say that the state must be neutral, meaning not merely that the state must be even-handed in its treatment of citizens, whatever their religion, but that the state itself must eschew every theological idea or religious association, we are also saying that the state is a sphere in which God must not be acknowledged as God. And that, of course, is a way of saying that, whatever deity there might be, it lacks any legitimate claim over the state – which is a theological statement, and one to which Catholics can by no means assent.

As we saw, Murray asked the council fathers to choose between a
state attempting to exercise public care of religious truth and a state
limited to public care of religious freedom; hence also between a
state willing to intervene in religious matters on a regular basis and
a state willing to intervene only "to maintain the essential exigencies
of the public order." He asked them to choose between the Leonine
demand for establishment and the requirement of religious neutrality. But these are false dilemmas if religious and theological neutrality is unattainable. Moreover, establishment is not the only
remaining alternative if the search for that sort of neutrality is abandoned. The other option is to seek a country built on sound moral
principles, including a robust sense of justice, in which there is an
open discussion as to where these principles come from, why they
are important, what they actually mean, and what arrangements will
best support them.

And what, then, if it turns out that public care of religious freedom requires at least some public care of religious truth? That decisions about the "essential exigencies" of public order, which depend
in turn on decisions about the common good and about the moral
order that undergirds it, require some theological or religious guidance or discernment? That care for the conditions that encourage
religious flourishing entails caring *both* for freedom of religion *and*
for some particular religion or religions? There is no obvious reason
to reject such conclusions out of hand, and these indeed seem to be
the conclusions of the council.[29]

Murray knew, of course, as did Maritain, that a moral foundation
is necessary for a just society and for authentic liberty. In his earlier
work he worried "that the moral footing has been eroded from
beneath the political principle of consent,"[30] and that the idea of "a
natural law that makes known to all of us the structure of the moral
universe in such wise that all of us are bound by it in a common obedience" has become all but moribund.[31] He feared the consequences
for liberal democracy, consequences already becoming evident even
in America. What he did not appear to reckon with adequately, however, is that this abandonment of natural law begins with abandonment of the collective responsibility to acknowledge God.[32]

These are deep waters. Both Murray and Maritain have been
accused by other Catholic thinkers of succumbing to a nature-grace
dualism at once injurious to the faith and, given the ever-more-rapid
erosion in view, politically impotent. I'll not try here to navigate that
debate.[33] My point is that the decisions for which Murray calls

inevitably entail overt or covert religious judgments. He does not wish to detach freedom from law, or law from morality. But how are we to detach morality from religion, "the moral universe" from its Maker and sovereign? How do we acknowledge this Maker, or refuse to acknowledge him, neutrally? Personhood, freedom, justice, moral order, the common good, the state as a limited good, God as the highest and necessary and qualifying good: these are not and cannot be religiously neutral concepts.[34]

So, for example, we may well agree with Murray, respecting the point at hand, that the state must be subject to strict limits "in what concerns religious freedom." The requirement for interference, he says, "is fourfold: that the violation of the public order be really serious; that legal or police intervention be really necessary; that regard be had for the privileged character of religious freedom, which is not simply to be equated with other civil rights; that the rule of jurisprudence of the free society be strictly observed, *scil.*, as much freedom as possible, as much coercion as necessary."[35] But in privileging religious freedom we are already making a religious judgment; and in deciding on what is "really serious" we may well have to make another such judgment.

A brief excursus is in order here: The limited state espoused by Murray professes neutrality in religious matters and coerces only under jurisprudential auspices and for grave reasons. This limited state, however, is not neutral as regards all *moral* matters. One admirer of Murray, Michael Perry (like Witte, a Woodruff Professor of Law at Emory), sees an inconsistency here. Perry is not content with a state in which there is freedom of thought, conscience, and religion. He calls for the recognition at law of "moral freedom" also.[36] This call is rooted not merely in skepticism about the political order – about governments or political majorities acting "as arbiters of moral truth"[37] – but in a doctrine of human dignity grounded ultimately, he admits, in religious belief. Perry wishes to prevent the state, via the corrective action of the judiciary, from imposing on the citizenry any dogma, whether religious or moral, or even the consequences of such dogma. And why not? Apparently because that would violate his own dogma – his religiously grounded dogma! – about human dignity.

This self-defeating amalgam of Mill and Murray should not be held against Murray, but it helps to expose the problem with Murray's own position. The state cannot act if it cannot judge, and it cannot judge without criteria for judgment. Murray wants these criteria to arise from natural law and not from religion. But natural law cannot be so neatly divided from religion. Do Catholics (and for that matter pagans such as Cicero) not believe that an elementary knowledge of God arises in and with the reasoning proper to natural law, that morality and religion are therefore intertwined? That together, not separately, they are culture-forming, society-forming, and so also state-forming?[38] The state, we may safely assert, cannot stand back from religion unless it stands back from morality also. But are we really to suppose that the state functions best when it concerns itself as little as possible with what is actually right or wrong, good or evil, conducive to happiness or unhappiness? Perhaps Murray is not really advising that. But arguably Perry sees the connection between the two better than Murray does, and so presses on with a demand for moral as well as religious freedom.

This moral freedom must serve to limit even further the impact of natural law on positive law, just as freedom of religion limits the impact of revealed law on positive law. The product, however, will not be a limited state but rather an unrestrained state – a state that does not see why it should not do whatever it wishes. (If, for example, it has a compelling "public order" reason to limit the population, why should it not enact, as China has, a one-child policy backed by forced abortion?) We may grant to both Murray and Perry that the state is neither the source of the moral or religious judgments we make nor responsible to see that we make the right judgments. It is tasked nevertheless with certain functions related to the reinforcement of those judgments. When, say, it enacts a law against one person killing another, absent certain mitigating circumstances, this is not mere pragmatism. The law is enacted because murder is an evil, not a good.[39] To both men we must insist that religion, morality, law, and freedom come as a package. If we say, and really mean, "Thou shalt not kill," we are only repeating what God has said. We have made a moral judgment that is also a religious judgment, and we expect the state to help us enforce it.

When Leo turns in *Libertas* §38 to "the system of those who admit indeed the duty of submitting to God, the Creator and Ruler of the world, inasmuch as all nature is dependent on His will, but who boldly reject all laws of faith and morals which are above natural reason," he repeats that this destroys the proper concord of church and state.[40] He treats this view under three forms, however: There are those who "wish the State to be separated from the Church wholly and entirely, so that with regard to every right of human society, in institutions, customs, and laws, the offices of State, and the education of youth, they would pay no more regard to the Church than if she did not exist; and, at most, would allow the citizens individually to attend to their religion in private if so minded" (§39). Leo rejects their position – one notes that it is close to Perry's position, and is indeed the prevalent and official position of many states today – but considers two more moderate approaches. The first of these makes more space for the Church yet contrives to "despoil her of the nature and rights of a perfect society, and maintain that it does not belong to her to legislate, to judge, or to punish, but only to exhort, to advise, and to rule her subjects in accordance with their own consent and will;" which has the effect of aggrandizing "the power of the civil government to such extent as to subject the Church of God to the empire and sway of the State, like any voluntary association of citizens" (§40). This too – one notes that it is close to Murray's position in certain respects – Leo rejects, as per *Immortale dei*. And, finally, there are "those who, while they do not approve the separation of Church and State, think nevertheless that the Church ought to adapt herself to the times and conform to what is required by the modern system of government" (§41). "Such an opinion is sound," he allows, "if it is to be understood of some equitable adjustment consistent with truth and justice; in so far, namely, that the Church, in the hope of some great good, may show herself indulgent, and may conform to the times in so far as her sacred office permits. But it is not so in regard to practices and doctrines which a perversion of morals and a warped judgment have unlawfully introduced. Religion, truth, and justice must ever be maintained." While this begs some questions, and does not fully satisfy Murray's arguments and concerns, or Perry's for that matter, it may be suggested to both that their own proposals do not make clear how truth and justice are to be maintained where religion is altogether excluded from consideration by the state.

My own view, briefly put, is much like Fr Murray's. The state functions best when it recognizes its own limits, and these limits come from the following sources: it is limited by its natural and human resources; it is limited by other states, taken singly or together; it is limited by the natural law; it is limited by the natural family and, just so, by its citizenry; and it is limited by God, both providentially through the above and by virtue of the *evangelium* announced by the Church. To fail to appreciate any one of these limits causes a state to flourish only artificially, and finally to fail. This failure is particularly severe, as Murray argued in *We Hold These Truths* and as I do in *Ascension Theology*, if the state secretly or openly tries to emulate the *libertas ecclesiae*.[41] Where then do we differ? I am with Leo in supposing that the Church that makes the announcement is itself a political body – in Leo's parlance, a *societas perfecta* – of which the state is obligated, in view of God's exaltation of Jesus Christ, to take political account, as I shall now try to say.

A COMMON ESCHATOLOGICAL DEFICIT

Would it be wrong to suggest that the later Murray, not the Murray of *We Hold These Truths* but the sixties Murray, seems more dated than Leo? Leo is zealous in his resistance of the doctrine of the One, Murray in his attempt to de-politicize the Church and de-sacralize the state. But, throughout the West, the "neutral" state has only become more bold in imposing on society its own vision of man. Liberal democracy has become increasingly illiberal, at least where Judeo-Christian religion is concerned. The former chief rabbi of Britain, Jonathan Sacks, called last year in New York for a new alliance of Jews and Christians to stem where possible the tides of secularism that are corroding the moral underpinnings of Western society.[42] It is not difficult, I think, to make the case that we are still poised in the long moment of decision, identified by Leo, respecting the nature of human autonomy. Will man acknowledge God or will he not? Will he interpret his autonomy as a gift from God and for God, or as something that can only be exercised in denial of God? Does he want his freedom as a "freedom for" or only as a "freedom from"?[43]

John Paul II – that apostle of hope and of the love that casts out fear – and Benedict also – that apostle of reason – sounded many Leonine notes as the blush of optimism, which is sometimes confused with hope, faded from the post-conciliar Church. Murray, had he lived so long, would have been sympathetic, I think. Nevertheless, I am led to the conclusion that in his *Dignitatis* phase he misconstrues the secular order and the kind of neutrality that belongs to that order, and with it the freedom of the Church.[44] More importantly, he unintentionally undermines Catholic faith in the lordship of the ascended Christ: the Κύριος Ἰησοῦς set over against Κύριος Καίσαρ (Caesar is Lord).

I make haste to explain, lest you mistake me for a LeFebvrist. By "LeFebvrist" I mean all those – schismatic or otherwise – who hold to what is sometimes called the "social kingship" doctrine, according to which Christ rules over human society as such, it being the Church's business to declare this rule and indeed to demand that society and the state recognize it. Adherents of this doctrine object to the council's minimalism and propose instead a maximalism that outstrips even Leonine ideals.

Thaddeus Kozinski, for example, directs us back to *Immortale dei*, and to a passage well outside the comfort zone of most Catholics today in liberal democracies: "For men living together in society are under the power of God no less than individuals are, and society, no less than individuals, owes gratitude to God who gave it being and maintains it and whose ever-bounteous goodness enriches it with countless blessings. Since, then, no one is allowed to be remiss in the service due to God, and since the chief duty of all men is to cling to religion in both its preaching and practice – not such religion as they may have a preference for, but the religion which God enjoins, and which certain and most clear marks show to be the only one true religion – it is a public crime to act as though there were no God."[45] A public crime? If so, then one of which the state, along with society, ought somehow to be conscious, though not perhaps in the way it was conscious in the good old days when such crimes, if committed by the baptized, were punishable not only by the Church but by the state.[46]

All of this seems inconceivable to us today, though in Canada it is but thirty-odd years since we acknowledged in our Charter a connection between the rule of law and the supremacy of God. That connection, already somewhat obscure, is all but broken now. For in *Saguenay* the Supreme Court not only reinforced "the duty of neutrality" by forbidding the town council to commence its meetings with a prayer, it undertook to neutralize the Charter preamble. "The reference to the supremacy of God," it said, "cannot lead to an interpretation of freedom of conscience and religion that authorizes the state to consciously profess a theistic faith."[47]

Now we may certainly ask whether this reading of the preamble is not rather counterintuitive. And does it not imply that, whatever deity there may be, it lacks any legitimate claim on the state? What is that, if not a theological profession? The state, on closer examination, is not so neutral as it pretends to be! Surely Catholics must point this out. For their own faith compels them to admit that societies are under the power of God, that people banded together in society are under obligation to give thanks to God, and to give thanks appropriately rather than idolatrously. But the social kingship doctrine says still more than this. It says that in the Church, the mystical body of Christ, Christ himself is fully present in and for the world. And it wants both civil society and the state to recognize and subject itself to Christ in his Church. For this it is prepared to work and wait, however long such a submission may take. Christendom, alas, may be a past era, but a still greater Christendom is yet to come.[48]

Well, perhaps it is. Who knows? The decision of one generation is not necessarily the decision of the next. Leo himself dared hope for better days, and for renewed concord between the Two.[49] On my view, however, disciples of Murray and their LeFebvrist opponents make a common mistake, though they make it differently. Both fail to place the doctrine of the Two in its proper framework, the framework determined for it by the ascension of Jesus. In consequence, the former fail to see that the state cannot be neutral, and the latter fail to see that the state is not, and ought not to be, an extension or instrument of the Church. Either way, the doctrine of the Two breaks down because of an eschatological deficit.

The LeFebvrists perceive that religious indifference is possible only if the state can function without being guided by any substantive vision of man. And what kind of state is that, if not a state whose vision is, rather, a vision of the state itself? A state, that is, for whom man is merely instrumental – a means, not an end? In which sphere can the state operate without presuming or implying a great deal about man: in the economy, in the military, in education, in health care, in human rights, in geopolitics? Can it really be maintained that its laws and its legal traditions function altogether independently of the answers to big questions about man and his nature? Was there ever a state that could ignore justice altogether, or take no interest in public mores with respect to sex, wealth, or death? And is such territory not also claimed by religion? I give you one word, though I could give you others, to demonstrate the nonsense of state neutrality: abortion.

These things the LeFebvrists know, and they know that in Jesus Christ, who sits at God's right hand, God has already shown man his end: his social and political end, not only some vague "spiritual" end. Yet the LeFebvrists do not understand that in the *saeculum*, in this bracketed age, Christ is both present and absent. They know that the kingdom of God is on the way, but have not grasped fully the fact that it is not on the way along *our* way. "This gospel of the kingdom will be preached throughout the whole world, as a testimony to all nations," declares Jesus, "and then the end will come." But it will not come by some gradual submission of the secular powers to the Church. It will come when Christ himself comes, confronting both the Church and the world in his true glory.[50]

To Murray and his followers, on the other hand, it must be insisted that *homo religiosus* and *homo politicus* are not two different creatures; otherwise put, that there is no sphere of human activity that can be isolated from the challenge posed to humanity by God's exaltation of the man, Jesus Christ, to the seat of "all authority in heaven and on earth."[51] The Church, if it is to be the Church, cannot but say to society at large, and so also to the state that exists to serve society, "Jesus is Lord!" It cannot but call on man, both individually and collectively, to serve the Lord with thanksgiving. To concede a neutral state, meaning a state rightly and properly indifferent to matters of religion – even while, for obscure reasons, acknowledging that religion is a fundamental good – is to posit some part of man, some sphere of human activity, some aspect of human sociality, that has not been redeemed by Christ, will not be saved by Christ, and hence cannot be claimed as subject by Christ.

Which is wrong, quite fundamentally wrong. It is the very error – although Fr Murray would be horrified to hear me say so – that the 1934 Synod of Barmen had to confront, on the Protestant side, in the German Christian movement. It is the error that Catholic dissenters such as Bishop von Galen had to confront when opposing Nazi demands on the Church. The point is put quite concisely in Article 2 of Barmen: "Just as Jesus Christ is the pledge of the forgiveness of all our sins, just so – and with the same earnestness – is he also God's mighty claim on our whole life; in him we encounter a joyous liberation from the godless claims of this world to free and thankful service to his creatures. *We repudiate the false teaching that there are areas of our life in which we belong not to Jesus Christ but to another lord*, areas in which we do not need justification and sanctification through him."[52]

This is the inescapable political implication of the Christian faith. It is Christian secularism. The state does not address the Church or the Christian citizen with an independent authority capable of over-ruling the law of God, whether as natural law or as the law of Christ. The state, indeed, does not address any citizen with such an author-ity. The state performs a limited service (both to God and to civil society) and can lay claim only to a limited and derivative jurisdic-tion. Where it steps beyond that, or presumes to have its authority without being under authority, it does so without any moral warrant and its laws are not morally binding, as Leo declares in his encyclical *On the Nature of Human Liberty*. The rule of law is tied to the supremacy of God.[53]

It is easy to reply, of course, that the Nazi state was anything but neutral. Was it not the very epitome of an ideological and hence an oppressive state? Did it not seduce Christians while at the same time embracing its own sinister brand of neo-paganism? This is all too true. It is also beside the point, which is this: Either the state demar-cates an area of human life that requires no redemption and has been left untouched by God's intervention in Jesus Christ, or it does not. Either it has its authority from God or it does not. To say that it does not, is not to honour the state but to dishonour it, for it is to place this sphere of activity beyond the pale not only of God's judgment but also of God's affirmation in Christ. And this, in the present age, is precisely to leave it open to inhabitation by ideological demons.[54]

SEEKING A BETTER COUNTRY

So: Advocates of the neutral state and the "social kingship" propo-nents are both operating with an eschatological deficit that attri-butes far too much to the *saeculum*. This deficit declares itself either in an idealization of the secular state as something perfectly vacant of religious instincts or convictions – a house swept and empty, to borrow Jesus' image[55] – or in an idealization of the secular church: a church that is aware of no meaningful absence of Christ and hence fancies itself capable of directing the state as if it were Christ. What do things look like if the eschatological deficit is overcome?

We need not concern ourselves further with *how* it is overcome, except to say that any tendency to neglect the doctrine of the two ages and the two cities, and to go straight to the doctrine of two rulers, must also be overcome.[56] For otherwise the conditions remain for pitting these rulers or authorities against each other in a false competition through the conflation of world and church into a single society. (Thus already the Carolingian formulation: "Two there are by whom the *Church* is ruled."[57]) A re-sourced eschatology reminds us that in the *saeculum* the city of God and the city of man, though they coexist and co-operate, must always be distinguished *qua* cities or societies. Each has its own hierarchy, with its own powers and responsibilities, though one extends into heaven and the other (whatever its claims) does not. One is eternal, though its secular form is temporal and provisional; the other is not eternal. One is a supernatural reality, whose facticity is a unique work of the Spirit in connection with the ascension of Jesus Christ; the other is merely mundane. The one therefore confronts the other in a way that other religious communities do not; that is, with an authority and a form of liberty – the *libertas ecclesiae* – that is *sui generis*.

When there is no eschatological deficit in the Church's own thinking, when it is fully cognizant *both* of its Lord's unassailable authority over the whole man *and* of its belonging to a kingdom not of this world, then it knows what real liberty is and by its free actions it creates worldly analogues to its own freedom. "Silver and gold have I none," says Peter to the lame beggar; "but such as I have, I give thee: in the name of Jesus Christ of Nazareth, rise up and walk!"[58]

The *libertas ecclesiae*, in other words, is not just a species of the *libertas religionis* that Catholics and non-Catholics may claim. It is indeed something transcendent, as Murray says. This means that it does not require and should not desire the force of the state in its service, for the state has no tools adequate to it. What the Church asks of the state, when there is no eschatological deficit – a deficit even Leo ran, as Paul VI seems to acknowledge[59] – is first of all the reciprocating graces of the state as regards space for the Church within the city of man: space for its houses of worship, for its hospitals, for its schools, for its members to live in good conscience as citizens of both cities.

For the most part, this is the freedom of religion for which everyone may ask, since Christians have asked for it. The *libertas ecclesiae* is the deepest well-spring of the *libertas religionis* and of like civil liberties, and their proper guarantor. It is by virtue of this freedom – freedom *through* religion, freedom through Christ – that we have discovered freedom *of* religion. Where the former flourishes, the latter also flourishes.[60]

But the *libertas ecclesiae* is more, and does more, than that; and what it is and does, *pace* Fr Murray, is not something apolitical of which the state need take no particular account.[61] The *libertas ecclesiae* creates in the world a new situation, in which people recognize in God and his Christ, and hence in the Church of Christ, an authority higher than the state, a fact that will from time to time generate conflicts of jurisdiction over "one and the same thing," even though that thing (the curriculum of Loyola High School, say) is always "differently related" to the two authorities just because those authorities are concerned with tasks belonging to distinct societies and ages. Here the Church asks the state for something that ordinary freedom of religion does not necessarily entail. It asks the state to acknowledge that it commands this higher allegiance and to act accordingly; that is, out of respect for the Church *qua* Church. It asks the state to refrain from making or applying laws that interfere with the mission of the Church and not merely with the person or persons to whom the mission is directed. It asks the state to respect the Church's canon law. This it does not do for other religious institutions, not merely because it does not speak for those institutions but because it does not regard them as having the same kind of authority. And it does not think the state should regard them as having the same kind of authority.

Errors of judgment have certainly been made here. Our "Carolingian" past still haunts us; so do corruptions such as those witnessed recently in the sexual abuse or financial scandals. That, however, is no reason to soft-pedal the doctrine of the Two, which is not a doctrine of the Many. Nor is there a reason in the brazen denial of that doctrine by the modern Western state, which is playing now its trump card, its doctrine of neutrality – the latest version of the doctrine of the One. Even the incredulity of colleagues and neighbours, who have been so thoroughly catechized in (and who have so thoroughly imbibed) the state doctrine, ought not to deter us. For the doctrine of the Two is simply the gospel proclaimed to *homo politicus*. Tyrants may fear it and try to suppress it, but people of good will and those who govern modestly have nothing to fear. The doctrine of the Two is good news of a Master Architect who is building a better city and a better country in the midst of ours, but not at the expense of ours; a Master "whose mysterious action heals everything human of its fatal weakness, transfigures it and fills it with hope, truth and beauty."

In Canada we have taken as a motto *desiderantes meliorem patriam*. This sounds the note of transfiguration, drawn from Hebrews 11, a text that refers to those who put their hope in the heavenly city of which God himself is the builder. And, of course, the main motto on our coat of arms, *a mari usque ad mare*, is taken from Psalm 72, where it contains a messianic reference to the one whose dominion shall be over the whole world and whose kingdom shall have no end. No one in their right mind confuses Canada with that kingdom. Yet those who seek a better country by announcing a kingdom not of this world may also seek a better country in this world, in the *saeculum*, as our mottos suggest. They will do so (if following the path marked out by Vatican II) not by demanding establishment for the Church or by insisting that the state translate the teaching of the Church into the law of the land, so as to enforce conformity, but by inviting the city of man to organize itself in a way reflective of, or at least open to, the truth about human sociality revealed in the city of God.

Since they belong to the city of God, they know that the city of man is not their abiding home, and they do not seek to force their will upon it.[62] They do not even demand a crucifix on the wall of the legislature. But they do labour to show the state what justice is, and mercy. And how to craft positive law that faithfully reflects natural law – including the fact that it is good for man to acknowledge and honour God, and bad for him to ignore or deny God. They ask the state to pass no law that violates natural law or that does violence to the teaching of the Church and to the responsibilities of the faithful.[63] And if they are not heard, they serve God and their neighbour, if need be, through the discipline of non-violent civil disobedience to the state.[64]

They know that seeking a better country in the *saeculum* requires, whether they themselves are a minority or a majority, a polity in which people of different beliefs can live together in peace. But they also know that there can be no peace among men who cannot acknowledge God thankfully and who will not submit even to that which reason reveals about God. To take the opposite view – the view that peace requires a religiously "neutral" state and a naked public square – is not to seek a *better* country, but to seek a decidedly *different* one than our forebears thought they were seeking. It is to build a nation devoid of eschatological hope and so also of political humility.[65]

Can a Revolution be Neutral?

EXPERT WITNESS REPORT

Professor Douglas Farrow

Re: *Loyola High School et John Zucchi*
c. Michelle Courchesne,
en sa qualité de ministre de l'Éducation,
du Loisir et du Sport

Cour supérieure, district de Montréal,
Nº 500-17-045278-085

Sous la présidence de: L'honorable Gérard Dugré, J.C.S.

Author's note: What follows is the text of an official document
(Exhibit P–7, dated 12 December 2008) submitted to the Quebec
Superior Court at the request of Loyola High School in advance of
testimony given on 9–10 June 2009. Loyola, a Jesuit institution,
sued the Minister of Education, on both administrative and constitutional grounds, for refusing its request for an equivalency exemption from the new Ethics and Religious Culture curriculum in order
that it might continue to teach its own material in its own way.
This report examines the philosophical underpinnings of the government's program and the implications of its mandatory pedagogy, which bring it into significant conflict with the principles of a
Catholic education and indeed with the Catholic faith. It also considers the impact upon civil liberty and religious freedom. For the
record, a judgment in favour of Loyola was delivered by Justice
Dugré on 18 June 2010. It was overturned by the Court of Appeal
on 4 December 2012. The Supreme Court of Canada ruled in
favour of Loyola on 19 March 2015.*

* These judgments can be viewed at scc–csc.lexum.com
(see Case Information file 35201) or at www.mcgill.ca/prpp.

INTRODUCTION

In this report I intend to make four closely related points: first, that
the Ethics and Religious Culture (ERC) program represents a significant transfer of power from civil society to the state; second, that its
ambitious goals belie any claim to neutrality; third, that the ERC
program is intended to provide formation (i.e., to cultivate a world
view and a way of thinking and acting consistent with that world
view) and not merely information, and that the formation it hopes
to provide is at points incompatible with a Catholic formation;
fourth, that the imposition of this curriculum (with its mandatory
pedagogy) on Catholic schools constitutes, from the perspective of
the Catholic Church, a breach of fundamental rights as well as a defeat
for certain of the program's own objectives in recognizing diversity.

Little of this should be controversial, since there are reliable sources
available with which to substantiate these claims. My primary
sources will include the Proulx report (though it will be assumed
that the history and background of the ERC program are familiar to
the Court), documents from the Ministry web site, ERC materials,
and official Catholic documents; secondary sources will include various statements and commentaries (with special attention to the
analysis of Georges Leroux). The following outline will be employed:

1 The ERC "revolution"
2 Can a revolution be neutral?
3 Education as formation: compatibilities and incompatibilities
4 Imposition of the ERC program as a threat to religious liberty

It may be allowed that variations can be found, whether in
Ministry documents or in Church documents, respecting some of the
points at issue; but this does not, in my judgment, undermine the
conclusions or prevent the informed observer from acknowledging
that the imposition of the program on Catholic schools raises fundamental questions about the civil liberties and freedoms recognized in
section 2a of the *Canadian Charter of Rights and Freedoms* and in
sections 3 and 41 of the Québec charter.

1   THE ERC "REVOLUTION"

ERC is a very ambitious program. Professor Leroux is the foremost
philosopher and apologist for the program, and we may safely follow

his lead in describing it. He claims that it is the "only truly novel" program in the recent reform of public education. Indeed, he insists that "no one can truly gauge the magnitude of change under way" and that "someone looking in from the outside on the transformation in progress could say we are preparing a sort of revolution."[1]

The revolution in question can only be understood by recognizing that ERC is designed to fill a void, or rather two related voids, one moral and the other religious. The first void is created in part by the lamentable fact (if fact it is) that "literary culture is no longer the vector for the moralization of youth, and even less so for their introduction to thought."[2] The second void is generated by the end of confessional education in the schools and, more generally, by what Leroux calls "a deconfessionalized society."

To deconfessionalize means to interrupt and even to disenfranchise. It means to break "with the structure of religious denominations and faith, in order to gain access in school, as everywhere else in the public sphere, to a non-denominational, secular space. That break cannot erase the past, but it also cannot help being a true interruption. Public schools will no longer be the setting for any confessionality whatsoever, and we must take the full measure of the break with the past. But this non-denominational space is nonetheless not destined to become empty, a space whose neutrality would require complete indifference to everything moral, spiritual and religious. The positive aspect of this movement must now challenge us more than the impact of the break in communities of believers, which are called on, for their part, to face the challenge of reconstruction of denominational transmission in their own institutions."[3]

In other words, it now falls to the state rather than to the churches and synagogues, etc., to take the lead in equipping our youth to deal with "the considerable issues, both moral and religious, facing the contemporary world." The ERC program "does not intend to leave empty the place for the religious and the symbolic, but to fill it another way. It also assumes, as resolutely as possible, responsibility for the education of all young people to face the moral issues of these times."[4]

This is indeed a revolution. If the state (or the Ministry on behalf of the state) is to assume responsibility for equipping young people to face the moral issues of our times, it will have to assume responsibility also for determining what those issues are and how they should be presented. If it does not intend to leave empty the place of the religious and the symbolic in the schools, it will have to decide how and with what that space should be filled. What was once the task of the family and of the religious community – which formerly worked in cooperation with the schools as per the original wording of Article 41 of the Québec *Charter of Human Rights and Freedoms* – has now become the task of the state. Otherwise put, the revolution transfers to the state some of the most fundamental responsibilities of civil society.[5]

That might not be Professor Leroux's preferred way of putting it. Still, when he insists that "Québec's choice is radical and absolutely unprecedented," he points to just such a transfer. Québec will not adopt either the communitarian model followed in many other states or the republican model adopted by France. The former leaves schools – even public schools – free to craft moral and religious education in a manner consonant with the communities in which the schools are found; the latter eschews formal education in those subjects and entrusts the schools only with the task of studying the kind of literature that is capable of raising some of their fundamental concerns. Québec's choice is for a new model that puts moral and religious education in the schools wholly into the hands of the Ministry; that is, of the state or its agents.

Some argue that this choice was itself made in a revolutionary way, when Article 41 was summarily altered without public consultation.[6] In any case, there is general agreement that its effects will be revolutionary. The religious and moral formation of the youth of Québec will not be neglected but transformed – transformed by the state's assumption of responsibility for it, and so also of the right to shape the vision that guides and governs it.

2   CAN A REVOLUTION BE NEUTRAL?

"The need to secularize public schools in order to respect each person's human rights," says one Ministry document, "did not mean that the schools no longer had to deal with the students' spiritual development ... To educate is, first and foremost, to train human beings."[7]

This ambitious goal – to effect, so far as schooling is able, the spiritual formation of human beings – explains the determination to combine religious and ethical instruction in the ERC program: "Seeking to assume responsibility for the transmission of norms – and that means not limiting ourselves to the transmission of basic knowledge such as language, mathematics and science – we decided to fill the gap left by deconfessionalization, not with one project, but with two concomitant projects for the transmission of norms."[8]

There was, as Professor Leroux admits, some considerable internal resistance to this decision, doubtless because the linking of ethics and religion makes it unambiguously clear that the object of the ERC remains the transmission of norms. The program is not intended merely to *in*form students about religion, but in the context of informing them about religion to help form and shape them both as human beings and as citizens.

The new program, in other words, is not revolutionary because it eschews the transmission of norms, but because it continues, even under the conditions of deconfessionalization, to embrace and insist upon the transmission of norms. It is revolutionary because it assumes that burden and does not shy from carrying it, though it handles it very differently than did confessional education: "We believe that moral and religious knowledge must be explicitly transmitted, not suppressed, and we believe that transmission must reflect the pluralism of our culture."[9]

This credo of the ERC revolution raises very important questions. How can the ERC program achieve the transmission of norms in a manner that reflects in an unbiased way the variety of religious and ethical commitments that can be found in contemporary Québec society? How far, in other words, can the ERC revolution hope to achieve or maintain neutrality in matters of religion and ethics if it really wants to form and not merely to inform human beings? And does it really intend neutrality?

Here we should observe that there is an unresolved tension at the heart of the program, generated by the assumption, on the one hand, that deconfessionalization belongs to the pursuit of a neutral secular space, and by the commitment, on the other hand, to a robust educational philosophy that recognizes the importance of human formation through the transmission of norms.[10] This tension did not exist before "deconfessionalization," and it is vital that we grasp it.

In order to do so we must consider more closely the ERC's underlying philosophy, which Leroux has identified under the revealing rubric of *normative pluralism*: "The first reason that we, the Government and all those who have supported it, judged that it is necessary, even essential, to draw up the course of ethics and religious culture, is normative pluralism. It is essential that diversified experience, both on the moral and the religious level, be valued in its diversity."[11]

Philosophically, pluralism indicates a refusal to accept a single organizing idea or basic principle. Politically, it is closely related to multiculturalism, which denies that public policy should favour the dominant culture. But pluralism does have a normative aspect. Put positively (as by Harvard's Pluralism Project) it is "the engagement that creates a common society" from the cultural and religious diversity we see all around us. Put negatively (as by Avigail Eisenberg) pluralism guarantees "that no one principle, ideal, or way of life can dominate."[12] To speak of *normative* pluralism is presumably to emphasize, in the present context, that valuing diverse moral and religious practices or perspectives is to become the norm.

This presents us with something of a conundrum: Pluralism may celebrate the fact that different ethnic and religious or cultural groups bump up against each other in the public sphere. It may celebrate the multicultural reality of a country with a high rate of immigration from diverse places. There is no conundrum there; nor does one need to be a pluralist in order to join the celebration. But if pluralism – as a political philosophy or educational strategy, not as a cultural landscape – is to guarantee the engagement that creates a common society, and if indeed it is to do so by policing the engagement in an attempt to see that no one principle or ideal dominates, what then are we to make of pluralism itself? Is its very normativity not in fact its self-contradiction?

This conundrum appeared already with the Proulx report, which champions moral and religious diversity in just such a way as to demand ideological conformity. "We never weary of admiring the intelligence of the report's analysis of the challenges of pluralism," remarks Leroux,[13] but his response is far from universal. In a forty-page analysis of the report, Peter Lauwers [now a justice of the Ontario Court of Appeal] astutely observes: "It is no small irony that it trumpets pluralism in Québec's society but then prescribes uniformity in public education as the appropriate antidote."[14]

It is worth noting that pluralism (as a philosophy or strategy) was one category employed in a threefold typology developed in the field of religious studies by Alan Race in the early 1980s. Its counterparts were exclusivism and inclusivism. One of the leading exponents of that typology, Professor Gavin D'Costa, has since acknowledged its faulty logic and renounced it on the very sensible grounds that the pluralist himself "is surely, and can only be, an exclusivist," because the pluralist is just as determined as anyone else to present his view as the right one and to see it prevail.[15]

In the present case, if I understand it properly, what is at issue is whether the pluralist philosophy, and its pedagogical correlatives, should prevail by force of law. That is, whether it should be imposed upon those who do not share it or think it sound; and whether the hegemony of pluralism, backed by government fiat, should extend even into the realm of religious schools. I will say more about that in the final section. All that needs to be said here is that its imposition cannot be justified in the name of some putative "neutrality" that is characteristic of pluralism. Pluralism is not neutral, nor, as we shall see, is the ERC program that has taken pluralism as its foundation.[16]

From the beginning the ERC revolution was inspired by a passionate commitment to normative pluralism. Its proponents have not been neutral about normative pluralism, in other words, nor should we expect them to be. (It would be an odd revolution if it were produced by the uncommitted!) But is normative pluralism really, as they claim, neutral in its approach to religion? Of course not. That is one reason why people *are* passionate about it, whether they be for it or against it. Normative pluralism is neutral towards religion only in the sense that it has made itself the *norma normans* to which all religions, including Catholicism, must submit.

This submission, if the revolution succeeds, will have its consequences for the next generation. "Our children will be better than us," says Leroux, because they will be "more open to religious and moral diversity and more committed to normative pluralism. They will believe that it is preferable to be plural [diverse] than homogeneous."[17] They will, however, be entirely homogeneous in at least one sense – they will all be normative pluralists!

Seen in this light, normative pluralism is about suppressing diversity, not supporting it. It tends to monoculturalism, not multiculturalism or even "interculturalism."[18] It is more Rousseauvian than Rawlsian, more statist than democratic.[19] It has a place for any religious culture that cedes to the state final authority over religious culture, and no place for any that does not. A revealing footnote in the main ERC consultation document actually indicates that the purpose of the program is to "allow Québec students to develop a religious culture *consistent with ministerial orientations*."[20]

Can this commitment to normative pluralism as the necessary foundation or prerequisite for the study of religion and ethics fail to bias the presentation of Catholic religion and morals? Must it not operate as a lens that filters rather than as a mirror that reflects? Can it possibly incorporate the transmission of Catholic norms into its own normative intentions without somehow distorting or falsifying the former?[21] Does it not, after all, see itself as a substitute for the traditional Catholic procedures and norms?

The tension at the heart of the program, to put it another way, is the tension between a program that retains the historic Catholic mandate to provide a robust education and a program that nevertheless jettisons certain basic Catholic ideas about what a robust education should look like. This may or may not be a good thing – society should be free to argue about that, in school and out – but it is hardly a neutral thing, and it would be disingenuous to present it as such in hopes of justifying its imposition on Catholics.

3   EDUCATION AS FORMATION:
COMPATIBILITIES AND INCOMPATIBILITIES

"To educate is, first and foremost, to train human beings." Or, as Vatican II put it: "True education is directed towards the formation of the human person in view of his final end and the good of that society to which he belongs and in the duties of which he will, as an adult, have a share."[22]

But what is a human being? No answer to this can be neutral when it rises to the level of moral and religious discourse. Catholic schools exist because the Catholic Church believes that shaping the humanity of its own youth, and of others who wish to participate in the process, is its right and responsibility. The Catholic Church, however, has some quite specific ideas about what a human being is, and therefore about what a proper education in religion and ethics is.

Catholic ideas about education are thus partly consonant with those that appear to guide the ERC program, and partly dissonant. They support the two main objectives of the ERC program, namely, "the recognition of others and the pursuit of the common good."[23] They support the notion that education should aim at the development of mature independent judgment, as the Second Vatican Council asserted.[24] They support the search for moral principles, for a better understanding of Québec's religious heritage, and for awareness of the main features of a broad range of world religions. They confirm and do not contradict the Committee's "opinion that giving students opportunities to develop an integrative perspective on traditions different from their own is necessary for a true recognition of others and an informed understanding of religion." They raise no quibble respecting the three competencies.[25] However, they call for a different approach, a different pedagogy, and for attention to other and still higher objectives.

The reason for that is simple: Catholics believe in God. They do not approach education as if the human person did not have God as his or her final end. They do not understand the secular as a space, or rather a time (secular derives from *saeculum*), in which God is not to be considered or in which belief in God somehow does not matter, or in which one belief is just as good as another. If Catholics are committed in principle to the recognition of others, the first and foremost thing to be recognized in the other is the fact that this other is a creature of God's, loved by God. If they are committed in principle to pursuit of the common good, the first and foremost thing to be said about that good is that (if it really is good) it leads ultimately to God, the source of all good. When Catholics speak of human autonomy, they do not set this autonomy over against the law of God or the law of nature as made by God; they speak of it rather as a function of the image of God.[26]

Some of the things that are said about the ERC's "open and secular" program cannot be said, then, of a Catholic approach to moral and religious education. It is falsely claimed of the former that "it does not espouse any particular set of beliefs or moral references,"[27] but of the latter the opposite may be said. It is open not because it espouses nothing in particular, but because in its own particularity it is capable of recognizing the particularity of the other. It is not, and does not intend to be, institutionally neutral.[28] It does intend to encourage teachers and parents "to accompany students on a spiritual quest," and "to present the history of doctrines and religions," and various other things that are formally eschewed by the ERC program. It intends to examine both its own and other world views critically, but *not* to maintain distance from its own world view and convictions – as if that were either possible or desirable.[29] It does not impose, but it does propose. It guides and models. If it didn't, it wouldn't be Catholic.

Catholicism "takes diversity into account," as the ERC program also wants to do. It is certainly not against diversity. Its trinitarian theology and its account of creation provide a solid foundation for respect for the many and not merely for the one, for the different and not merely for the same. That is one reason why societies shaped by the Church have generally welcomed immigrants, and why the

Church itself is arguably the best global illustration of diversity in unity and unity in diversity. The Church is a partner in dialogue at an astonishing number of borders and intersections in the modern world, as it was in the mediaeval world. Studies of its schools have shown that this characteristic stands out.[30] But its approach both to dialogue and to education is different from that of the Ministry's normative pluralists, who wish to impose a program that (they say) proposes nothing.

According to canon law, "since true education must strive for complete formation of the human person that looks to his or her final end as well as to the common good of societies, children and youth are to be nurtured in such a way that they are able to develop their physical, moral, and intellectual talents harmoniously, acquire a more perfect sense of responsibility and right use of freedom, and are formed to participate actively in social life."[31] The appeal to a final end – the only part of this that the ERC has dropped – is decisive. "It is clear," says the Church, "that the school has to review its entire programme of formation, both its content *and the methods used*, in the light of that vision of the reality from which it draws its inspiration and on which it depends. Either implicit or explicit reference to a determined attitude to life (*Weltanschauung*) is unavoidable in education because it comes into every decision that is made."[32]

With this in mind, we may expand just a little on a few of the differences that must be respected if a Catholic school is to be authentically Catholic in the formation it offers.

First, the Catholic school is fully committed to the view that human dignity lies in human ends, not merely in human autonomy (which enables human beings willingly and rationally to seek their proper ends). In its moral and religious education, then, it cannot be content to examine the ways in which different societies and different groups within society articulate their values and norms, or arrange their religious symbols, or handle the motifs of "tolerance, justice, human ambivalence [and] the future of humanity."[33] All of this it will want to do, but not at the expense of asking students, at the very heart of their ethical reflection, to contemplate the right ordering of ends; or of asking them, at the heart of their religious education, to think about God as the End of ends.

Second, the Catholic school is fully committed to the view that reason, to be and remain reasonable in its highest pursuits, requires faith and the community of faith as its guide and support.[34] ERC literature, for its part, shows traces of a facile and frankly indefensible dichotomy between faith and reason, which plays into its tendency to regard the selection of ethical principles and the making of religious commitments chiefly as a form of self-expression or self-definition. This issue obviously goes to the core of curricular and pedagogical differences, since Catholicism admits no such dichotomy and therefore regards both ethics and religion as something more than personal or corporate self-expression.[35]

Third, the Catholic school does not set its "obligation to the present" over against its obligation to the past.[36] Unlike the new ERC school, it continues to see in its faithfulness to its heritage the most important gift it can make to society today. It believes in transmission not merely so that Québecers, in pondering their present or their future, will have some recollection of their past, but because *what* is transmitted is regarded as essential for the present and the future – just as essential as it was in and for the past.

Fourth, the Catholic school does not adhere to individualism, either philosophically or pedagogically. It seeks the formation of human beings, and it agrees on "the primacy of the individual over institutions," as one Committee brief puts it[37] – only it does not understand humans as individuals but as persons in community, because it understands God as triune and personal. Which is to say, it is not stuck in some modern or postmodern paradigm that presents "each student as a unique, autonomous individual" who must, on the one hand, be protected from the influence of his teachers lest his autonomy be stunted; and who, on the other hand, must be taught by those same teachers, their reticence notwithstanding, how to be properly open to "diverse values, beliefs, and cultures."[38] It is free rather to see itself as "a community whose values are communicated through the interpersonal and sincere relationships of its members,"[39] and as a place where students learn "to form their own judgments in the light of the truth" – a truth that, to be taught, must be lived.[40]

Fifth, the Catholic school does not believe, as the Ministry apparently does, that people should be forced to be free. "By grouping all the students together, rather than dividing them into groups according to their beliefs, and by promoting the development of attitudes of tolerance, respect and openness, we are preparing them to live in a pluralist and democratic society."[41] Or as Professor Leroux puts it: "We agree to give young people the freedom that results from the

knowledge of traditions – their own and those of all others – and
that is what we have chosen to do by providing that education in a
normative framework."[42] The latter statement is more acceptable to
a Catholic way of thinking, but in the *normative* lies a problem: a
problem respecting the conflict of norms just outlined; a problem,
therefore, respecting religious liberty.

4   IMPOSITION OF THE ERC PROGRAM
AS A THREAT TO RELIGIOUS LIBERTY

The right to educate one's offspring in a manner consonant with
one's beliefs is regarded by the Catholic Church as an indispensable
element of religious freedom. This right, as the Church understands
it, goes beyond the right of parents to teach their own children at
home or of religious communities to educate their members without
government interference. It includes the right to establish schools
devoted to a Catholic ethos and world view.

The Catholic Church has both law and official teaching on this
matter, which can be found in a number of places. The Code of
Canon Law includes the following canons:

793 §1. Parents and those who take their place are bound by the
obligation and possess the right of educating their offspring.
Catholic parents also have the duty and right of choosing
those means and institutions through which they can provide
more suitably for the Catholic education of their children,
according to local circumstances.
800 §1. The Church has the right to establish and direct schools of
any discipline, type, and level.
803 §2. The instruction and education in a Catholic school must be
grounded in the principles of Catholic doctrine; teachers are to
be outstanding in correct doctrine and integrity of life.[43]

The Pontifical Council on the Family has produced a Charter of
the Rights of the Family, [44] which includes the following article:

5 c) Parents have the right to ensure that their children are not
compelled to attend classes which are not in agreement with
their own moral and religious convictions. In particular, sex
education is a basic right of the parents and must always be

carried out under their close supervision, whether at home or in educational centers chosen and controlled by them.

The Sacred Congregation for Catholic Education has set out in *The Catholic School* a fuller treatment of the subject that contains, *inter alia*, these affirmations:

[8] In her encounter with differing cultures and with man's progressive achievements, the Church proclaims the faith and reveals "to all ages the transcendent goal which alone gives life its full meaning". She establishes her own schools because she considers them as a privileged means of promoting the formation of the whole man, since the school is a centre in which a specific concept of the world, of man, and of history is developed and conveyed.

[13] The Church upholds the principle of a plurality of school systems in order to safeguard her objectives in the face of cultural pluralism. In other words, she encourages the co-existence and, if possible, the cooperation of diverse educational institutions which will allow young people to be formed by value judgments based on a specific view of the world and to be trained to take an active part in the construction of a community through which the building of society itself is promoted.

[14] Thus, while policies and opportunities differ from place to place, the Catholic school has its place in any national school system. By offering such an alternative the Church wishes to respond to the obvious need for cooperation in a society characterised by cultural pluralism. Moreover, in this way she helps to promote that freedom of teaching which champions and guarantees freedom of conscience and the parental right to choose the school best suited to parents' educational purpose.

[15] Finally, the Church is absolutely convinced that the educational aims of the Catholic school in the world of today perform an essential and unique service for the Church herself. It is, in fact, through the school that she participates in the dialogue of culture with her own positive contribution to the cause of the total formation of man. The absence of the Catholic

school would be a great loss for civilisation and for the natural
and supernatural destiny of man.

Speaking at Castel Gandolfo on 25 September 2008, Pope Benedict
XVI insisted that "the Catholic school is an expression of the right
of all citizens to freedom of education, and the corresponding duty
of solidarity in the building of civil society" (Zenit News Service).
More than a century earlier, Pope Leo XIII, addressing the Manitoba
school question in his encyclical, *Affari vos*, argued as follows:

> Justice and reason then demand that the school shall supply our
> scholars not only with a scientific system of instruction but also
> a body of moral teaching which, as we have said, is in harmony
> with the principles of their religion, without which, far from
> being of use, education can be nothing but harmful. From this
> comes the necessity of having Catholic masters and reading
> books and text books approved by the Bishops, of being free to
> regulate the school in a manner which shall be in full accord
> with the profession of the Catholic faith as well as with all the
> duties which flow from it. Furthermore, it is the inherent right of
> a father's position to see in what institutions his children shall be
> educated, and what masters shall teach them moral precepts.
> When, therefore, Catholics demand, as it is their duty to demand
> and work, that the teaching given by schoolmasters shall be in
> harmony with the religion of their children, they are contending
> justly. And nothing could be more unjust than to compel them to
> choose an alternative, or to allow the children to grow up in
> ignorance or to throw them amid an environment which consti-
> tutes a manifest danger for the supreme interests of their souls.
> These principles of judgment and action which are based upon
> truth and justice, and which form the safeguards of public as
> well as private interests, it is unlawful to call in question or in
> any way to abandon.[45]

Thus also Cardinal Ouellet, who, in addressing the Québec school
question, has argued that the imposition of the ERC program is an
undue burden on the Church in its own responsibility respecting
"the transmission of our religious heritage":

> Without considering the primacy of the right of parents and their
> clearly expressed desire to retain the freedom of choice between

confessional and moral teaching, the state is suppressing confessional teaching and imposing an obligatory course of ethics and religious culture in both public and private schools. No European nation has ever adopted such a radical approach, which revolutionizes the convictions and religious freedom of the citizens. This leads to the profound dissatisfaction and sense of powerlessness that many families feel ... Will the operation of refocusing the ethical and religious formation of citizens by means of this obligatory course be able to salvage minimal points of reference to ensure a harmonious common life? I doubt it, and I am convinced of the contrary, because this operation is conducted at the expense of the religious freedom of the citizen, especially the freedom of the Catholic majority.[46]

Similarly, albeit in a different tone of voice, the "Statement from the Assembly of Québec Catholic Bishops on the Ethics and Religious Culture Program": "The Assembly of Québec Catholic Bishops has always expressed its preference for respecting parents' choices in matters concerning moral and religious education. For this reason, it has favored a system of options between confessional instruction and a non-religious moral instruction. This freedom of choice will disappear once the new program is implemented. In our eyes this represents a loss and we conclude that we must remain very vigilant regarding the fundamental respect of freedom of conscience within the newly created context."[47]

Likewise the "Report of the English Speaking Catholic Council on the Proposed Ethics and Religious Culture Program": "The treatment of religious rights and freedoms betrays a basic flaw. The project completely screens out the fundamental human rights of parents from religious education. The article on parental rights in the Quebec Charter of Human Rights acknowledges the unique rights of parents to transmit their moral and religious traditions to their children: 'Parents,' article 41 states, 'have a right to give their children a religious and moral education in keeping with their convictions.'"[48]

There can be no doubt, then, that from the perspective of the Catholic Church the imposition of a program the objectives of which are acceptable, but the philosophical presuppositions and pedagogy of which are unacceptable, constitutes an infringement both of parental freedom of choice and of fundamental religious freedom.

Professor Leroux, for one, appears to take some account of this. "Communities of believers," he says, "are called on, for their part, to face the challenge of reconstruction of denominational transmission *in their own institutions*" (emphasis mine). And yet he adds, as if in recognition of the problem at hand: "We can already foresee long debates about reasonable accommodation and even legal challenges under our charters."[49] Such foresight does not require a prophetic gift, but only a recognition that the new program, if mandatory, does indeed suffer from a basic flaw in its treatment of religious rights and freedoms. To ask a Catholic institution such as Loyola to face the challenge of reconstruction, while at the same time imposing upon it the ERC curriculum, is to ask it to make bricks without straw.

The precise nature and limits of religious rights and freedoms are not altogether settled, of course, which is hardly surprising given that the definition of religion is itself a difficult matter and that the grounds for restricting religious expression are always prudential.[50] But if freedom of religion does not include the right of religious communities to establish their own schools, and in those schools to teach religion and ethics with the breadth and competence prescribed by the Ministry but in a manner consonant with the beliefs of that community, then freedom of religion is an almost meaningless concept. Either that, or the community in question – for reasons good or bad – has been denied freedom of religion.

Moreover, if the right to see that one's own children are educated in a manner consonant with one's religious beliefs is denied by the state, then the state has arrogated to itself one of the primary responsibilities and privileges of parenthood. Indeed, it has called into question who or what has primary responsibility for the children – their parents or the state itself. In that case it has turned its back on the *Universal Declaration of Human Rights*, which does not view the family as a creature of the state but as something still more fundamental than the state. The *Universal Declaration* insists that "the family is the natural and fundamental group unit of society and is entitled to protection by society and the State," and expressly recognizes that parents "have a prior right to choose the kind of education that shall be given to their children."[51]

Universal imposition of the ERC program is a serious obstacle to "democracy and parental choice"[52] in Québec. Not only does it deprive parents of their right to choose an authentically Catholic (or Jewish, etc.) education for their children, it fundamentally subverts the democratic process by subjecting all young citizens to a compulsory spiritual formation designed and delivered according to a state-approved ideology.[53]

When the matter is put in this light, it is not at all clear that the ERC model represents, as Leroux maintains, a wholly unprecedented choice. It may differ from what he calls the Republican model of contemporary France, but it bears some resemblance to the high-handed approach of an earlier era in French history and – most ironically – to the failed policies of the British regime in Québec in the period between the Treaty of Paris and the Quebec Act.[54] In its attack on religious liberty it also bears comparison with certain draconian measures adopted in authoritarian states and, lately, in various western jurisdictions from the UK to California. To claim that it is unprecedented is to deflect attention from the question that ought to be asked, *viz.*, whether its precedents are ones that Quebec should be emulating.[55]

CONCLUSION

We return in conclusion to our point of departure. Professor Leroux speaks of deconfessionalization as a break or rupture with the past, and of a spiritual and ethical void that must be filled by the ERC program. Cardinal Ouellet, however, maintains that there was already a break of a more fundamental kind, of which deconfessionalization and the ERC revolution are themselves symptoms: "The real problem in Quebec is the spiritual vacuum created by a religious and cultural rupture, a substantial loss of memory, leading to a crisis of the family and education, leaving citizens confused, demoralized, prone to instability and relying on transient and superficial values. This spiritual and symbolic void inside Quebec culture disperses its vital energy and creates insecurity, for want of roots in and continuity with the sacramental and evangelical values that have nurtured it since its beginning."[56]

Who really has the measure of the problem – the Church or the champions of the ERC program? That can and should be debated. Should the Ministry takes sides in this debate? To some extent that may be unavoidable, though arguably it should be avoided as far as possible. But has the Ministry any right to impose the ERC solution on the Church, by dominating the study of ethics and religion in the Church's own educational institutions? Surely not. The imposition of the new curriculum, which dictates even to private and religious schools how moral and religious issues are to be framed and communicated, is an unreasonable restriction on religious freedom that is in no way justified by the state's proper concern for the maintenance of good order through universal access to a high quality education.

In so far as it suppresses debate in and between schools by preventing religious schools from being true to their own charters and mandates, it serves only to undermine educational interests as well. The two main objectives of the program, as we have noted, are "the recognition of others and the pursuit of the common good." These objectives might have been lifted straight out of *Dignitatis humanae* or any number of other Catholic documents, yet the imposition of the program on Catholic schools implies the *non*-recognition of the Catholic voice, which must now be filtered by the Ministry, to the great detriment of its distinctive contribution to the common good.[57]

The more general goals of the Québec Education Program – namely, "the construction of identity, the construction of world-view and empowerment" – also stand to suffer if Catholics are denied the right to work at these goals in an authentically Catholic way. It is difficult, in fact, to resist the conclusion that the universal imposition of ERC is intended to frustrate the construction of a solid Catholic identity and world view, unless perchance it is intended to frustrate some other identity or world view, with the frustration of the Catholic as collateral damage.

At all events, both past history and present research suggest that non-Catholics, too, will be impacted negatively by a universally mandated ERC program: not only because it has similar implications for their own pursuit of these goals, but because the Catholic loss is already their loss. A public order argument, properly developed, would not justify the suppression of the right to religious freedom that belongs to Catholic families and citizens, and by extension to their schools; on the contrary, it would support the fullest exercise of that right, which has yielded, and continues to yield, positive results for those societies in which it has been respected.[58]

Nor should the right in question be reduced to freedom of conscience, and so to a question of individual autonomy. That is what some urge, thinking to strike a blow for libertarian ideas or, conversely, that a public order argument might then be brought to bear. But such a move falsely conflates the distinct elements of what the *Universal Declaration of Human Rights* speaks of as "the right to freedom of thought, conscience and religion."[59] This tends in turn to an elision of the communal and public dimensions of this threefold freedom – especially the familial and religious dimensions, which are typically expressed in the formation and choice of educational institutions such as Loyola High School.[60]

What is particularly insidious about the universal imposition of the ERC program is that it undermines all three constituent freedoms. It does so by purporting to defend the first of them, but in such a way as to seize from parents the primary responsibility for cultivating that freedom,[61] and from the Catholic Church its educational mission. Against this stands the claim of *Dignitatis humanae* that parents "have the right to determine, in accordance with their own religious beliefs, the kind of religious education that their children are to receive," and that "the rights of parents are violated if their children are forced to attend lessons or instructions which are not in agreement with their religious beliefs."[62] Against it stands also the claim that "the Catholic school forms part of the saving mission of the Church, especially for education in the faith."[63] Against it stands indeed Canada's obligation as spelled out in articles 10 and 13 of the *International Covenant on Economic, Social and Cultural Rights*,[64] and the desire of Québec society to preserve and enhance liberty of thought, liberty of conscience, and liberty in religion.

Notes

1 Biblical quotations will be from the *Revised Standard Version* unless otherwise indicated.
2 Here, however, the forty days (cf. Jonah 3:4) symbolize the time between the ascension of Jesus and his parousia, on which I have written elsewhere.
3 Revelation 21:26.
4 Revelation 21:24.
5 For Christians, of course, neither is the divine confined, as for Epicureans, to the *intermundia*, nor is it identifiable, as for Stoics and many moderns as well, with the world or world-process. The divine is the living and speaking God himself, the God of the patriarchs and prophets, "the God and Father of our Lord Jesus Christ." It is this incurably Jewish view of God that renders "the real work of political theology" (*pace* Paul W. Kahn, *Political Theology: Four New Chapters on the Concept of Sovereignty* [New York: Columbia University Press, 2011], 120) something done in a transcendent and not merely an immanent frame.
6 *Religion, Law, and the Growth of Constitutional Thought: 1150–1650* (Cambridge: Cambridge University Press, 1982), 1.
7 I think this is harder for political theology than, say, for philosophical theology, but it is not easy there, either; cf. Douglas Farrow, "Theology and Philosophy: Inhabiting the Borderlands," *Nova et Vetera* 11, no. 3 (2013): 673–706. (All references to *Nova et Vetera* will be to the English edition.)
8 This article (Douglas Farrow, "Baking Bricks for Babel?", *Nova et Vetera* 8, no. 4 [2010]: 745–62) was occasioned by the appearance in 2009 of Benedict's controversial encyclical, *Caritas in veritate*.

9 Douglas Farrow, "The Audacity of the State," *Touchstone* 23, no. 1 (2010): 28–35.

10 "Church," when capitalized (as often in chapter 5, for example), will refer to the Roman Catholic Church in distinction from the eastern churches in impaired communion or the ecclesial communities of the "separated brethren." The preference for the lower case as the default position owes much to the genre of the present essays, and nothing to doubt about either the supernatural dimension of ecclesial existence or *Lumen gentium*'s *"subsistit in"* (§8). That there can be no entirely satisfactory or fixed usage of the capital in a work like this must be granted.

CHAPTER ONE

1 Epimenides, fragment from an AD ninth-century Syriac commentary on Acts by Isho'dad of Merv, which is our only extant source (http://en.wikipedia.org/wiki/Epimenides).

2 From a 1990 interview with Nathan Gardels ("From the East: A Sense of Responsibility"), as it appears in *New Perspectives Quarterly* 21, no. 4 (2004), on the subject of Miłosz's 1995 "The Fate of the Religious Imagination" (www.digitalnpq.org/archive/2004_fall/28_milosz.html). I have substituted "resurfaced" for "been resurrected," for the sake of consistency with his metaphor.

3 My apologies to anyone reading this who may be Cretan by origin; the literal sense is not in view here.

4 This and the following quotations are drawn from his article, "Human Rights: The Midlife Crisis," *The New York Review of Books*, 20 May 1999, 58–62.

5 My colleague, Arvind Sharma, has attempted something along those lines in various drafts of an expanded charter of human rights according to the world's religions, but this project tends, on my view, to overreach itself. See also the South African Charter of Religious Rights and Freedoms (http://acsi.co.za/charter-religious-rights).

6 Michael Ignatieff, *Human Rights as Politics and Idolatry*, ed. Amy Gutmann. With commentary by K. Anthony Appiah, David A. Hollinger, Thomas W. Laqueur, and Diane F. Orentlicher. Princeton: Princeton University Press, 2001.

7 See Daniel Cere, "The Problem of 'Nature' in Family Law," in *The Jurisprudence of Marriage and Other Intimate Relationships*, ed. Scott FitzGibbon, Lynn Wardle, and Scott Loveless (Getzville, NY: William S.

Hein & Co., 2010): "In the course of the committee debates, all references to 'nature' were weeded out of the UDHR document, except for one. The most dramatic casualty was the deletion of the reference to 'nature' in article 1, which affirmed that all persons are 'endowed *by nature* with reason and conscience' (emphasis added). By Dec.10th 1948, the date of ratification, the only reference to nature left standing in the Universal Declaration was the affirmation of the 'natural and fundamental' character of the family ... Charles Malik of Lebanon proposed new wording that eliminated any reference to the role of state law and defined the family as 'a natural and fundamental group unit of society.' Malik argued that rights language on marriage and the family should not be framed so as to imply that conjugal society is a creature of state law subject to 'the caprice of men.'"

8 The golden rule (to use its seventeenth-century moniker) is often traced back to Confucius, c. 500 BC, but it shows up in one form or another in many ancient cultures. For example, in this positive Egyptian form more than a millennium earlier: "Now this is the command: Do to the doer to cause that he do thus to you." Or this negative Egyptian form about the time of Confucius: "That which you hate to be done to you, do not do to another." In the *Crito,* Socrates even says, "One should never do wrong in return, nor mistreat any man, no matter how one has been mistreated by him" (49c), and this is very close to Jesus' reading of it. The command, as received from Jesus, exceeds all of these, however: "So whatever you wish that men would do to you, do so to them; for this is the law and the prophets" (Matthew 7:12).

9 See Alberto Giubilini and Francesca Minerva, "After-birth Abortion: Why should the baby live?" *Journal of Medical Ethics* 39, no. 5 (2013):261–3.

10 In Ignatieff's words: "The Universal Declaration enunciates rights; it doesn't explain why people have them." Communist and some non-communist delegations, at the time of the drafting, rejected explicitly any reference to human beings as created in God's image. Even the fortifying qualification, "by nature," failed to pass muster. So, concludes Ignatieff, "secularism has become the *lingua franca* of global human rights, as English has become the *lingua franca* of the global economy. Both serve as lowest common denominators, enabling people to pretend to share more than they actually do" ("Human Rights: The Midlife Crisis," 58). Cf. Michael J. Perry's analysis in chapter 3 of *Toward a Theory of Human Rights* (Cambridge: Cambridge University Press, 2007), although Perry draws a different conclusion, maintaining the importance of a religious foundation for human rights.

11 Michael Ignatieff, *The Rights Revolution* (Toronto: House of Anansi Press, 2007), 107.

12 Conor Gearty, "Human Rights after Darwin: Is a General Theory of Human Rights Now Possible?" (7 May 2009, MSc Human Rights Alumni Lecture, London School of Economics).

13 A note on terminology: The word "right" (Old English *riht*) comes from the Latin *rectus*, "ruled," which comes in turn, says the *New Oxford American Dictionary* (NOAD), from "an Indo-European root denoting movement in a straight line." From *rectus* we also get "rectitude," of course, which indicates "straightness": that is, conformity to the proper standard, being governed by what should govern, being "true" in that sense. (Anselm, at *De Veritate* 12, has "truth," "rectitude," and "justice" as mutually defining terms.) But behind the word "right," as used in the expression "human rights," is another Latin word, *ius*, which indicates what is binding and a matter of duty. (The verbal root, *iuro*, means to swear or take an oath.) *Ius* can mean "law," but more broadly it means what is fair or equitable, what is objectively right or just. (From the adjective *iustus* we have our word "just," and from the noun *iustitia* our word "justice;" thus, for example, in Aquinas at ST 2–2.57.3, *ius naturale* is translated as "natural right," or at 57.1, *ius est obiectum iustitiae* is rendered "right is the object of justice.") NOAD tells us, based on common usage, that a right is "a moral or legal entitlement to have or obtain something or to act in a certain way." Thus also *The American Heritage Dictionary of the English Language*: "*Right* refers to a just claim, legally, morally, or traditionally: [e.g.,] *the right of free speech*." Much of what we call "justice" is a defence of such entitlements. If the entitlement in question is a universal right, rather than a royal prerogative, say, or a prerogative of parliament or of some other specific office or entity or person – if, that is, it transcends any local custom or covenant or contract – then we may say that it is an entitlement that belongs to human persons simply by virtue of the fact that they *are* human persons (provided, of course, that we have not rejected the "essentialist" notion that a human person *is* anything in particular).

14 Galatians 3:28, perhaps the biblical text most quoted in our time.

15 Translation *per* Henry Bettenson and Chris Maunder, *Documents of the Christian Church* (Oxford: Oxford University Press 2011, 4th ed.), 54. The crucial phrase, for present purposes, is *consubstantialem nobis eundem secundum humanitatem*, "of one substance with us according to his humanity," which posits a common human nature, united and dignified by the divine self-investment in it.

16 Larry Siedentop's recent book, *Inventing the Individual: the Origins of
Western Liberalism* (Cambridge, MA: Harvard University Press, 2014)
traces important aspects of the history to which I have alluded, in its pre-
Reformation phase, stressing eventually the role of William of Ockham,
whose understanding of moral autonomy he credits for "the birth of lib-
eral secularism" with its emphasis on "equality and reciprocity" (316f.).
While Ockham's contribution must not be underestimated, it is also
problematic, as we will observe in this chapter (see also chapter 3).
In *The Reformation of Rights: Law, Religion, and Human Rights in
Early Modern Calvinism* (Cambrige: Cambridge University Press, 2007,
12), John Witte Jr highlights Protestant contributions, emphasizing
Milton's role:

> While scores of sturdy English Calvinist rights theorists emerged in
> seventeenth-century England, it was the great poet and political philoso-
> pher John Milton who provided the most interesting integrative theory
> of rights and liberties. While some of Milton's ideas strayed beyond
> Calvinist conventions, most of his political ideas remained within the
> tradition and indeed extended it. Citing Calvin, Beza, and an array of
> Dutch, Scottish, and English Calvinists, Milton argued that each person
> is created in the image of God with "a perennial craving" to love God,
> neighbor, and self. Each person has the law of God written on his and
> her heart, mind, and conscience, and rewritten in Scripture, most nota-
> bly in the Decalogue. Each person is a fallen and fallible creature in per-
> petual need of divine grace and forgiveness which is given freely to all
> who ask for it. Each person is a communal creature, naturally inclined
> to form private, domestic, ecclesiastical, and political associations. Each
> such association is created by a consensual covenant or contract that
> defines its form and function and the rights and powers of its members,
> all subject to the limits of natural law. Each association is headed by an
> authority who rules for the sake of his subjects and who must be
> resisted if he becomes abusive or tyrannical. All such resistance must be
> as moderate, orderly, and peaceable as possible, but it may rise to revolt
> and regicide if necessary in the political sphere.

See also Witte's "Rights, Resistance, and Revolution in the Western
Tradition: Early Protestant Foundations," *Law and History Review* 26,
no. 3 (Fall 2008): 545–70. But perhaps it is to Oliver and Joan
O'Donovan's *From Irenaeus to Grotius: A Sourcebook in Christian
Political Thought, 100–1625* (Grand Rapids, MI: Eerdmans, 1999) that
one should turn if one desires to follow this history at first hand. We will
come to their own theoretical contribution shortly.

17 Locke's "life, liberty, and property" or the UDHR's "life, liberty and security of person" (art. 3; cf. the Canadian Bill of Rights) are expressions that do not include the word "happiness," yet this word is very significant because it orders all the rest to ultimate ends and thus makes the political secondary rather than primary.

18 16 April 1963, at p. 7 (Martin Luther King, Jr., Research and Education Institute: http://mlk-kppo1.stanford.edu:5801/transcription/document_images/undecided/630416-019.pdf).

19 *Dignitatis humanae*, §15 (trans. Laurence Ryan; ed. Austin P. Flannery, *Documents of Vatican II* [Grand Rapids, MI: Eerdmans, 1975], 812).

20 See Augustine, *De Trinitate*, book 13.

21 See *The Solzhenitsyn Reader: New and Essential Writings, 1947–2005*, ed. Edward E. Ericson Jr and Daniel J. Mahoney (Wilmington, DE: ISI Books, 2006), 566.

22 As reported by LifeSite News on 22 March 2012 (www.lifesitenews.com/news/your-gods-wrong-judge-erupts-in-angry-tirade-sends-pro-life-activist-back-t).

23 John Paul elaborates this contrast between what we say in our society and what we do:

> On the one hand, the various declarations of human rights and the many initiatives inspired by these declarations show that at the global level there is a growing moral sensitivity, more alert to acknowledging the value and dignity of every individual as a human being, without any distinction of race, nationality, religion, political opinion or social class.
>
> On the other hand, these noble proclamations are unfortunately contradicted by a tragic repudiation of them in practice. This denial is still more distressing, indeed more scandalous, precisely because it is occurring in a society which makes the affirmation and protection of human rights its primary objective and its boast. How can these repeated affirmations of principle be reconciled with the continual increase and widespread justification of attacks on human life? How can we reconcile these declarations with the refusal to accept those who are weak and needy, or elderly, or those who have just been conceived? These attacks go directly against respect for life and they represent a direct threat to the entire culture of human rights. It is a threat capable, in the end, of jeopardizing the very meaning of democratic coexistence. (*Evangelium vitae*, §18)

24 Tom Campbell, *Rights: A Critical Introduction* (London: Routledge, 2006), 5. There are today many critics of human rights in secularist circles,

some of whom are following a trajectory away from the concept
altogether. Here, however, we will look instead to theological critiques.

25 In particular, Hobbes' "redefinition of natural right, over against the
scholastic mainstream, as each individual's *unrestrained liberty* 'to use his
own power and to act for his self-preservation, so asserting both the radical priority of natural right to natural law and the radical separation of
natural right from social obligation'." Joan Lockwood O'Donovan,
"Rights, Law and Political Community: A Theological and Historical
Perspective," *Transformation* 20, no. 1 (2003): 35.

26 See Joan Lockwood O'Donovan, "Historical Prolegomena to a
Theological Review of 'Human Rights,'" *Studies in Christian Ethics* 9, no. 2
(1996): 52–65, where she notes the "progressive antagonism between the
older Christian tradition of political right and the newer voluntarist, indi-
vidualist and subjectivist orientations" and examines three constituent elements of the latter: property rights, contracts, and freedom of choice. By
her account, the growth of a "proprietary concept of subjective right,"
based on the sovereign ownership of one's self and one's capacities rather
than on natural or divine law, led to a disjunction between natural right
and social obligation and to an "economic or market model of social relationships." The Puritan and Whig idea of an exchange of natural for civil
rights also contributed to the "reduction of public law and the common
good it enforces to private law and private good." Freedom – understood
as emancipation from external constraints, whether spiritual or material,
for the pursuit of self-referential ends – eventually emerged as the highest
goal in a society where subjective rights is "the only coherent public moral
language." But such concepts are incompatible, she thinks, with "the revit-
alised striving in contemporary society for the substance of community,
reciprocity, equity, and public trust." They are also inconsistent with "the
Christian doctrines that are regularly invoked to support the generic concept of human rights: those of the *imago dei*, the divine-human covenant,
and sinful humanity's justification and freedom in Christ." Why then, she
asks, are Christian thinkers "willing to adopt a child of such questionable
parentage"? Could it be that in interpreting these doctrines they have
relied too much on the premises of classical liberal anthropology?

27 O'Donovan, "Rights, Law and Political Community," 38. Here and
elsewhere she offers a compact genealogy (disputable in certain details) for
the subjective rights-based culture that has taken root in modernity at the
expense of one based on moral order, a culture in which *ius* no longer
means what is objectively right or just, but only what the individual can
claim for himself as his "right."

28 On natural rights, cf. Nicholas Wolterstorff, *Justice: Rights and Wrongs* (Princeton: Princeton University Press, 2008), 31ff. and Oliver O'Donovan, *The Desire of the Nations* (Cambridge: Cambridge University Press, 1996), 247f.

29 Oliver O'Donovan, "The Language of Rights and Conceptual History," *Journal of Religious Ethics* 37, no. 2 (2009), 195. O'Donovan asks whether "the evolution of a plural-rights concept indicate[s], in fact, a civilizational mutation in the practical outworking of which we are still caught up, which has as its end the overthrowing of our traditional conceptions and practices of justice-as-right" (196) and has indeed contributed to "the subversion of working orders of law and justice" (194).

30 O'Donovan, "The Language of Rights," 202f. "In saying this, we bring to light the underlying affinity between the rights project and the modern tradition prevailing in the liberal West since the seventeenth century (which is that of grounding political community in the wills of the individuals who compose it). On the ground floor of multiple rights is the ontological assertion that each human being is irreducibly *one*, not interchangeable with any other. We come into the world not as sons and daughter of Adam and Eve, brothers and sisters under the skin, but like Walt Whitman's 'ships sailing the seas, each with its special flag or ship-signal.'"

31 O'Donovan, "The Language of Rights," 202, 204.

32 See Wolterstorff, *Justice*, 390ff.; cf. Ignatieff, who worries about a false emphasis on human rights before and unless God goes missing.

33 "Over" because it may place the person outside any corporate judgment; "under" because it may leave the whole burden to a theological judgment on which we cannot reach agreement.

34 In a subsequent book, *Justice in Love* (Grand Rapids, MI: Eerdmans, 2011), Wolterstorff brings this round to a reconciliation of justice and love, but consideration of that must be left to another time.

35 O'Donovan, "The Language of Rights," 204f. My own view is that he is too hard on the Universal Declaration, and places too much emphasis on it as a watershed moment in the shift from created order and natural law to this negative anthropology and free-floating positive law. He may also be too hard on Wolterstorff.

36 "May this human worth, which serves as a foundation for individual rights, actually belong to a general account of human nature? Is it a merely contingent truth that God's worth-conferring love is conferred on *each* member of the human species, or is the love of God to 'one and all' connected, after all, with the fact that 'one and all' are members *of the human race*? Wolterstorff believes in human nature. *Can human nature*

actually impose its form on justice conceived as rights?" (O'Donovan, "The Language of Rights," 205f., emphasis in last sentence mine).

37 Wolterstorff, *Justice,* 360; cf. 129.

38 Commenting on the International Theological Commission's "The Search for a Universal Ethics: A New Look at the Natural Law," in "The Situation of Natural Law in Catholic Theology," *Nova et Vetera* 9, no. 3 (2011), 668f., Hittinger writes: "When the ITC expresses the 'urgent' need to reach common foundations (of a natural law sort) for the human rights project, it will have to anticipate a response that, on its view, is terribly inadequate if not irrational. Namely, the renewed claim of rights to liberty within this indeterminate 'immanent' condition. These rights will be invoked against customs, positive laws, and the natural law insofar as they are norms antecedent to choice and consent."

39 *De iis, quae appelantur iura hominis, satis audiit multitudo: audiat aliquando de iuribus Dei* (Leo XIII, *Tametsi futura prospicientibus,* §13; cf. Wolterstorff 366).

40 Karol Wojtyla, *Love and Responsibility* (San Francisco: Ignatius Press, 1993), 41.

41 According to Hittinger ("The Situation of Natural Law," 658): "John XXIII's *Pacem in terris* (1963) enumerated some two dozen human rights grounded in natural law. To accommodate the expanding field of social doctrine, the revised Code of Canon Law (1983) states: 'The Church has the right always and everywhere to proclaim moral principles, even in respect of the social order, and to make judgments about any human matter in so far as this is required by fundamental human rights or the salvation of souls'" (canon 747, §2). On the other hand, David S. Yeago observes that O'Donovan-like concerns are also present among Catholics, who sometimes worry that recent popes – John Paul II, for one – "took on board too much of modern liberalism along with the discourse of rights." Surely it is a difficult task "to separate modern 'rights' from an individualistic voluntarism that undermines the very idea of a 'created order' that we cannot flout without disaster" ("Modern But Not Liberal," *First Things,* June/July 2012, 28).

42 Leo XIII, *Tametsi futura prospicientibus,* §3; cf. Augustine, *De Trinitate* 13.13.

43 See Singer's *Practical Ethics,* 2nd ed. (Cambridge: Cambridge University Press, 1993), chapter 4.

44 Wolterstorff unfortunately overlooks the trinitarian features of a Christian analysis. In fact, his book contains but a single reference to the Trinity, and that a negative one, in dismissal of a point by Barth.

45 "Justice [*iustitia*] consists in the firm and constant will to give God and neighbour their due [*ius*]" (*Catechism,* §1836; cf. Aquinas, *Summa Theologica* 2–2.58.1 and also Augustine, *De moribus ecclesiae catholicae et de moribus Manichaeorum,* §25).

46 In other words, that it rests on a pure individualism rather than on a genuine personalism (cf. John Paul II, *Gratissimam sane,* §14).

47 Eucharistic Prayer (preface), Roman Missal.

48 Singer (*Practical Ethics,* 11) thinks that "ethics takes a universal point of view," and from "the point of view of the universe" (334) – a "lofty standpoint" indeed! – God, apparently, may be left out of account. Singer's ethical man appears to be the very antithesis of eucharistic man. Not so with Wolterstorff, of course. But perhaps we must be a little critical of him, also, for thinking that being loved by God translates into a right to be loved by me. Would it not be better to remain on the God-creature axis rather than to return to the creature-creature axis? To be sure, the two great commandments begin with the one and move to the other. But the command to love my neighbour as myself does not entail my neighbour's right to be so loved, only the impossibility of my being like God, and so fulfilling my own vocation, in any other way. And it is, after all, my neighbour whom I am to love, not (except in the sense indicated by Thomas at *Summa Theologica* 2–2.23.1 ad 2) every fellow human – which would be an impossibility, at least in this life, except as a mere abstraction; but love is not abstract.

49 "The more extensive operation of liberty implies that a more complete subjection and affection towards our Liberator had been implanted within us. For he did not set us free for this purpose, that we should depart from Him – no one, indeed, while placed out of reach of the Lord's benefits, has power to procure for himself the means of salvation – but that the more we receive his grace, the more we should love him. Now the more we have loved him, the more glory shall we receive from him, when we are continually in the presence of the Father." Irenaeus, *Against Heresies* 4.13.3; see further my treatment of this theme in *Ascension Theology* (London: T&T Clark: 2011), 66ff.

50 *Resurrection and Moral Order: An Outline for Evangelical Ethics* (Grand Rapids, MI: Eerdmans, 1986), 76. Wolterstorff's insights could also be refined, and corrected, by relocating them in this context.

51 In point of fact, generous hearings were granted to earlier versions of this chapter, which were read to highly diverse audiences at the University of St Thomas (New Brunswick) and McGill University. For this I am grateful,

as I am to Dr Ryan Topping, who asked me to address the subject. The
present question did arise, naturally.

52 It was Christ, Leo observes at §3, who taught us "that the meaning of
human life, the supreme law, the end of all things was this: that we come
from God and must return to Him. From this first principle the consciousness of human dignity was revived: men's hearts realised the universal
brotherhood: as a consequence, human rights and duties were either
perfected or even newly created, whilst on all sides were evoked virtues
undreamt of in pagan philosophy. Thus men's aims, life, habits and customs received a new direction. As the knowledge of the Redeemer spread
far and wide and His power, which destroyeth ignorance and former vices,
penetrated into the very life-blood of the nations, such a change came
about that the face of the world was entirely altered by the creation of a
Christian civilisation."

53 *Solzhenitsyn Reader*, 583.

54 See Rom. 1:18ff. Man also ceases to be free; for freedom depends on
morality, and morality on justice, and justice on religion; that is, on justice
towards God.

55 Leo XIII, *Tametsi futura prospicientibus*, §7.

56 Ibid., §13.

CHAPTER TWO

1 Jean-Jacques Rousseau, *On the Social Contract, with Geneva Manuscript
and Political Economy*; ed. R. D. Masters, trans. J. R. Masters (New York:
St. Martin's, 1978), IV.8 (p. 131).

2 In *Hyde v. Hyde and Woodmansee* (1866 [L.R.] 1 P. & D. 130) Lord
Penzance posed *inter alia* this question: "What, then, is the nature of this
institution as understood in Christendom? Its incidents vary in different
countries, but what are its essential elements and invariable features?" His
answer was entirely correct: "If it be of common acceptance and existence,
it must needs (however varied in different countries in its minor incidents)
have some pervading identity and universal basis. I conceive that marriage,
as understood in Christendom, may for this purpose be defined as the
voluntary union for life of one man and one woman, to the exclusion of
all others."

3 *Nuptiae sunt coniunctio maris et feminae et consortium omnis vitae,
divini et humani iuris communicatio* (Digest 23.2.1).

4 *Summa Sententiarum* 7.6 (authorship disputed); quoted by Aquinas, *Supplementum* 44.3, ad. 4.

5 One may consult the Yogyakarta Principles for particulars (www. yogyakartaprinciples.org). This undifferentiated man, who has lost sexual complementarity, is now known, in an Orwellian turn of phrase, as capable of genuine sexual "diversity."

6 The condition that is of most concern is when the speech in question is "directed at behaviour that is integral to and inseparable from the identity of the group" being vilified (*Saskatchewan Human Rights Commission v. William Whatcott* [2013 SCC 11] at 122).

7 I am indebted in my phrasing here to Fr Thomas Guarino. It should be added that this bleak view of man represents a swing of the pendulum between an (alleged) essentialism that *reduces* a person to their sex and an anti-essentialism that denies the relevance of sex.

8 No one doubts that our bodies are sexed by chromosomal structures and reproductive organs, as by the hormonal system – by a physical reality that is given, not chosen. That, however, is for some but a barrier to be overcome. For matter, it seems, must be made entirely pliable to spirit, the realm of nature to the realm of freedom. We are not bound to any general design in nature, but may act in accordance with, indeed determine for ourselves, our own individual natures or identities. We are not, so to say, a little lower than the angels (Psalm 8) but rather a little higher; for we are, each of us, self-made.

9 This substantive problem has deep and tangled roots in mediaeval and modern nominalism. It is far from new to think that a categorical term has no actual referent. Its current manifestation in the realm of sexuality, however, is quite striking. In Sweden, for example, he (*han*) and she (*hon*) are now accompanied by the gender-blind *hen*, equally useful to those who don't feel comfortable making gender decisions and to those who wish to make sure they don't feel comfortable.

10 What I mean by "flag of convenience" is that they are not very interested in the difficulties of people who struggle sexually or socially to feel comfortable in their bodies. Nor indeed do they give much thought to the institution of marriage – that crumbling stronghold of gender stereotyping. Their real goal is to dissolve the whole nexus of sexual mores, thus rendering the very notion of deviancy moot. They are, in short, ethical nihilists, which cannot be said of others fighting under the "trans" flag. Unlike these others, they mean to be transgressive for transgression's sake, until the very possibility of transgression has been exhausted.

11 Christianly considered, this entailed monogamy.

12 Aquinas, *Supplementum* 49.3.

13 Aquinas, *Supplementum* 49.2.

14 See *Supplementum* 42.1.

15 See further *Supplementum* 42.2–3, and 49. This is not based solely on theological reason, of course, but on dominical teaching (cf. Matthew 5:31f. and 19:3–12 with Luke 16:18 and 1 Corinthians 7:10f.). Neither dominical teaching nor theological reason, however, rules out the annulment of what was said to have been a valid marriage when in fact it was not.

16 Augustine, *On Marriage and Concupiscence* 1.19; cf. 1.11ff.

17 "For in the resurrection they neither marry nor are given in marriage, but are [in that respect] like angels in heaven" (Matthew 22:30). Hence the celibate vocation is prized alongside marriage as equally necessary to the church's witness to ultimate human fulfillment (see again Matt. 19:10–12).

18 Council of Trent, Session 24. See: Norman P. Tanner, ed., *Decrees of the Ecumenical Councils* (London: Sheed and Ward, 1990), II:754.

19 Trent, Session 24, Canons on the Reform of Marriage, chapter 9 (Tanner, *Decrees* II:759); with which cf. Article 16 of the *Universal Declaration of Human Rights*.

20 There is a certain irony here, as some have remarked, given the fact that, among males, exclusivity is not a common feature, or even a common goal, of stable same-sex partnerships.

21 See further *Nation of Bastards: Essays on the End of Marriage* (Toronto: BPS Books, 2007), 63ff., which discusses *inter alia* the musings of Canada's chief justice on this subject.

22 F. C. DeCoste, "Courting Leviathan: Limited Government and Social Freedom in Reference Re Same-Sex Marriage," *Alberta Law Review* 42 (2005): 1099–122.

23 See "Marriage and Freedom: The Splendor of Truth in a Time of Denial," in *Nova et Vetera* 11, No. 4 (2013): 1137–54. Cf. John Milbank, "Gay Marriage and the Future of Human Sexuality," 13 March 2012 (Australian Broadcasting Corporation: www.abc.net.au/religion/articles/2012/03/13/3452229.htm).

24 John Milbank, "The Impossibility of Gay Marriage and the Threat of Biopolitical Control," 23 April 2013 (Australian Broadcasting Corporation: www.abc.net.au/religion/articles/2013/04/23/3743531.htm).

25 There was, I am told on good authority, an international conspiracy of sorts to make Canada a kind of crucible for same-sex marriage; whatever the truth of that, Canada has become such, though the experiment is still in its early stages.

26 See further Douglas Farrow, et al., "Thirteen Theses on Marriage," *First Things,* October 2012, 23–31. Cf. my article, "Why fight same-sex marriage?," *Touchstone,* January/February 2012, 24–31.

27 The "potentially" and "in principle" must not be overlooked. There are, of course, people whose circumstances make marriage difficult, if not impossible, even where it is deemed desirable. These circumstances may be economic or social or political or professional. They may also be medical. In combination and by association they may produce a phenotype (to use that loaded term) into which marriage does not easily fit. There are irregularities in nature, including chromosomal and hormonal irregularities that have an impact on sexual desire and on sexual function, and so on suitability for marriage. An irregularity, however, is just that. However difficult and burdensome it may be, and however demanding the personal or professional support required of a compassionate society, it doesn't, as some are trying to claim, create a new and different sex or category of human being. Even complete androgen insensitivity syndrome doesn't make a male into a female, though it results in female external genitalia; true gonadal intersex, as some call it, is a much more striking phenomenon, but it is the phenomenon of chromosomal doubling; again, it does not amount to a third sex. If it did – which is to say, if man were not essentially male and female – the "discrimination" or rights argument I have just presented, and my refutation of it, would have to be different.

28 See further "Rights and Recognition," in Daniel Cere and Douglas Farrow, eds, *Divorcing Marriage* (Montreal: McGill-Queen's University Press, 2004), 97–119, especially section 1.

29 See Robert P. George, "What Few Deny Gay Marriage Will Do," First Thoughts, 16 April 2013 (www.firstthings.com/blogs/firstthoughts/2013/04/what-few-deny-gay-marriage-will-do/).

30 This without prejudice to the proposal that has been put forward in various places that clergy, in witnessing marriage on behalf of the state, should refuse to use forms that by their very terminology falsify marriage.

31 Sherif Girgis, Ryan T. Anderson, Robert P. George, *What is Marriage? Man and Woman: A Defense* (New York: Encounter Books, 2012), 55. See further my review of this book in the September 2014 issue of *Touchstone.*

32 Ibid. 70; quoting Ellen Willis, "Can marriage be saved? A Forum," *The Nation,* 5 July 2004, 16.

33 Thus Michael J. Perry, in chapter 7 of *Toward a Theory of Human Rights: Religion, Law, Courts* (Cambridge: Cambridge University Press, 2007).

34 Or confined to a couple of pages, as in *The Meaning of Marriage: Family, State, Market Morals,* ed. Robert P. George and Jean Bethke Elshtain

(Dallas: Spence Publishing Company, 2006); but cf. Robert R. Reilly, *Making Gay Okay: How Rationalizing Homosexual Behaviour Is Changing Everything* (San Francisco: Ignatius Press, 2014).

35 This in defiance of the fact that the neo-sexual revolution rolls on. To heterosexual and homosexual (which replaced male and female) it has lately added "cis" and "trans" as an operative binary, distinguishing those who are, or are not, comfortable with the sex assigned to them at birth and with the gender roles imposed upon them. There is to be no "cisnormativity," of course, just as there is to be no heteronormativity.

36 Sirach 42:24f.

37 Cf. John Paul II, *Familiaris consortio* (1981), §31ff.

38 See section 3. "Contraception and Chastity," based on an address to the Bristol Newman Circle and an article in issue no. 7 of *The Human World* (1972), was published by the Catholic Truth Society in 1975. It is available, with an introduction, in Janet E. Smith, ed., *Why Humane Vitae was Right: A Reader* (San Francisco: Ignatius Press, 1993), 119–46. The earlier essay, "You can have sex without children: Christianity and the New Offer," appeared in the proceedings of the 1968 Canadian Centenary Theological Congress, which was held in Toronto.

39 Certainly it creates a myriad of bioethical problems, some of them insoluble – what to do with frozen embryos, for example – as the procreative, in turn, is isolated through new reproductive technologies. See further *Donum vitae* (Congregation for the Doctrine of the Faith, 1987) and *Dignitatis personae* (Congregation for the Doctrine of the Faith, 2008).

40 Many today seem to have forgotten that "Christianity was at odds with the heathen world, not only about fornication, infanticide and idolatry; but also about marriage" (Anscombe, "Contraception and Chastity," 1). They also seem to have forgotten that Jesus deepened even the requirements of the Mosaic covenant when he drove his questioners back to the divine design in creation itself: "Have you not read that he who made them from the beginning made them male and female, and said, 'For this reason a man shall leave his father and mother and be joined to his wife, and the two shall become one'? So they are no longer two but one. What therefore God has joined together, let no man put asunder." (Matthew 19:4–6) Cf. Robert A. Gagnon, *The Bible and Homosexual Practice: Texts and Hermeneutics* (Nashville: Abingdon Press, 2001), 187ff.

41 I am alluding, of course, to Romans 1:18ff. Paul would be the first to tell us that today's attack on sexual morality, which is also an attack on the body itself, is *ipso facto* an attack on the Creator and on man's vocation to honour God as God and to give thanks to him. Irenaeus would tell us

pretty much the same thing, for in important ways the struggle in which the church now finds herself reprises the life and death struggle with gnosticism that took place in the second century. Now, as then, sexuality is not really the *primary* battlefield, though it is an enormously important battlefield. At the heart of the matter are questions about God. Is the God who made this world, and who made man male and female, the true God? Shall we render thanks to him for and with our bodies, or shall we not?

42 John XXIII, *Ad Petri cathedram* (1959), §58.

43 John Witte Jr, *From Sacrament to Contract: Marriage, Religion, and Law in the Western Tradition* (Louisville: Westminster John Knox Press, 1997), 209.

44 Witte, *From Sacrament to Contract*, 215.

45 "The two shall become one flesh: Reclaiming Marriage. A Statement by Evangelicals and Catholics Together." *First Things*, March 2015, 25–31.

46 On Rousseau, see my chapter, "Of Secularity and Civil Religion," in Douglas Farrow, ed., *Recognizing Religion in a Secular Society: Essays in Pluralism, Religion, and Public Policy* (Montreal: McGill-Queen's University Press. 2004). As for St John, recall *Ad Petri cathedram*, §130: "There is never any need, therefore, to turn to proponents of doctrines condemned by the Church; for they only draw men on with false promises and when they obtain control of the state, try boldly and unscrupulously to deprive men of their supreme spiritual goods – the Christian commandments, Christian hope, and Christian faith. Those who adhere to the doctrines these men propose, minimize or eliminate all that our present age and our modern civilization hold dearest: true liberty and the authentic dignity of the human person. Thus they attempt to destroy the bases of Christianity and civilization." Cf. §§137–141, in which he seeks to support his persecuted brethren who hold fast to the truth. See also *Pacem in terris* (1963), §51, in which he marks with Aquinas the foundation and the limits of state authority: "Since the right to command is required by the moral order and has its source in God, it follows that, if civil authorities pass laws or command anything opposed to the moral order and consequently contrary to the will of God, neither the laws made nor the authorizations granted can be binding on the consciences of the citizens, since 'God has more right to be obeyed than men.' Otherwise, authority breaks down completely and results in shameful abuse." (Needless to say, my allusion above to Daniel and friends is intended to reinforce the distinction between civil disobedience for the sake of divine law and moral order, which is a disobedience accompanied by righteous suffering, and the

strong-arm tactics, with or without the sanction of civil law, employed by
those who set themselves against that order.)

CHAPTER THREE

1 Second Vatican Council, Session 9, *Dignitatis humanae* (Declaration on
   Religious Freedom, 1965), §1. In: Norman P. Tanner, ed., *Decrees of the
   Ecumenical Councils* (London: Sheed and Ward, 1990), II:1001f. Larry
   Siedentop traces the origins of this demand in *Inventing the Individual:
   the Origins of Western Liberalism* (Cambridge, MA: Harvard University
   Press, 2014).
2 *Loyola High School, et al. v. Attorney General of Quebec* (2015 SCC 12).
3 The quotation (here translated from the French) is drawn from an address
   by Leroux to the *Fédération des établissements de l'enseignement privé*
   on 3 May 2007, cited in a commentary for *Le Devoir* by Jean Morse-
   Chevrier ("Gare au pluralisme normatif dans les cours d'éthique et de
   culture religieuse," 4 June 2007).
4 See the appendix to the present volume, "Can a revolution be neutral?"
5 Thus Avigail Eisenberg, in a review of David Miller and Michael Walzer,
   eds., *Pluralism, Justice, and Equality* (Oxford: Oxford University Press,
   1995) in *American Political Science Review* 90, no. 3 (1996), 636.
6 Hence the school's announcement on the eve of the judgment: "Regardless
   of tomorrow's ruling, we wish to stress that Loyola will remain true to its
   founding principles and mission." (Letter to Stakeholders, 18 March 2015)
7 Québec Superior Court, Case No. 500-17-045278-085, 18 June 2010,
   par. 15 (translation available at www.mcgill.ca/prpp/). In point of fact,
   Loyola for many years had been teaching a comprehensive ethics and
   world religions curriculum of its own.
8 Par. 326.
9 Par. 331. Actually, the Inquisition's demands of Galileo were rather more
   nuanced than the Ministry's demands of Loyola, though the analogy is
   especially apt given the conflicted role of the Jesuit order in that conflict.
   See, for example, Peter Hess and Paul Allen, *Catholicism and Science*
   (Westport, CT: Greenwood Press, 2008), 41–54; cf. Rivka Feldhay, *Galileo
   and the Church: Political Inquisition or Critical Dialogue?* (Cambridge:
   Cambridge University Press, 1995).
10 "In our view, it would be insufficient to merely grant an exemption for
   Loyola to teach Catholicism from a Catholic perspective, while requiring
   an unmodified curriculum and a neutral posture in all other aspects of the

program. Binding Loyola to a secular perspective at all times, other than during their discussion of the Catholic religion, offers scant protection to Loyola's freedom of religion, and would be unworkable in practice" (*Loyola,* par. 154). The school, for example, "does not want its teachers to be forced to remain neutral – or more realistically, mum – in the face of ethical positions that do not accord with the Catholic faith. Rather, Loyola proposes to have its teachers facilitate respectful and open-minded debate, where all positions are presented, but where students evaluate ethics and morals not in a vacuum but with knowledge of the Catholic perspective" (par. 155).

11 Par. 156 and 159.

12 Par. 160.

13 In fairness, it must be acknowledged that Loyola contributed to this confusion by narrowing its argument before the court, as Justice Abella notes at par. 31, to the question of its right to teach about Catholicism and about ethics from a Catholic perpective and in a Catholic manner. This narrower focus certainly drew attention to the unreasonable nature of the Ministry's demand, but it also obscured the larger issue. The result was a less generous remedy than that proposed by the minority.

14 As, for example: "a 'neutral' and 'objective' way" (par. 72) as opposed to "from a religious perspective" or in a religious way (par. 70) – as if the latter is inherently incapable of being objective. At par. 78, however, Abella J. backs away from that contrast: "Nor is asking Loyola's teachers to teach other religions and ethical positions as objectively as possible a requirement that they shed their own beliefs."

15 Par. 45–7 reveal what I am calling the "neo-catholic" assumptions and aspirations that are operative here: "Because it allows communities with different values and practices to peacefully co-exist, a secular state also supports pluralism" (par. 46).

16 Nor does Abella J. pause to ask whether, in these matters, there *is* any such a thing as a neutral point of view.

17 Par. 75.

18 Quoted in *Loyola* at par. 43f. from Richard Moon, "Freedom of Religion Under the *Charter of Rights*: The Limits of State Neutrality" (2012), 45 *U.B.C. L. Rev.* 497, 498f., emphasis added.

19 Par. 160–162, emphasis added.

20 Here is the remark in full, from the editorial that launched *First Things*: "Pluralism is a much abused term. It is often suggested that, because we are a pluralistic society, we must play down our differences, pretending that our deepest differences make no difference. That, in our judgment,

is not pluralism at all. It is the opposite of pluralism. It is the monism of indifference." ("Putting First Things First," *First Things*, March 1990; reprinted March 2015, pp. 17–19)

21 [1996] 1 S.C.R. 825, at par. 91.

22 This, historically speaking, is just the opposite of the founding, which did indeed involve a diversity of views and hence of compromises among them. But it is the compromises that count, not the mere fact of diversity – otherwise, there could have been no founding. This applies as much to religion, by the way, as to any other matter. What Laurence Moore said of America is apropos, despite the very great differences between the two countries: "the full extension of religious tolerance ... was more the product of conditions of pluralism which no one sect had the power to overcome as of an abstract belief in the value of pluralism." R. Laurence Moore, *Religious Outsiders and the Making of Americans* (Oxford: Oxford University Press, 1986), 205.

23 In the *Loyola* hearing, Justice Abella more than once asked whether the state has a role to play in promoting a variety of truths. Perhaps she meant a variety of *approaches* to truth. If not, she would seem to have presupposed the disunity of truth, and as such the cessation of any meaningful search for truth even by the court. But even with that correction in place, her question still reproduces this problematic aspect of *Ross,* as does the judgment she authored.

24 For a fuller account, see Mary Anne Waldron, *Free to Believe: Rethinking Freedom of Conscience and Religion in Canada* (Toronto: University of Toronto Press, 2013), 110–13.

25 *Carter v. Canada* (2015 SCC 5), emphasis added. The response in question is first a feeling (fear of suffering) and then an action (suicide). The court thinks the prohibition of assisted suicide violates the principles of fundamental justice because it "has the effect of forcing some individuals to take their own lives prematurely, for fear that they would be incapable of doing so when they reached the point where suffering was intolerable." The court raises at par. 2 and takes up at par. 54 (ff.) the relation between autonomy and dignity, on the one hand, and the sanctity of life on the other. But by this very hendiadys, "dignity and autonomy," it prejudges the whole question. Dignity is found in autonomy, and autonomy is threatened by the denial of (lethal) "aid in dying." It then sets up a false quality/quantity analysis respecting the value and sanctity of life that permits it to evade the question as to whether suicide itself has a moral objectivity that might function as a reference point for dignity and so for fundamental justice. Or, rather, it assumes that the function is a positive one, just because

suicide addresses fear, and that the freedom to commit suicide at the time
of one's choosing is just what dignity and justice require. Quoting the trial
judge, it asserts that this freedom is "very important to [one's] sense of
dignity" (par. 68). It concerns itself not at all with whether fear of temporal suffering, as a complusive force, is good or evil, or with questions
about the nature of human autonomy. It does not even concern itself with
the social consequences of its judgment. No further illustration is required,
surely, of the fact that (for the culture represented by this court) the sense
of dignity which *Dignitatis humanae* says "has been impressing itself more
and more deeply on the consciousness of contemporary man" is no longer
tethered to anything the council fathers would have recognized as proper
to man. The concept of man has changed. Man does not stand, and never
will stand, *coram Deo*. His dignity is self-derived and his judgment
self-authenticating.

26 See "On Free Will" [*De Libero Arbitrio*, c. 1085], in *Anselm of
Canterbury: The Major Works*, ed. Brian Davies and G. R. Evans (Oxford:
Oxford University Press, 1998), 175–92. According to Anselm, were the
will only a will to happiness it would not be free in the way that it is free,
for then it could stray only through ignorance, not through sin, but it does
also stray through sin. On the other hand, were it only a will to justice, it
would pursue justice slavishly rather than for the sake of happiness. It
would seek only to fulfill the law for its own sake, as Kant later urged.
And this would not be freedom, even if it were autonomy. For the man
who is neither happy nor on the way to happiness is in bondage to whatever makes him unhappy. But if, as formed and moved by God, the will is
a will to happiness and also a will to justice, then things are very different.
For the pursuit of happiness must always be exercised either for or against
justice, and of justice either for or against happiness. Freedom begins by
virtue of the will's being situated by God at this intersection. Freedom
develops and advances as the will chooses to occupy this intersection
rather than seeking, vainly, to escape it. It seeks to escape when it tries to
pursue happiness without the first and primal justice, the justice of obedience to God – as Adam and Eve did, and the Serpent before them.

27 See J.S. Mill, *On Liberty*, chapter 3, which will be cited here from the collection *Utilitarianism, On Liberty, and Considerations on Representative
Government*, ed. H.B. Acton (London: J.M. Dent & Sons, 1972).

28 By shifting the focus from kinds of things (*genera*) to individual things,
from being *qua* analogical participation to being *qua* mere facticity, from
a concern with ends (*teloi*) to a concern with immediacy, nominalism
made many important contributions to science and to culture, but it also

distorted much in science and culture, and indeed in our grasp of human nature, as Anselm had already perceived that it would.

29 Siedentop (*Inventing the Individual*, 315) is right to praise Ockham for defending the freedoms necessary to sustain the sphere of conscience, including "what might be called its 'conscientious mistakes' of judgement," and for resisting the assumption "that morality can be enforced." Nevertheless, there is much that is problematic about Ockham's conception both of divine and of human freedom. Cf., for example, Servais Pinckaers, *The Sources of Christian Ethics*, trans. Mary Thomas Noble (Edinburgh: T&T Clark, 1995), 328ff., and Michael Allen Gillespie, *The Theological Origins of Modernity* (Chicago: University of Chicago Press, 2008), 22–30.

30 Mill, *On Liberty*, 114.

31 See Georges Leroux, *Éthique, culture religieuse, dialogue: arguments pour un programme* (Montréal: Éditions Fides, 2007), 20f. Leroux seems to think of this as a rite of passage for Quebec. It is *par la voix de l'Etat* that the people will begin to express themselves. It is under the state's tutelage, not the Church's, that they will learn to speak in their own voices.

32 The case of Dr Bogdan Chazan, in Poland, comes to mind. The Associated Press (9 July 2014) reported that he was fined and removed from his post as head of a Warsaw maternity hospital over a refusal to refer for abortion. The particulars of any given case may be complicated, of course, but the problem is becoming systemic. A couple of months earlier, *The Tablet* (27 May 2014) quoted Dr Charles O'Donnell in a frank address to the Catholic Medical Association: "To be a sound Catholic regarding sexual ethics it is not possible to train as a consultant obstetrician and gynecologist." The best advice he could offer aspiring British obstetricians was to emigrate (www.thetablet.co.uk/news/840/0/catholic-doctors-who-follow-church-teaching-advised-to-emigrate-rather-than-train-in-britain-). Midwives in the United Kingdom are faced with a similar dilemma, since the Supreme Court ruled on 17 December 2014 that accommodation of conscientious objection to abortion will apply only to actual participation in abortion procedures, and that midwives may not refuse to delegate or perform a supervisory or supportive role in these procedures. Some North American jurisdictions are headed in the same direction.

33 One of the most insidious features of Quebec's new euthanasia law, Bill 52, is its pretence of allowing conscientious objection while demanding referrals. The same is true of the new *Professional Obligations and Human Rights* policy (2015) of the College of Physicians and Surgeons of Ontario, by which no genuine conscientious objector could abide. In

Carter the Supreme Court has stopped short of demanding referrals, saying only that "the *Charter* rights of patients and physicians will need to be reconciled in any legislative and regulatory response to this judgment" (par. 132). But they *cannot* be reconciled, just because there arises here an absolute moral disagreement which generates not relative but, rather, conflicting "rights."

34 Those who wish to dispense with freedom of religion in favour of freedom of conscience do well to bear in mind that attacks on the one quickly lead to attacks on the other. That is because conformity of behaviour is the true object of attacks on the one as well as the other.

35 The Supreme Court of Louisiana (2013-C-2879) recently ordered a Catholic priest to break the seal of the confessional; a priest's oath would require him, as the diocese of Baton Rouge pointed out, to subject himself to prison rather than to do so.

36 "Luckily," says Michael Novak ("A New Conversation among Civilizations," 20 March 2002, www.aei.org/publication/a-new-conversation-among-civilizations), "these had been translated into Syriac by St. Ephrem of Syria" in the fourth century. From Syriac they were translated into Arabic in the ninth century, and put to good use by Ibn Sina, at the turn of the new millennium. Averroes wrote important commentaries on them in the conquered Spanish territories a little while later. It was through contact with the work of Averroes and of his Jewish counterpart in Cordoba, Maimonides, that the West began to recover Aristotle. Through the Crusades (which began in 1095), new manuscripts of Aristotle were also discovered and brought back to the West, making possible some reconstruction of the Greek texts.

37 Hans Thijssen, "Condemnation of 1277," *The Stanford Encyclopedia of Philosophy* (Winter 2013 edition), ed. E. Zalta (http://plato.stanford.edu/archives/win2013/entries/condemnation). "Nowadays," says Thijssen, "scholars agree that there were no medieval authors who entertained the philosophically absurd theory that two contradictory propositions – one derived from philosophical investigation, the other from Christian revelation – can both be true at the same time. Rather, Tempier's reproach should be taken as an attempt to ridicule the hermeneutical practice of commentators to evaluate a doctrine … from a philosophical point of view … and from faith." That, however, is an equally unsatisfactory formulation of the problem, which we will not pursue here. See also Bartosz Brożek, *The Double Truth Controversy* (Kraków: Copernicus Center Press, 2010).

38 *The Gazette*, 16 May 2014.

39 Ibid., 19 June 2014.

40 CTV News, 2 June 2014.

41 *The Montreal Star*, 25 May 1972.

42 The language is borrowed from *Syndicat Northcrest v. Amselem* (2004 SCC 47), par. 39: "In essence, religion is about freely and deeply held personal convictions or beliefs connected to an individual's spiritual faith and integrally linked to one's self-definition and spiritual fulfilment, the practices of which allow individuals to foster a connection with the divine or with the subject or object of that spiritual faith."

43 The latter is the view that the ERC program adopts, and that Loyola High School rejects. Logically, of course, there is a third possibility, *viz.*, that politics rather than religion belongs to the realm of the irrational; this may, alas, be true in the present case.

44 *National Post*, 21 June 2014.

45 Were this just a political game, such as we see all the time in Ottawa, as in Westminster or Washington, or an academic game, such as sophists have always engaged in for profit, we might treat it less seriously. Unfortunately, it is a game in which the courts have also become involved. Moreover, it is a "game" in which not only livelihoods but lives are at stake.

46 As the learned sociologist of religion, Armando Salvatore, has shown in his book *The Public Sphere: Liberal Modernity, Catholicism, Islam* (New York: Palgrave, 2007), the very idea has been detached from the intricate particularities of the older Mediterranean and European traditions that gave birth to it – traditions that do not divide so neatly between what is public and what is private. It has been made over into the special possession of liberal modernity, where the newly minted polarity between "inwardness" and "publicness" effectively "obscures the relational delicacy of the social bond" (259).

47 In this light, suggests Salvatore, we may understand Habermas's lament respecting the "over-institutionalization and bureaucratization of publicness." See further *The Public Sphere*, 252ff.

48 Michael J. Sandel, "The Procedural Republic and the Unencumbered Self," *Political Theory* 12, no. 1 (1984): 81–96.

49 J.S. Mill, *On Liberty*, chapter 3 (Acton 114f., 119).

50 Thus does John Locke's earlier emphasis on the community, rather than the ruler, becoming "Umpire by settled, standing Rules, indifferent, and the same to all Parties" (*Second Treatise*, §87) still lead to Leviathan, if by a somewhat different route.

51 In "The Problem of Pluralist Authority" (*Political Studies* 2013) Muñiz-Fraticelli leans on Joseph Raz, who combines liberal perfectionism with

moral pluralism and legal positivism, but distances himself from Raz's strictly functionalist or instrumentalist view of authority, which does not fully address the problem internal to the political pluralist tradition; *viz.*, that arguments undermining the absolute authority of the state also undermine the authority of religious and professional associations, thus tending to antinomianism. Like Raz, Muñiz-Fraticelli wants to avoid both the impasse that results from having multiple legitimate sources of authority and the antinomian resolution of such conflicts through appeal to individual conscience. For his part, he proposes a new balance between the state and private associations by recognizing the dependence of the latter on the former for the necessary institutional conditions under which they help to establish and even to constitute the individual's reasons or goals. The conflict between the state and external authorities is thus internalized in the state, which has both a first-order and a second-order authority, one commanding the citizen over against the authority of associations and the other abetting those associations. See further Victor Muñiz-Fraticelli, *The Structure of Pluralism* (Oxford: Oxford University Press, 2014).

52 Richard W. Garnett, "'The Freedom of the Church': (Towards) An Exposition, Translation, and Defense," *Journal of Contemporary Legal Issues* 33 (2013) (SSRN pre-publication version, p. 15), quoting Perry Dane, "The Maps of Sovereignty: A Meditation," *Cardozo Law Review* 12 (1991): 959. Garnett also reminds us of Harold Berman's remark in *Law and Revolution* (Cambridge, MA: Harvard University Press, 1983), 10: "Perhaps the most distinctive characteristic of the Western legal tradition is the coexistence and competition within the same community of diverse jurisdictions and diverse legal systems. It is this plurality of jurisdictions and legal systems that makes the supremacy of law both necessary and possible." (We will return to Garnett in chapter 4, where our concerns overlap further.)

53 Muñiz-Fraticelli treats the question of authority in chapter 8 of *The Structure of Pluralism*; with which compare chapter 8 of Oliver O'Donovan's *The Ways of Judgment* (Grand Rapids, MI: Eerdmans, 2005), a quite different world of discourse.

54 Cf. Garnett, "'The Freedom of the Church,'" 37: "Even if it stops short of attacking non-state authorities as 'worms within the entrails' of the body politic, and even if its powers are constitutionally conferred, enumerated, and limited, the state seems likely to regard non-state authority as provisionally and by concession held and exercised, and also to attempt to guarantee that more and more of this authority is exercised in accord with the same norms that (appropriately) govern the state itself."

55 Cf. Robert P. George, "Natural Law," *Harvard Journal of Law and Public Policy* 31, no. 1 (2008): 171–95. Muñiz-Fraticelli acknowledges "the many problems inherent in an argument anchored on foundational plurality, incommensurability, and tragic loss" (*The Structure of Pluralism,* vii). But what about the problem inherent in the very expression, "foundational plurality"?

56 Cf. Avery Cardinal Dulles, "John Paul II and Religious Freedom: Themes from Vatican II," *The* Thomist 65 (April 2001): 161–78. Dulles shows that *Dignitatis* develops the Church's thinking about the grounding of freedom in truth and so also in responsibility, rather than merely echoing non-theological calls for freedom. See further chapter 4 and, especially, chapter 5 of the present volume.

57 Leo XIII, *Libertas praestantissimum,* §37.

58 Ibid., §7.

59 Ibid., §16; see §6f., §10f., §15f.

60 Ibid., §35.

61 *Gaudium et spes* (Constitution on the Church in the Modern World, 1965) §22 should govern our reading not only of that document but of *Dignitatis humanae.* Its logic is the logic of intersection, of overlap, of convergence and divergence: "For by His incarnation the Son of God has united Himself in some fashion with every man. He worked with human hands, He thought with a human mind, acted by human choice, and loved with a human heart ... In Him God reconciled us to Himself and among ourselves; from bondage to the devil and sin He delivered us ... By suffering for us He not only provided us with an example for our imitation, He blazed a trail, and if we follow it, life and death are made holy and take on a new meaning."

62 *Gaudium et spes,* §39. See that entire paragraph for the logic of intersection or overlap as it pertains to the political life; cf. also §43, where we read: "This council exhorts Christians, as citizens of two cities, to strive to discharge their earthly duties conscientiously and in response to the Gospel spirit. They are mistaken who, knowing that we have here no abiding city but seek one which is to come, think that they may therefore shirk their earthly responsibilities. For they are forgetting that by the faith itself they are more obliged than ever to measure up to these duties, each according to his proper vocation. Nor, on the contrary, are they any less wide of the mark who think that religion consists in acts of worship alone and in the discharge of certain moral obligations, and who imagine they can plunge themselves into earthly affairs in such a way as to imply that these are altogether divorced from the religious life. This split

between the faith which many profess and their daily lives deserves to be counted among the more serious errors of our age." See further my remarks on this in "Baking Bricks for Babel?" (*Nova et Vetera* 8, no. 4 [2010], 759ff.) and, more systematically, in chapter six of *Ascension Theology* (London: T&T Clark, 2011).

63 I use the word "proffered" advisedly, since it has not as yet been accepted or attempted in practice.

64 In his 1997 paper, "The Idea of Public Reason Revisited," which concludes the expanded edition of *Political Liberalism* (New York: Columbia University Press, 2005), John Rawls describes "the well-ordered constitutional democratic society" of his book as "one in which the dominant and controlling citizens affirm and act from irreconcilable yet reasonable comprehensive doctrines," doctrines that "in turn support reasonable political conceptions ... which specify the basic rights, liberties, and opportunities of citizens in society's basic structure" (expanded edition, 490). This only makes clear that he has been chasing his tail all along. The well-ordered society is well ordered because it is the product of world views that, though incompatible in one way or another, all support basic rights, liberties, and opportunities. Fine. But what qualifies as basic? And do reasonable comprehensive doctrines support reasonable political conceptions, or do reasonable political conceptions generate a family of reasonable comprehensive doctrines? Who decides, in any case, what is reasonable? Or that democracy has a better claim to reasonableness than monarchy, say? Rawls never gets to grips with the fact that political liberalism, though intending to be much more modest than comprehensive liberalism, is in the end equally self-referential, and thus itself implicitly comprehensive. It has the advantage of recognizing the hubris in comprehensive liberalism, but the disadvantage of thinking it has solved the problem simply by positing a reasonable pluralism of such doctrines and offering to mediate between them. That in order to do so it has to disentangle political justice even more completely from higher forms or conceptions of justice is already sufficient reason to be suspicious of its offer.

65 See Rawls, *Political Liberalism*, liii, n. 31. As we might expect, Dr O'Donnell (supra, n. 32) is far more realistic in this matter than Dr Rawls; but what sort of public reason requires principled obstetricians to emigrate?

66 Taylor's open secularism is much to be preferred to the closed or militant secularism that he has done so much to contest. But is it premised on a misconstrual of the immanent frame as a kind of baseline for modern society? "What I have been describing as the immanent frame is common

to all of us in the modern West, or at least that is what I am trying to por-
tray. Some of us want to live it as open to something beyond; some live it
as closed. It is something which permits closure, without demanding it."
(Charles Taylor, *A Secular Age* [Cambridge, MA: The Belknap Press,
2007], 543f.) The theologian would say that there is a nature/grace problem here. Taylor's way of putting things implies, quite rightly, the harmony
of nature and grace. However, it overlooks the church's claim that any
"sloughing off" of the transcendent, to use his expression, is not a mere
(self-imposed) confinement to the natural realm, but at the same time its
falsification: as if nature were not itself oriented to grace or in need of
grace; as if unaided reason were not responsible to recognize that God
exists; as if society, built now "from the bottom up," could decline to rise
any higher than itself without vesting in itself – that is, usurping – any
transcendent authority. Which is to say, Taylor posits as common ground
what is not in fact common. It detracts nothing from the richness of his
genealogy and phenomenology of modernity to admit that here it is theologically deficient, both descriptively and analytically (*per* his response to
Stanley Hauerwas and Romand Coles in "Challenging Issues about the
Secular Age," *Modern Theology* 26, no. 3 [2010], at 410ff). And does this
deficiency not account, at least in part, for the fact that his "management
of diversity" model of governance remains quite Rawlsian? With the later
Rawls, and even more decisively, he rejects "containment" of religion –
very popular in Quebec! – as a proper approach to secularism. He wants a
society in which we have liberty to express the beliefs that are at the core
of our identities and world views; indeed, a society in which "maximum
input" at this level is encouraged. (*A Secular Age* may be his own best
attempt at such encouragement.) At the same time, he remains committed
to the neutrality of the state in all such matters – a necessary neutrality, he
thinks, if it is to negotiate the deep diversity of its citizens and their associations. But is it necessary? Is it even possible? Is it not already a sloughing-
off of the transcendent and, as such, a closed rather than an open
rendering? Or can the statesman achieve a neutrality (not to be confused
with mere "even-handedness") that the philosopher and the historian, as
Taylor readily admits, cannot?

67 In chapter 4 of *Utilitarianism*, Mill (Acton 33) claims that "each person's
happiness is a good to that person, and the general happiness, therefore, a
good to the aggregate of all persons." But the "therefore" is neither justified nor justifiable, and "the general happiness" neither specified nor speci-
fiable. Even individual happiness eludes definition, though it is what
everyone desires. Now happiness may indeed be "the sole end of human

action, and the promotion of it the test by which to judge of all human conduct" (36), but if we can't say what it is, we really haven't said anything at all. By contrast, see Augustine, *De Trinitate* 13.6ff.

68 In such a context, rights begin to trump responsibilities, and society itself is reconceived in procedural or statist terms that ultimately undermine rights. Against this, Benedict XVI calls in *Caritas in veritate* (2009) "for a renewed reflection on how rights presuppose duties" and on the hierarchy of goods to which rights belong:

> Nowadays we are witnessing a grave inconsistency. On the one hand, appeals are made to alleged rights, arbitrary and non-essential in nature, accompanied by the demand that they be recognized and promoted by public structures, while, on the other hand, elementary and basic rights remain unacknowledged and are violated in much of the world ... [I]ndividual rights, when detached from a framework of duties which grants them their full meaning, can run wild, leading to an escalation of demands which is effectively unlimited and indiscriminate ... *Duties set a limit on rights because they point to the anthropological and ethical framework of which rights are a part,* in this way ensuring that they do not become licence. Duties thereby reinforce rights and call for their defence and promotion as a task to be undertaken in the service of the common good. Otherwise, if the only basis of human rights is to be found in the deliberations of an assembly of citizens, those rights can be changed at any time, and so the duty to respect and pursue them fades from the common consciousness. (§43, emphasis added)

69 Cf. Augustine, *De Moribus Ecclesiae*, §§4–56.

70 Anyone inclined to doubt this should consult Augustine, *De Civitate Dei*, 19.

71 Matthew 5:14.

72 On these controversial claims, see further chapter 5, "Catholics and the Neutral State."

73 *R. v. Big M Drug Mart Ltd.*, 1985 1 SCR 295:

> The *Lord's Day Act* to the extent that it binds all to a sectarian Christian ideal, works a form of coercion inimical to the spirit of the *Charter*. The Act gives the appearance of discrimination against non-Christian Canadians. Religious values rooted in Christian morality are translated into a positive law binding on believers and non-believers alike. Non-Christians are prohibited for religious reasons from carrying out otherwise lawful, moral and normal activities. Any law, purely religious in purpose, which denies non-Christians the right to work on Sunday denies them the right to practise their religion and infringes their religious freedom. The protection of one religion and the concomitant

non-protection of others imports a disparate impact destructive of the religious freedom of society. The power to compel, on religious grounds, the universal observance of the day of rest preferred by one religion is not consistent with the preservation and enhancement of the multi-cultural heritage of Canadians recognized in s. 27 of the *Charter.*

74 Jesus said, "You shall know the truth, and the truth shall set you free." Today we say, "A free man makes his own truth." And then we say: "You are not free to acknowledge the truth, even where your conscience or your religion reminds you of the claims of truth, if that truth offends your neighbour or interferes with his preferences and choices."

75 See Waldron, *Free to Believe,* 26–53. Her critique of *Big M* is focused on the advent of a phony right not to be offended, which supplants genuine freedom of conscience and religion to the detriment of democracy, but she also questions *inter alia* the rejection of any legislation with a religious purpose.

76 In "Church, State, and Charter: Canada's Hidden Establishment Clause" (*Tulsa Journal of Comparative and International Law* 14, no. 1 [2006]: 25–52), Jeremy Patrick follows those who trace this trajectory from as far back as the 1854 *Clergy Reserves Act.* Be that as it may – the Charter surely marks a turning of sorts – he is correct in contending that "church and state cases decided under the Charter's religious freedom guarantee appear strikingly similar in result and reasoning to those decided under the American Constitution's Establishment Clause," and that "neutrality is increasingly viewed as the only legitimate and appropriate relationship between government and religion" (51). (Cf. Justice Abella's comments in *Loyola* at par. 43f., which make plain that this is her view; about this putative neutrality more will be said in chapter 5.)

77 Patrick proposes "that the preamble, like the Charter itself, is liberal in the best sense of the word," reflecting the conception "that religion ('the supremacy of God') and government ('the rule of law') have their respective spheres and that an intermingling of the two is dangerous for each of them" (ibid. 50f.). I am among those who have argued otherwise, and I can only see in this "tentative" suggestion a fine piece of wishful thinking.

78 *Pace* Patrick 39f. and 48f., and certain of the legal decisions referenced there.

79 It must be disputed that "a prohibition on state support for religion is an important instrumental means of achieving religious freedom in the narrow sense" (Patrick, "Church, State, and Charter," 45).

80 Leo XIII, *Affari vos* (1897), §4. Note well that Leo's intervention achieved very little, as measured by law. In the end, Catholics were deprived of their

tax-funded schools, to the benefit of the Protestant majority. (There are a number of ironies here, including those that appear when one begins to speculate about what Charter jurisprudence might have done for the Catholic cause and hence for the subsequent shape of federalism and indeed for politics in Quebec, which today are devoted to a still more draconian de-confessionalization.) With *Affari vos* compare the 2009 letter on religious education in the schools from Cardinal Grocholewski, prefect of the Congregation for Catholic Education, available at www. vatican.va/roman_curia/congregations/ccatheduc/documents/rc_con_ ccatheduc_doc_20090505_circ-insegn-relig_en.html.

81 The acceptance in Catholic schools of recent health curricula, for example, suggests that (despite the trauma of the residential schools *débâcle*) little has been learned about protecting children, unless teaching them how to give consent to sexual activity at an ever-earlier age is counted as progress. It is indeed a kind of progress – in what Pope Francis called the "ideological colonisation that we have to be careful about that is trying to destroy the family" (Reuters, Manila, 16 January 2015).

82 See "A Rising Tide Lifts All Boats: Measuring Non-Government School Effects in Service of the Canadian Public Good," Cardus Education Survey (Phase One) 2012, Executive Summary, p. 6: "Separate Catholic Schools, for almost every measure including religious, produce similar results to graduates of public schools. Whereas evangelical Protestant schools and religious home education graduates reflect attributes of religious conviction, spiritual formation, and practices that one would expect of those who are religiously motivated (with schooling effects having contributed positively to those results), graduates of separate Catholic schools appear almost identical to those of public schools in every measure."

83 *S.L. v. Commission scolaire des Chênes et La procureure générale du Québec* (2009 QCCS 3875), in which Catholic parents were refused permission to withdraw their children from ERC classes in public schools. See further www.mcgill.ca/prpp/.

84 Par. 162.

85 When Ireland adopted "gay marriage" by popular referendum, Archbishop Diarmuid Martin remarked (23 May 2015) that most of those "who voted Yes are products of our Cathholic schools." But where is the will to reform those schools? See George Weigel, *Evangelical Catholicism: Deep Reform in the 21st-Century Church* (New York: Basic Books, 2013), 228ff.; cf. Ryan Topping, *Rebuilding Catholic Culture* (Manchester, NH: Sophia institute Press, 2012) and Stratford Caldecott, *Beauty in the Word: Rethinking the Foundations of Education* (Tacoma, WA: Angelico Press, 2012).

CHAPTER FOUR

1 Robert Bellah, "A Reply to my Critics," *First Things* (June/July 2013), 54.
   This goes somewhat beyond the tradition of James Madison, who warned
   that all rights are imperilled to the extent that this particular one is (see
   Stephen D. Smith, *The Rise and Decline of American Religious Freedom*
   [Cambridge, MA: Harvard University Press, 2014], 169f. and 213, n. 5).
   Cf. Jean Bethke Elshtain, "Persons, Politics, and a Catholic Understanding
   of Human Rights," in *Recognizing Religion in a Secular Society: Essays in
   Pluralism, Religion and Public Policy*, ed. D. Farrow (Montreal: McGill-
   Queen's University Press, 2004), 76ff.

2 Brian Leiter, *Why Tolerate Religion?* (Princeton: Princeton University
   Press, 2012), 7. See also, for example, James W. Nickel, "Who Needs
   Freedom of Religion?," *University of Colorado Law Review* 76 (2005):
   941, and Micah Schwartzman, "What If Religion Is Not Special?,"
   Chicago Law Review 79 (2012): 1351.

3 Christopher L. Eisgruber and Lawrence G. Sager, *Religious Freedom and
   the Constitution* (Cambridge, MA: Harvard University Press, 2007), 6.

4 Stephen D. Smith, "Discourse in the Dusk: The Twilight of Religious
   Freedom," *Harvard Law Review* 122 (2009): 1869. This is a review essay
   in response to Kent Greenawalt's *Religion and the Constitution*, vol. 2:
   Establishment and Fairness (Princeton, NJ: Princeton University Press,
   2008). The quotation is from the abstract of the review, available at
   papers.ssrn.com/sol3/papers.cfm?abstract_id=1431556.

5 And in a certain sense it must, for "the constraints of modern secular
   discourse," if accepted, preclude any principled explanation as to "why
   government sometimes *must*, sometimes *may*, and sometimes must *not*
   give religion special treatment" (Smith, "Discourse in the Dusk," 1905).

6 Here is the quotation (Bellah, "Reply," 54) in full: "Freedom of religion is
   the very first commitment of civil society, going back to its origins in the
   eighteenth century. All the other freedoms that civil society requires, such
   as freedom of speech, of the press, of association, and so forth, are extrapolations from that one central freedom, the freedom of religion. For a
   long time the Catholic Church supported the idea of an established church
   and was doubtful about religious freedom, but several of the central documents of Vatican II indicate a strong affirmation of religious freedom."

7 Cf. "The Freedom of the Church": (Towards) An Exposition, Translation,
   and Defense," *Journal of Contemporary Legal Issues* 21 (2013): 33, in
   which Richard Garnett replies more extensively to these charges, as laid
   by Richard Schragger and Micah Schwartzman in "Against Religious

Institutionalism," *Virginia Law Review* 99 (2013): 917. I agree with Garnett, who naturally takes some comfort in the judgment of the US Supreme Court in *Hosanna-Tabor,* that the charges smack of "shopworn Rawlsian liberalism," but see below, n. 51.

8 Second Vatican Council, Session 9, *Dignitatis humanae* (Declaration on Religious Freedom, 1965), §3 (Norman P. Tanner, ed., *Decrees of the Ecumenical Councils* [London: Sheed and Ward, 1990], 2: 1003).

9 On the Incarnation of the Word of God §27, in St Athanasius: Select Works and Letters, *Nicene and Post-Nicene Fathers of the Christian Church,* ed. Philip Schaff and Henry Wace (Grand Rapids, MI: Eerdmans, 1980), 4:50f.

10 Lactantius, *De mortibus persecutorum,* §34; trans. Department of History, University of Pennsylvania (http://origin.web.fordham.edu/halsall/source/edict-milan.asp).

11 Lactantius, *De mortibus persecutorum,* §48.

12 Brian Tierney, *The Crisis of Church and State: 1050–1300* (Toronto: University of Toronto Press, 1988), attends in much detail to the lay investiture controversy, but more attention is owed to the earlier periods. One notes, for example, the influential claim of Lactantius that "religion cannot be imposed by force" (*Divinarum Institutionum* 5.20), or of Augustine that "when force is applied, the will cannot be aroused" (*In Iohannis Evangelium tractatus* 26.2). As Robert Louis Wilken ("In Defense of Constantine," *First Things* 112 [April 2001]: 36–40) observes of Lactantius: "This is the first theological rationale for religious freedom, because it is the first rationale to be rooted in the nature of God and of devotion to God."

13 *Duo quippe sunt, imperator auguste, quibus principaliter mundus hic regitur: auctoritas sacra pontificum et regalis potestas.*

14 J.C. Murray, *We Hold These Truths* (Kansas City: Sheed and Ward, 1960), 202 (following Gerd Tellenbach).

15 Murray, *We Hold These Truths,* 203.

16 "This concept, the *res sacra in temporalibus,* had all the newness of Christianity itself. It embraces all those things which are part of the temporal life of man, at the same time that, by reason of their Christian mode of existence, or by reason of their finality, they transcend the limited purposes of the political order and are thus invested with a certain sacredness." (Ibid.)

17 *Dignitatis humanae,* §5. Cf. Leo's warning (*Rerum novarum* §14) against that "most pernicious error" whereby the state interferes, without just cause, in the sphere of the family.

18 Murray, *We Hold These Truths*, 205.

19 "The political experiment of modernity has essentially consisted in an effort to find and install in the world a secular substitute for all that the Christian tradition has meant by the pregnant phrase, the 'freedom of the Church.'" (Ibid., 201.)

20 Ibid., 205f.

21 From Marsilius onward "it has been an attempt to carry on the liberal tradition of Western politics, whose roots were in the Christian revolution, but now on a new revolutionary basis – a rejection of the Gelasian thesis, 'Two there are,' which had been the dynamic of the Christian revolution." (Ibid., 206.)

22 The heresy in question was basically Nestorian, with an interesting political twist. The divinity and humanity of Christ were correlated with his kingship and priesthood respectively, the latter being subordinated to the former. This effectively reversed Gelasius' claim that of the two offices "by which this world is chiefly ruled" the priestly office was the weightier. See further Oliver O'Donovan and Joan Lockwood O'Donovan, eds., *From Irenaeus to Grotius: A Sourcebook in Christian Political Thought, 100–1625* (Grand Rapids, MI: Eerdmans, 1999), 250ff.

23 The *cuius regio, eius religio* settlement of the Peace of Augsburg (1555) was formalized in the Peace of Westphalia (1648), but these treaties were rejected by Innocent in *Zelo domus dei* as "null, void, invalid, iniquitous, unjust, damnable, reprobate, inane, empty of meaning and effect for all time."

24 Murray, *We Hold These Truths*, 208.

25 Ibid., 209. Murray continues:

Professor Hocking has put the matter thus: "Outside the Marxist orbit the prevalent disposition of the secular state in recent years has been less to combat the church than to carry on a slow empirical demonstration of the state's full equivalence in picturing the attainable good life, and its superior pertinence to actual issues. As this demonstration gains force the expectation grows that it will be the church, not the state, that will wither away. Where the fields of church and state impinge on each other, as in education and correction, the church will in time appear superfluous. Where they are different, the church will be quietly ignored and dropped as irrelevant." This, says Hocking, is the "secular hypothesis." It is, he adds, the premise of the "experiment we call 'modernity.'" (Ibid., 209.)

26 Ibid., 210f.

27 Ibid., 210.

28 Ibid., 214.
29 It should be noted that Murray, in chapter 2, goes to great lengths to
   exempt the American founding from this charge. Gerald Bradley ("Beyond
   Murray's Articles of Peace and Faith," in K. Grasso and R. Hunt, eds, *The
   Thought of John Courtney Murray* [Grand Rapids, MI: Eerdmans, 1992],
   181–204) suggests, however, that the story of the First Amendment's religion clause is improperly told there, as Murray tries to make the founding
   principles more palatable to Catholics. Alternatively, we might suggest that
   Murray tried to rescue the religion clauses from their Protestant milieu for
   the sake of the American experiment itself. Either way, there is a problem.
   On the one reading – since Murray could hardly replace their Protestant
   content with something Catholic – he tried instead to suspend the religion
   clauses above any theological judgment at all, to make them "articles of
   peace" rather than of dogma. This all-too-Hobbsean ploy backfires, as
   Bradley notices; by making too little of politics, it ends up making too
   much. On the other reading, he did in fact try to replace that content with
   something Catholic, by re-contextualizing the religion clauses within the
   Church's (European) contest with Jacobinism. When he says that "the
   American thesis is simply political," rather than philosophical and theological like the Jacobin thesis, he immediately explains himself by saying that
   it belongs to "the Christian political tradition" that respects, rather than
   undermines, the doctrine of the Two (*We Hold These Truths*, 69). And
   what tradition is that, if not a Catholic one? Yet it is one thing to say that
   the religion clauses are deeply indebted to this doctrine and this tradition,
   and quite another to claim that they properly embody it. Bradley is right to
   think that they do not. Moreover, Murray's argument from the American
   experience, as Bradley again observes, looks very weak today, given the
   steady advance of the very "juridical omnipotence and omnicompetence
   of the state" to which Murray (ibid., 68), like the founders, so objected.
30 Murray, *We Hold These Truths*, 216f., employing Hocking's phrase.
31 To borrow the title of William Cavanaugh's book (Oxford University
   Press, 2009).
32 As F. Russell Hittinger puts it, "Vatican I's basic proposition concerned
   whether the liberty of the Church had to be answered in terms of its unity
   and whether its unity required communion with the bishop of Rome. In
   short, Vatican I concluded that Catholic bishops were not functionaries of
   the state or of national churches." "The Declaration on Religious Liberty,
   Dignitatis humanae," in *Vatican II: Renewal Within Tradition*, ed.
   Matthew Lamb and Matthew Levering (Oxford: Oxford University Press,
   2008), 360.

33 Where a capacity is impaired by physical or mental defect its exercise is also impaired, but the freedom still exists in principle because the inherent dignity of the person is not, on the Catholic view, diminished by the circumstance of physical or mental impairment.

34 *Dignitatis humanae*, §6.

35 Ibid., §9.

36 Ibid., §12.

37 Ibid., §13. (Tanner 2:1009, initial capital and emphasis added).

38 Of course, it is often just where these improper restrictions are imposed that the church most effectively achieves its evangelical mandate. As Lactantius observed, "the religion of God is increased the more it is oppressed" (*Divinarum Institutionum* 5.20).

39 See the *Catechism of the Catholic Church*, §2109: "The right to religious liberty can of itself be neither unlimited nor limited only by a 'public order' conceived in a positivist or naturalist manner. The 'due limits' which are inherent in it must be determined for each social situation by political prudence, according to the requirements of the common good, and ratified by the civil authority in accordance with 'legal principles which are in conformity with the objective moral order.'"

40 It has a long record of attempting this, even into the twentieth century, as for example in its encouragement of the Quebec state to take repressive measures against Protestant sects.

41 The literature on this problem is still expanding, particularly in the wake of Benedict XVI's 2005 address to the Roman Curia. See for example Martin Rhonheimer, "Benedict XVI's 'Hermeneutic of Reform' and Religious Freedom," *Nova et Vetera* 9, no. 4 (2011): 1029–54, and responses by Thomas Pink et al. See also Pink, "Conscience and Coercion," *First Things* (Aug./Sept. 2012): 45–51.

42 John 8:32.

43 It is necessary here to distinguish between two kinds of religious freedom: the concrete kind belonging to Christianity, as a defining feature thereof, and the more abstract kind that we have in mind when we say, for example, that "everyone has the following fundamental freedoms: freedom of conscience and religion" (*Constitution Act*, 1982). The second or abstract kind, where it is at all reliable, is a product and consequence of the first or concrete kind. Freedom of religion – that is, freedom to pursue the religion we inherit or the religion to which we have converted, or to pursue no religion at all, without improper interference from others and especially from the state – arises from, and can only be sustained by, the freedom produced through religion and, quite specifically, the Catholic religion.

44 "FIRST, We have granted to God, and by this our present Charter have confirmed, for Us and our Heirs for ever, that the Church of England shall be free, and shall have all her whole Rights and Liberties inviolable ... "

45 Quoted from www.vatican.va/archive/hist_councils/ii_vatican_council/ documents/vat-ii_decl_19651207_dignitatis-humanae_en.html (cf. Tanner 2:1009).

46 This is not to say that the latter is not mediated in some sense by Christ, "through whom are all things" (1 Cor. 8.6). Archbishop LeFebvre, however, objected to the statement, *libertas ecclesiae est principium fundamentale*, because he believed it did not go far enough. The state itself was obligated to confess the "social royalty" of Christ, who is Lord of all and not merely Lord of the Church. The council, however, as Hittinger observes, had chosen not to attempt to address this matter directly, for it could not very well do that without undertaking to complete the whole task of *De Ecclesia Christi* – leftover business from Vatican I that remains just that.

47 One must not miss the "also" in the final sentence quoted above from §13: "The Church also claims freedom for herself in her character as a society of men." The Latin is even clearer that this is a distinct claim: "*Libertatem pariter sibi vindicat ecclesia prout est etiam societas hominum ... .*"

48 *Dignitatis humanae*, §4. In Canada, the *Loyola* decision (2015 SCC 12) affirms the social and corporate dimensions of religious freedom, though the majority does not go as far as the minority (cf. par. 60 and par. 89–100).

49 *Dignitatis humanae* §7. This stipulation, notes Hittinger ("Declaration," 368), was included at the behest of Bishop Karol Wojtyla, who knew rather a lot about restrictions on religious and civil liberties that amounted to violations of human dignity and of the natural law.

50 Section 7 reads as follows (www.vatican.va):

The right to religious freedom is exercised in human society: hence its exercise is subject to certain regulatory norms. In the use of all freedoms the moral principle of personal and social responsibility is to be observed. In the exercise of their rights, individual men and social groups are bound by the moral law to have respect both for the rights of others and for their own duties toward others and for the common welfare of all. Men are to deal with their fellows in justice and civility. Furthermore, society has the right to defend itself against possible abuses committed on the pretext of freedom of religion. It is the special duty of government to provide this protection. However, government is not to act in an arbitrary fashion or in an unfair spirit of partisanship.

Its action is to be controlled by juridical norms which are in conformity with the objective moral order [*ordini morali objectivo conformes*]. These norms arise out of the need for the effective safeguard of the rights of all citizens and for the peaceful settlement of conflicts of rights, also out of the need for an adequate care of genuine public peace, which comes about when men live together in good order and in true justice, and finally out of the need for a proper guardianship of public morality. These matters constitute the basic component of the common welfare: they are what is meant by public order. For the rest, the usages of society are to be the usages of freedom in their full range: that is, the freedom of man is to be respected as far as possible and is not to be curtailed except when and insofar as necessary.

51 Schragger and Schwartzman suppose that the unsolved difficulty of religious institutionalism is how to multiply the freedom of the church; otherwise put, how to turn a particular claim into a pluralistic one, how to move from "two there are" to "many there are," or how not to equivocate with the word "church." John Inazu ("The Freedom of the Church [New Revised Standard Version]," *Journal of Contemporary Legal Issues* 21 (2013): 365) is right to be dissatisfied with Garnett's response, which seems to grant the framing of the question:

The strong claims that undergird the freedom of the church depend upon a thick account of church that may not be generalizable to "religious institution" or "religious organization." Consider, for example, Garnett's claim that "[t]he 'freedom of the church' idea presumes and proposes that religion is special – or more precisely, that religious institutions, communities, and authorities are and should be differentiated both from political authorities and from non-state institutions and voluntary associations generally." The problem with Garnett's reasoning is that the freedom of the church has nothing to say about "religious institutions, communities, and authorities." Its theological anchor is an ontological claim about the reality of Jesus Christ embodied in the church on earth, which presumes nothing about the special nature of "religion."

Unfortunately Inazu, in marshaling Barth, Bonhoeffer, and Hauerwas to the support of a "thicker" (Protestant) account, does not get far in reframing the question – that is, in getting it turned the right way round. The idea that religion is special, or that religious freedom is important, presupposes the freedom of the church.

52 J.C. Murray, "The Issue of Church and State at Vatican Council II," *Theological Studies* 27, no. 4 (1966), 590; cf. Hittinger, "Declaration," 373. Already in 1964, while the council was still deliberating, Murray put

forward for general consideration a document of his own – "The Problem of Religious Freedom," *Theological Studies* 25, no. 4 (1964): 503–75) – that contrasted the view he wished the council fathers to abandon with the view he wished them to adopt. But it is too much to claim that they did adopt it. We will take this up again in chapter 5.

53 "For to say there is an authority higher than the state implies a jurisdictional limit but not necessarily an epistemological deficit" (Hittinger, "Declaration," n. 38).

54 *Dignitatis humanae* §1; see Hittinger, "Declaration," 365.

55 In saying (as he does in "The Issue of Church and State at Vatican Council II") that "the autonomy of the secular orders requires that, within this order and in the face of its constituted organs of government, the Church should present her claim to freedom on these secular grounds – in the name of the human person," Murray effectively denies that the *libertas ecclesiae* has any real purchase on the secular order. But in fact the church confronts both the state and the human person with an authority higher than either.

56 Stephen Smith, "Discourse in the Dusk," 1883 (cf. 1887). He identifies John Garvey and Richard Garnett as examples of those who are swimming against the stream here – as is Smith himself, of course. Rare is the legal scholar who admits "that government ultimately cannot avoid making judgments about theological issues" (1902, n. 141).

CHAPTER FIVE

1 R. J. Neuhaus, *The Naked Public Square: Religion and Democracy in America* (Grand Rapids, MI: Eerdmans, 1988).

2 Oliver O'Donovan, *The Desire of the Nations: Rediscovering the Roots of Political Theology* (Cambridge: Cambridge University Press, 1996), 195.

3 "The corresponding term to 'secular' is not 'sacred', nor 'spiritual', but 'eternal'" (O'Donovan, *Desire of the Nations*, 211). Larry Siedentop is correct in saying that secularism, properly understood, does not imply "indifference or unbelief." He overloads the term, however, by assigning it the task of "identif[ying] the conditions in which authentic beliefs should be formed and defended," based on a commitment to equal liberty that "puts a premium on conscience rather than the 'blind' following of rules." *Inventing the Individual: the Origins of Western Liberalism* (Cambridge, MA: Harvard University Press, 2014), 361.

4 O'Donovan has extended this feature of *Desire of the Nations* into *The Ways of Judgment* (Grand Rapids: Eerdmans, 2005) and other works. Even critics of his project often acknowledge it as the most important work of political theology in our generation. Many of them, unfortunately, are either unwilling or unable to reckon with its christological claims, which require them to do something other and more than what Paul Kahn, engaging Carl Schmitt, wrongly describes as "the real work of political theology," which, Kahn says, "is done in giving a theoretical expression to those understandings that already inform a community's self-understanding." *Political Theology: Four New Chapters on the Concept of Sovereignty* (New York: Columbia University Press, 2011), 120. Schmitt and Kahn are right, however, that even that task soon exposes the theological transpositions made by "secular" political theorists.

5 *Duo quippe sunt, imperator auguste, quibus principaliter mundus hic regitur: auctoritas sacra pontificum et regalis potestas.* Letter to Emperor Anastasius, AD 494; translation modified from Oliver and Joan O'Donovan, *From Irenaeus to Grotius: A Sourcebook in Christian Political Thought* (Grand Rapids, MI: Eerdmans, 1999), 179.

6 I have offered my own account of this in chapter 9 of *Recognizing Religion in a Secular Society: Essays in Pluralism, Religion, and Public Policy* (Montreal: McGill-Queens University Press, 2004).

7 In *Immortale dei* (1885) Leo XIII appeals to Gregory at §34: "On the question of the separation of Church and State the same Pontiff writes [in *Mirari vos*] as follows: 'Nor can We hope for happier results either for religion or for the civil government from the wishes of those who desire that the Church be separated from the State, and the concord between the secular and ecclesiastical authority be dissolved. It is clear that these men, who yearn for a shameless liberty, live in dread of an agreement which has always been fraught with good, and advantageous alike to sacred and civil interests.'" In the following paragraph Leo insists that "in matters ... of mixed jurisdiction, it is in the highest degree consonant to nature, as also to the designs of God, that so far from one of the powers separating itself from the other, or still less coming into conflict with it, complete harmony, such as is suited to the end for which each power exists, should be preserved between them."

8 *Immortale dei,* §13.

9 J.C. Murray, "Leo XIII on Church and State," *Theological Studies* 14, no. 4 (1953), 28f.; cf. p. 10: "The basic conflict concerned the order of

reality itself – the nature of truth, the norm of morality, the scope of reason, the meaning of freedom, and the mutual relations of freedom and authority, liberty and law. On this level a naturalistic rationalism challenged the Christian metaphysic. The disagreement was over the very nature and destiny of man."

10 Murray, "Leo XIII," 29f. "The secularization of politics had ensued on the assertion of man's absolute individual autonomy, as prolonged into the assertion of the absolute autonomy of political power." Leo's counter-assertion, as Murray points out, is summed up in *Libertas praestantissimum* (1888) §36: "that man, by a necessity of his nature, is wholly subject to the most faithful and ever enduring power of God; and that, as a consequence, any liberty, except that which consists in submission to God and in subjection to His will, is unintelligible."

11 Murray, "Leo XIII," 20ff.

12 See J.C. Murray, "The Issue of Church and State at Vatican Council II," *Theological Studies* 27, no. 4 (1966): 580–606.

13 Murray, "Church and State," 606. He asserts that "[t]he victories won in the West for the cause of constitutional government and the rights of man owed little to the Church, however much the 'leaven of the gospel' … may have contributed to the rise of the secular dynamism which, in fact, brought the 'free world' into existence" (601). Although this might be admitted when the matter is viewed through a quite narrow historical or constitutional window, it cannot be admitted generally, as my previous chapter shows.

14 The early American model eschews, not religion itself, but the establishment of religion; the state assumes religious principles and religious flourishing but seeks to remain in the background, as it were, so as not to interfere with that flourishing or curtail its scope. A Catholic may ask whether this principle is contrary to the teaching of Leo in *Libertas*, where he once again rejects the separation of church and state. But there, too, the context is a moral one; his problem is with those "who affirm that the morality of individuals is to be guided by the divine law, but not the morality of the State," as if "in public affairs the commands of God may be passed over, and may be entirely disregarded in the framing of laws." Leo insists, as many of the American founders would also insist, on "the absurdity of such a position." For "Nature herself proclaims the necessity of the State providing means and opportunities whereby the community may be enabled to live properly, that is to say, according to the laws of God" (§18; cf. 38ff.). We shall return to this below.

15 J.C. Murray, "The Problem of Religious Freedom," *Theological Studies* 25, no. 4 (1964), 571f.

16 Having stated that "all men are bound to seek the truth, especially in what concerns God and His Church, and to embrace the truth they come to know," the fathers are careful to observe and declare that "it is upon the human *conscience* that these obligations fall and exert their binding force" (*Dignitatis humanae*, §1, emphasis added). No external power, not even the Church, can displace the conscience. "The truth cannot impose itself except by virtue of its own truth, as it makes its entrance into the mind at once quietly and with power." The demand for religious freedom is, in turn, "a demand for immunity from coercion in civil society," another external power. "Therefore it leaves untouched [*integram relinquit*] traditional Catholic doctrine on the moral duty of men and societies toward the true religion and toward the one Church of Christ." This is the addition in question, and it serves to deflect any suggestion that support for religious freedom is support for religious relativism or – note the "and societies" – for political "indifferentism" in matters religious.

17 When protecting society from abuses in the guise of religious freedom, the state, as elsewhere, is to operate *secundum normas iuridicas, ordini morali obiectivo conformes* (*Dignitatis humanae*, §7).

18 F. Russell Hittinger, "The Declaration on Religious Liberty, *Dignitatis humanae*" (*Vatican II: Renewal Within Tradition*, ed. Matthew L. Lamb and Matthew Levering [Oxford: Oxford University Press 2008]: 359–82), p. 369:

> On the issue of the competence of government in *Dignitatis humanae*, article 3, the second schema, the *Declaratio prior*, said that the "State is not qualified [*ineptam esse*] to make judgments of truth in religious matters." After vigorous debate, this sentence was abandoned in the penultimate draft – and for good reason. First, it might have been construed to mean that government lacks even the epistemic warrant to judge that religion is good, thus undercutting the argument of *Dignitatis humanae* itself; second, it could obscure the responsibilities of government on mixed matters, such as marriage and abortion; third, it almost certainly would have favored the neutralist and indifferentist doctrines that *Dignitatis humanae* otherwise took such great pains to avoid. While it is true that it does not provide a detailed map of the acceptable range of government's cognizance of religion, *Dignitatis humanae* does not remove government altogether from the veridical order – that is, the order of truth – in matters religious.

19 Hittinger, "Declaration," 381, n. 56.
20 Murray, "Church and State," 591.
21 Colossians 1:16.
22 According to Murray ("Church and State," 592f.), "[t]he mandate of
   Christ empowers the Church to preach the gospel to every creature – to
   every man as a creature of God, to whom the divine message of salvation
   is addressed. To this empowerment or freedom of the Church there corresponds on the part of all men and all peoples an obligation to hear the
   word of God and to respond to it by faith as assent and consent. In this
   sense the content of the freedom of the Church is positive; it is a freedom
   'for' the preaching of the gospel." So far so good, but he continues:
   This discourse, however, moves in the transtemporal order of the history
   of salvation – the order of man's vertical relation, so to speak, to God
   acting and speaking in history through His Church. On the other hand,
   the technical issue of religious freedom rises in the juridical order, which
   is the order of horizontal interpersonal relations among men, between a
   man and organized society, and especially between the people – as individuals and as associated in communities, including religious communities – and the powers of government. As asserted in the interpersonal
   order of human rights, the freedom of the Church, whether as a community or as an authority, is and can only be negative in its content; it is a
   freedom "from" any manner of coercive constraint imposed by any secular power. As further guaranteed in the constitutional order of civil
   rights, the freedom of the Church consequently appears as an immunity.
   To confuse these two distinct orders of discourse, and the modes of
   freedom proper to each, is to run into inextricable difficulties.
   Murray then quotes but a single sentence of *Aux gouvernants* in support
   of his notion that in the political or juridical sphere the Church asks only
   for a negative freedom, the same freedom as any person or association of
   persons may ask for: that the state restrain itself from interfering in religious activity. The Church does not make a claim with any positive content; that is, it does not assert "that the government should use its power
   in furtherance of the Church's divine mission" (593). It asks "only liberty,
   the liberty to believe and to preach her faith, the freedom to love her God
   and serve Him." This is how he reads the statement from *Dignitatis* § 13,
   that "the Church should enjoy all the freedom of action it needs in order
   to care for the salvation of humanity."
23 *Aux gouvernants* (Address of Pope Paul VI to the Rulers, 8 December 1965).
24 Rather, "*Dignitatis humanae* offered a carefully calibrated silence on the
   establishment of religion." Moreover, the Catholic Church, says Hittinger

("Declaration," 366), "did not, and does not, believe that disestablishment is a principle superior to free exercise."

25 Address of Pope Paul VI during the last General Meeting of the Second Vatican Council, 7 December 1965 (http://w2.vatican.va/content/paul-vi/en/speeches/1965/documents/hf_p-vi_spe_19651207_epilogo-concilio.html); see Hittinger, "Declaration," 382, n. 58.

26 "Here," not in general; and cf. J. C. Murray, "The Problem of Mr. Rawls' Problem," in *Law and Philosophy*, ed. Sidney Hook (New York: New York University Press, 1964): 29–34.

27 Murray ("Church and State," 597f.) thinks church-state language is best transposed into the abstract terminology of "two social magnitudes," religion and government, and that "the sense of the Declaration [is] to say that governmental favor of religion formally means favor of the freedom of religion." But that abstraction and that equation would surely have met with the *non placet* of a good many bishops, and a papal veto as well. Church-state language is always concrete and can never be reduced to a religion-government abstraction without losing its substance. Nor does the history of salvation move in a "transtemporal" sphere that intersects the secular order only tangentially.

28 On this point critics such as Archbishop LeFebvre had the better of the argument. There were 70 *non placet* votes in the end (though it is not known how LeFebvre, who was a signatory to the document, voted).

29 Murray appears to bracket out, for present purposes, the fundamental political question as to the legitimacy of public authority and the source of its competence to care for these things. The chief source, according to both pope and council – the source that requires recognition even politically – is God himself, who is neither unknowable nor unknown. And the better God is known, the greater the competence with regard to the conditions that encourage religious flourishing.

30 J.C. Murray, *We Hold These Truths: Catholic Reflections on the American Proposition* (Kansas City: Sheed and Ward, 1960), 293.

31 Murray, *We Hold These Truths*, 40 (with reference to the American university in particular). In must be stressed that Murray by no means embraced the anti-religious neutralism that is popular today. In his introduction to *We Hold These Truths*, Walter Burghardt writes of Fr Murray's "effort to explore ... the civic consensus whereby a people acquires its identity and sense of purpose ... Reduced to its skeleton, the [American] consensus affirmed a free people under a limited government, guided by law and ultimately resting on the sovereignty of God." I am *not* claiming that Murray abandoned this perspective, but only that he failed in his later

work to articulate how his own brand of neutralism could connect the
rule of law to the supremacy of God.

32 "Some fixed ideas about God and human nature," as Alexis de Tocqueville
    insists, are indispensable to the daily conduct of our lives and to our
    health as a people. "I doubt," says he, "that man can ever support a com-
    plete religious independence and an entire political freedom at once; and
    I am brought to think that if he has no faith, he must serve, and if he is
    free, he must believe." "Religious peoples," he adds, are "naturally strong
    in precisely the spot where democratic peoples are weak; this makes very
    visible how important it is that they keep to their religion when becoming
    equal." (*Democracy in America* [trans. H.C. Mansfield and D. Winthrop;
    London: The Folio Society, 2002] II.1.5, 417ff., a passage that seems to
    draw on Exodus 32 as a paradigm.) Tocqueville saw the danger, especially
    in the democratic era, for religions that overstep the bounds and refuse "to
    confine themselves carefully to the sphere of religious matters," but spoke
    thus "from a purely human point of view," as a political advisor. He was
    not arguing for a church without any political doctrine or a state without
    any religious principles or assumptions.

33 See, for example, David L. Schindler, "Religious Freedom, Truth, and
    American Liberalism: Another Look at John Courtney Murray,"
    Communio 21, no. 4 (1994): 696–741. Schindler puts his finger on a key
    problem, namely, Murray's transposition of the Gelasian church-state
    dyarchy into a generic distinction between sacred and secular, or between
    civil society and religious community. He rightly observes that his con-
    strual of the nature-grace relation "tends to leave nature primitively
    neutral toward God" and to favour a "freedom from" over a "freedom
    for" approach that brackets the question of truth. Schindler, however,
    connects this to the dispute about whether man has both a natural and a
    supernatural end, which is not the best way to handle it. For one can
    distinguish these ends without drawing Murray's conclusions.

34 Tocqueville (*Democracy in America* II.1.7; cf. II.1.2) points to one
    theological temptation facing man in the age of equality, that is to say,
    a return to pantheism: "Among the different systems by whose aid philos-
    ophy endeavors to explain the universe I believe pantheism to be one of
    those most fitted to seduce the human mind in democratic times. Against
    it all who abide in their attachment to the true greatness of man should
    combine and struggle." (426) But he also points, unforgettably, to another
    threat, namely, that "immense tutelary power" (II.4.6, p. 663) that he
    feared would rise out of the petty vices and constricted virtues and

uncertain beliefs of democratic man, to rule over him in a benign yet suffocating tyranny (such as Dostoevsky also foresaw). This figure, in Tocqueville's great treatise, is the political substitute for God – God's reverse image, so to say, who also sees everything and sees to everything, but in such a way as to stifle rather than cultivate authentic freedom, substituting freedom *from* for freedom *for*.

35 Murray, "The Problem of Religious Freedom," 530.

36 See Michael J. Perry, *The Political Morality of Liberal Democracy* (Cambridge 2010), chap. 5, where he contends that "the right to *moral* freedom is a compelling extension of the right to *religious* freedom" (98), interpreting this proposed right as "the right to freedom to live one's life in harmony with one's moral convictions and commitments" (89). To affirm this right "is to reject the proposition that protecting the moral health of the citizenry is a legitimate governmental interest" (95). Perry appeals to Murray, who writes in *We Hold These Truths* (166): "[T]he moral aspirations of law are minimal. Law seeks to establish and maintain only that minimum of actualized morality that is necessary for the healthy functioning of the social order. It does not look to what is morally desirable, or attempt to remove every moral taint from the atmosphere of society. It enforces only what is minimally acceptable, and in this sense socially necessary." There's the rub, of course: what exactly is socially necessary? Murray continues: "Law and morality are indeed related, even though differentiated. That is, the premises of law are ultimately found in the moral law. And human legislation does look to the moralization of society. But, mindful of its own nature and mode of action, it must not moralize excessively; otherwise it tends to defeat even its own more modest aims, by bringing itself into contempt." All true, but the word "excessively" only raises the question again.

37 While I share Perry's disinclination to trust American or Canadian law, I do not share his confidence in its general trajectory. Nor, for that matter, do I share the confidence of his illustrious predecessor, Harold J. Berman, in the Lessingite (neo-Joachimite) doctrine that "we have entered a new age, the age of the Holy Spirit," wherein "a worldwide belief in the sanctity of spiritual values" will find its embodiment in a global jurisprudence for an authentic world community ("The Holy Spirit: The God of History," *The Living Pulpit*, April–June 2004, 33); though I do support the effort to advance the rule of law internationally in terms something like those of Fr Murray in "The Juridical Organization of the International Community" (*The New York Law Journal*, 9 October 1944: 813–14).

38 By definition, there is no such thing as private morality, and there is no
   such thing as private religion, either: morality or immorality, religion or
   irreligion, is a public interpretation of reality.

39 If we try to say why, we can appeal to the deleterious effects of murder;
   but we are really appealing to natural law and, in the end, to religion.
   Attempts to do otherwise have produced only a flattening and a narrowing of the concept of the person, an ever-more-arbitrary notion of human
   dignity, and the steady advance of a culture of death in which supposedly
   mitigating circumstances are expanded ever further, even to the justification of murder on a massive scale, as with abortion. And this in turn
   forces a curtailment of freedom of conscience and freedom of religion,
   such as we are currently witnessing in many Western nations and, more
   dramatically, in places such as China.

40 See n. 14 above.

41 That is, "to find and install in the world a secular substitute for all that the
   Christian tradition has meant by the pregnant phrase, the 'freedom of the
   Church'" (*We Hold These Truths*, 201); or, in Cardinal Ratzinger's words,
   with reference to the Enlightenment culture underlying this search, "to
   boast a universal pretense and conceive itself as complete in itself, not in
   need of some completion through other cultural factors" ("Cardinal
   Ratzinger on Europe's Crisis of Culture": text of a lecture on 1 April 2005
   at the Convent of Saint Scholastica in Subiaco, Italy, published online in
   translation at Zenit.org, 26–28 July 2005.) Ratzinger adds: "The real
   opposition that characterizes today's world is not that between various
   religious cultures, but that between the radical emancipation of man from
   God, from the roots of life, on one hand, and from the great religious cultures on the other. If there were to be a clash of cultures, it would not be
   because of a clash of the great religions – which have always struggled
   against one another, but which, in the end, have also always known how
   to live with one another – but it will be because of the clash between this
   radical emancipation of man and the great historical cultures."

42 The 2013 Erasmus Lecture by Rabbi Sacks was published under the title,
   "On Creative Minorities," in the January 2014 issue of *First Things*: 33–9.

43 Cf. George Weigel, "A Better Concept of Freedom," *First Things* (March
   2002): 14–20.

44 But is there not a hint of this problem in chapter 2 of *We Hold These
   Truths*? See again chapter 4 of the present volume, n. 29.

45 *Immortale dei*, §6.

46 Tales of the Inquisition (many of them false) cause us to shudder at the
   words "public crime," although Leo does say "public," not "punishable."

Thaddeus J. Kozinski ("Jacques Maritain, the HHS Mandate, and the Failure of American Pluralism," in the May/June 2012 issue of *The Angelus*) is critical of Maritain's and Murray's search for "a personalist democracy [that] would manifest the now ripe societal and political fruit of the Gospel's seed planted two thousand years ago in the city of Bethlehem," and in particular of their rejection of magisterial teaching about religious unity in favour of a doctrine of pragmatic pluralism supported by a "caricature" of *Dignitatis humanae*. "Such an attitude is not reconcilable with a belief in the absolute value of religious truth and its integral importance in every sphere of life, including the political." Kozinski's treatise on *The Political Problem of Religious Pluralism: And Why Philosophers Can't Solve It* (Lanham, MD: Lexington Books, 2010) engages Rawls, Maritain, and MacIntyre on the way to its conclusion that the state, like civil society, requires orientation to a comprehensive vision of the good, and hence a religious commitment. Cf. Robert P. Kraynak, who in *Christian Faith and Modern Democracy* (Notre Dame, IN: University of Notre Dame Press, 2001) likewise calls for the restoration in political thinking of "a hierarchy of ends," but appeals more cautiously, and rather more pessimistically, to Augustine and to Solzhenitsyn in support of a more strictly limited government under God, whether or not in the form of "a tempered version of democracy" (245f.).

47 *Mouvement laïque québécois v. Saguenay* (2015 SCC 16), par. 147. The following paragraph quotes Lorne Sossin ("The 'Supremacy of God,' Human Dignity and the Charter of Rights and Freedoms," [2003], 52 UNBLJ 227, 229): "The reference to the supremacy of God in the Charter *should not be construed so as to suggest one religion is favoured over another in Canada, nor that monotheism is more desirable than polytheism, nor that the God-fearing are entitled to greater rights and privileges than atheists or agnostics*" (emphasis added by the court). But Sossin's view, which evacuates the preamble of any real meaning, is not cited in conjunction with contrary views; nor is it defended. It is simply adopted by the court as congenial and made the law of the land.

48 Patrick McKinley Brennan, "Resisting the Grand Coalition in Favour of the *Status Quo* by Giving Full Scope to the *Libertas Ecclesiae*" (Villanova University School of Law Public Law and Legal Theory Working Paper No. 2013–3060), 11: "It comes down to this: if we believe that creation itself was for the sake of the Church, we can hardly make 'religious freedom' the ideal. We may well need to tolerate [it], for now ... as the best available *modus vivendi,* but it would be apostasy to renounce the ideal: the reign of Christ over all and the incorporation of all into his mystical

body. Christ came to bring salvation, not endless toleration." His concluding remark? "Creation was for the sake of the Church, Christ-continued-
in-the-world – not for the sake of 'religious freedom.' Christ is not
optional. '*Oportet illum regnare.*'" (41) It was Malebranche, of course,
who opened his treatise on nature and grace with the statement: "God,
being able to act only for his own glory, and being able to find it only in
himself, cannot have had any other plan in the creation of the world than
the establishment of his Church." (Nicolas Malebranche, *Treatise on
Nature and Grace*; trans. Patrick Riley [Oxford: Clarendon Press, 1992],
112). From this premise, social kingship theorists have drawn unwar-
ranted conclusions.

49 Thus *Praeclara gratulationis publicae* (On the Reunion of Christendom,
1894), in which Leo nonetheless is filled with foreboding of wars still to
come – and, as it happened, just around the corner. What he actually calls
for, however, *is* simply concord, through the renewal of virtue, both within
the Church and without; that, and the liberty of the Church, which "does
not covet power" or wish "to encroach on the rights of civil power." Thus
also Pius XI, in *Quas primas* (1925), which specifies the *Church* as the
kingdom of Christ (§12), while adding that "it would be a grave error, on
the other hand, to say that Christ has no authority whatever in civil
affairs, since, by virtue of the absolute empire over all creatures committed
to him by the Father, all things are in his power" (§17). Pius immediately
goes on to point out that Christ did not and does not exercise this power
over things temporal and material directly, but rather indirectly, investing
"the human authority of princes and rulers with a religious significance"
in the sense that the recognition of his own kingship inculcates a proper
respect for duly appointed authority (§19) and induces concord among
men and kingdoms (§20).

50 Matthew 24:14. There was good reason – good eschatological reason – for
the Feast of Christ the King, which Pius XI instituted in *Quas primas* for
the Sunday prior to All Saints, to be moved to the final Sunday of the litur-
gical year and to be renamed *D. N. Iesu Christi universorum Regis*. The
new *Calendarium romanum* promulgated by Paul VI's 1969 *motu proprio*,
Mysterii paschalis, intended that "the eschatological importance of this
Sunday [be] made clearer" (p. 63). Ignoring this, however, and drawing
support from a tendentious reading of *Quas primas* and of the Catechism
at §2105, Brennan extends his criticism in "Resisting the Grand
Coalition" (34f.): "*Dignitatis*, as I emphasized above, having declared that
it left untouched traditional Catholic teaching on the duty of individuals
and societies toward the one true religion and the Catholic Church, went

on to declare that the '*principium fundamentale*' governing all relations between the Church and public authorities and the whole civil order is the *libertas Ecclesiae*. To the extent that that proposition is true, however, it is so only if it be interpreted in light of traditional Catholic social teaching on which *Dignitatis* and the Council – but not the *Catechism* – are regrettably silent, viz., the social Kingship of Christ ... Murray aptly singled the Church out as a unique participation in the Incarnate Jesus. What Murray neglected to mention is the Church's participation – not to mention the state's different participation – in specifically the kingship, the royal *munus*, of the one Christ. If we speak more precisely and more fully than *Dignitatis* does, we must say that [here he quotes Archbishop Lefebvre, from a passage appearing in Michael Davies, *The Second Vatican Council and Religious Liberty* (Long Prairie: Neumann Press 1992), 181]: '[f]reedom is not *the* fundamental principle, nor *a* fundamental principle in the matter. The public law of the Church is founded on the State's duty to recognize the social royalty of Our Lord Jesus Christ! The fundamental principle which governs the relations between Church and State is the "He must reign" of St. Paul, *Oportet illum regnare* (I Cor. 15:25) – the reign that applies not only to the Church but must be the foundation of the temporal City.'"

51 Matthew 28:18.
52 Emphasis added. Article 5 of the Barmen Declaration (see E.H. Robertson, *Christians against Hitler* [London: SCM Press, 1962], 48ff.) is also apropos, and equally catholic in nature:

"Fear God. Honor the emperor." (1 Peter 2:17) The Bible tells us that according to divine arrangement the state has responsibility to provide for justice and peace in the yet unredeemed world, in which the Church also stands, according to the measure of human insight and human possibility, by the threat and use of force. The Church recognizes with thanks and reverence toward God the benevolence of this, his provision. She reminds men of God's Kingdom, God's commandment and righteousness, and thereby the responsibility of rulers and ruled. She trusts and obeys the power of the Word, through which God maintains all things. We repudiate the false teaching that the State can and should expand beyond its special responsibility to become the single and total order of human life, and also thereby fulfil the commission of the Church. We repudiate the false teaching that the Church can and should expand beyond its special responsibility to take on the characteristics, functions and dignities of the State, and thereby become itself an organ of the State.

53 "If, then, by anyone in authority, something be sanctioned out of conformity with the principles of right reason, and consequently hurtful to the
   commonwealth, such an enactment can have no binding force of law, as
   being no rule of justice, but certain to lead men away from that good
   which is the very end of civil society" (*Libertas* §10).

54 We have these demons in Quebec, too, of course, and we shall have to
   confront them. The notorious Bill 60, by which this dishonour to the state
   was proposed by the state, was not revived by the current government. But
   Bill 52, which requires medical personnel to make themselves guilty of
   mortal sin either by assisting in suicide or by referring patients to other
   personnel for this purpose, was not only revived but instantly passed with
   overwhelming support. This is demonic and all of a piece, intellectually,
   morally, and politically, with Nazism. Cf. Major Leo Alexander's remark
   in his report on "Medical Science Under Dictatorship" in *The New
   England Journal of Medicine* 241, no. 2 (14 July 1949), 44: "Whatever
   proportions these crimes finally assumed, it became evident to all who
   investigated them that they had started from small beginnings. The beginnings at first were merely a subtle shift in emphasis in the basic attitude of
   the physicians. It started with the acceptance of the attitude, basic in the
   euthanasia movement, that there is such a thing as life not worthy to be
   lived. This attitude in its early stages concerned itself merely with the
   severely and chronically sick. Gradually the sphere of those to be included
   in this category was enlarged to encompass the socially unproductive,
   the ideologically unwanted, the racially unwanted and finally all non-
   Germans. But it is important to realize that the infinitely small wedged-in
   lever from which this entire trend of mind received its impetus was the
   attitude toward the nonrehabilitable sick."

55 Matthew 12:43–45.

56 "The doctrine of the Two was, before all else, a doctrine of two ages. The
   passing age of the principalities and powers has overlapped with the coming age of God's Kingdom. The confrontation of the two societies, the
   more attenuated balance of the two rules and the inner dynamism of the
   two persons [a reference to Luther's version of the distinction between
   what we are calling *homo religiosus* and *homo politicus*] are all generated
   by this eschatological fusion." (O'Donovan, *Desire of the Nations*, 211)

57 A defective form that emerged in France long ago, in the Carolingian era,
   went like this: "Two there are by whom the *Church* is ruled as by princes."
   This form – this one city or society with two rulers form – is defective
   because it tends to divide that city against itself. It had very grave consequences for both the Church and the state throughout the last millennium,

although we have not focused on that here. Among those consequences was, eventually, the rejection of the Church that Gregory, Pius, and Leo were confronted with. Their response would have been more effective had they wrestled more openly with this aspect of the problem, as indeed would Murray's. The council's work, especially *Dignitatis humanae*, *Lumen gentium*, and *Ad gentes*, demonstrates that real progress has been made towards a recovery of the earlier, Gelasian form of the doctrine of the Two (not altogether unproblematic) and, better yet, of the Augustinian doctrine of the two cities, which is both more cautious and more flexible about the link between church and state in the *saeculum*.

58 Acts 3:6. Or as *Gaudium et spes* (Pastoral Constitution on the Church in the Modern World, 1965) puts it, rather prosaically, at §40: "Pursuing the saving purpose which is proper to her, the Church does not only communicate divine life to men but in some way casts the reflected light of that life over the entire earth, most of all by its healing and elevating impact on the dignity of the person, by the way in which it strengthens the seams of human society and imbues the everyday activity of men with a deeper meaning and importance."

59 In *Aux gouvernants* Paul continues: "In your earthly and temporal city, God constructs mysteriously His spiritual and eternal city, His Church. And what does this Church ask of you after close to 2,000 years of experiences of all kinds in her relations with you, the powers of the earth? What does the Church ask of you today? She tells you in one of the major documents of this council [*Dignitatis humanae*]: She asks of you only liberty, the liberty to believe and to preach her faith, the freedom to love her God and serve Him, the freedom to live and to bring to men her message of life. Do not fear her. She is made after the image of her Master, whose mysterious action does not interfere with your prerogatives but heals everything human of its fatal weakness, transfigures it and fills it with hope, truth and beauty."

60 Freedom *through* religion is historically prior to, and philosophically more fundamental than, freedom *of* religion. Paradoxically, then, freedom is a function of bonding. (*Religio*, argued Lactantius at *Divinarum Institutionum* 4.27, is derived from *religare*: "We are tied to God and bound to Him [*religati*] by the bond of piety, and it is from this, and not, as Cicero holds, from careful consideration [*relegendo*], that religion has received its name.") Which is to say, it is a function of love and the obedience of love. As Irenaeus points out in *Adversus Haereses*, "the more extensive operation of liberty implies that a more complete subjection and affection towards our Liberator has been implanted within us" (4.13).

61 Murray himself points us to *Gaudium et spes* §76: "The Church, by reason of her role and competence, is not identified in any way with the political community nor bound to any political system. She is at once a sign and a safeguard of the transcendent character of the human person." Murray ("Church and State," 602f.) thinks that this "brilliant phrase ... suggests the central significance of the Church for the political order. It suggests ... the essential basis of the Church's claim to freedom in the face of all public powers. It implies that the Church may neither be enclosed within the political order nor be denied her own mode of spiritual entrance into the political order. It indirectly asserts the rightful secularity of the secular order, at the same time that it asserts the necessary openness of the secular order to the transcendent values whose pursuit is proper to the human person." But it must be asked of Murray how the Church can be this sign and safeguard if it can only enter the juridical sphere of secular politics in the name of the person, rather than speaking *aux gouvernants* (and not merely to private citizens) in its own name and with its own authority, claiming a positive as well as a negative liberty.

62 Not even the social kingship people do that – at least, not at present. At present, they know, Catholics can aim only at a society that adopts as many Christian principles as possible and a state that acts accordingly. Yet they are not afraid to say – indeed, they regard this as magisterial teaching, found even in *Dignitatis* – that because "the natural law, as well as the Divine law, is authoritatively interpreted by and articulated only through the Catholic Church ... any state that desires the best for its citizens must privilege the freedom of the Catholic Church and formally cooperate with her mission, while also permitting and supporting the freedom of other religious communities insofar as they contribute to the common good and uphold public order" (Thaddeus Kozinski interview, available at www. zenit.org/en/articles/the-political-problem-of-religious-pluralism). But what is implied by "formally cooperate"? An established Church? For my part, I would say that Catholics are never obligated to call on the state to do what it *may* do, but need not necessarily do – what the Church indeed no longer encourages it to do – namely, to establish the Catholic religion constitutionally as the proper religion of the people.

63 They maintain, that is, the attitude of the Church itself, as articulated by Pius XI in *Ubi arcano* (1922), §64f.: "Although the Church is committed by God, first of all, to the attainment of spiritual and imperishable purposes, because of the very intimate and necessary connection of things one with another, such a mission serves likewise to advance the temporal prosperity of nations and individuals, even more so than if she were instituted

primarily to promote such ends. The Church does not desire, neither ought she to desire, to mix up without a just cause in the direction of purely civil affairs. On the other hand, she cannot permit or tolerate that the state use the pretext of certain laws or unjust regulations to do injury to the rights of an order superior to that of the state, to interfere with the constitution given the Church by Christ, or to violate the rights of God Himself over civil society."

64 Non-violent on their side! Here in Canada we need only think of Mary Wagner and Linda Gibbons to recognize violence from the side of the state. As for the Catholic who thinks she can offer her assent to the notion that the state is a sphere in which God need not be acknowledged as God, or step back from the resulting inhumanity of man to man, she ought to attend to Leo: "It is unlawful to follow one line of conduct in private life and another in public, respecting privately the authority of the Church, but publicly rejecting it; for this would amount to joining together good and evil, and to putting man in conflict with himself; whereas he ought always to be consistent, and never in the least point nor in any condition of life to swerve from Christian virtue" (*Immortale dei*, §47). With this unsubtle reminder I am not asking only, What has happened to the religious assent you, as a Catholic, owe to magisterial teaching? I am asking with Leo a still sharper question: What has happened to your confession of the lordship of Christ? Does *homo politicus* stand outside that lordship? Is there, or is there not, a sphere that Christ has not redeemed and to which he cannot lay claim?

65 To bring this closer to home: If the people of Quebec wish the crucifix removed from the National Assembly, let it be removed. What is done in that house too often mocks it anyway. But do not think the space will be left empty. Do not imagine that the house is thus swept clean. Do not think the naked public square will remain naked. No! Man will honour God and his Christ, or he will honour Antichrist. God has left no other option to man. The "neutral" state is just the state in transition from the one to the other.

APPENDIX

1 "The latest addition to the reform of elementary and secondary education, the Ethics and Religious Culture program, is also the only truly novel one" (Georges Leroux, "Ethics and Religious Culture: An Education Program for Québec Society," 29 November 2006, 3). Professor Leroux provides a

more expansive treatment of the program in *Éthique, culture religieuse, dialogue: Arguments pour un programme* (Montréal: Éditions Fides, 2007).

2 Leroux, "Ethics and Religious Culture," 17. Loyola, however, remains dedicated to literary culture.

3 Ibid., 5.

4 Ibid., 3.

5 Either that or it identifies civil society *with* the state, rather than with the nexus of voluntary associations and activities that are normally built on the foundations of the family, the religious communities, and the marketplace. There is an enormous body of literature on what constitutes civil society and on its relation to the state, but there appears to be a serious erosion of the distinction in ERC-related literature. If Leroux is right that "society is the guardian of spiritual and religious knowledge" ("Ethics and Religious Culture," 9f.), the question must be pressed as to what society is and how its duty is fulfilled. That is too large a question to tackle here, but it may at least be asked whether we are to assume that "society" speaks now primarily with the voice of government commissions and Ministry officials.

6 The gutting of Article 41 on 15 June 2005, after only twelve hours of *consultations particulières* and without a recorded vote – by any standards a mockery of the Charter's integrity – was noticed by too few (but see Spencer Boudreau et al., "Losing Faith in Education," *Montreal Gazette*, 20 November 2005). Article 41 no longer speaks of a right *d'exiger que, dans les établissements d'enseignement publics, leurs enfants reçoivent un enseignement religieux ou moral conforme à leurs convictions dans le cadre des programmes prévus par la loi.* It now reads: *Les parents ou les personnes qui en tiennent lieu ont le droit d'assurer l'éducation religieuse et morale de leurs enfants conformément à leurs convictions, dans le respect des droits de leurs enfants et de l'intérêt de ceux-ci.* See further n. 48 below.

7 Comité sur les affaires religieuses, *The Spiritual Development of Students: A Challenge for Secular Schools* (Brief to the Minister of Education, February 2007), 45. We must pass over the contentious question as to whether "the need to secularize public schools" can properly claim support from human-rights principles; we will come in due course to the more immediately germane question as to whether the imposition of the ERC program itself violates such principles where schools like Loyola are concerned.

8 Leroux, "Ethics and Religious Culture," 6.

9 Ibid., 13.

10 In Leroux's own words ("Ethics and Religious Culture," 14): "On the one hand, a determination to gather for transmission the normative heritage, both moral and religious, of Québec history, a heritage of great riches; on the other, the political determination to make the pluralist social and cultural experience a success in a non-religious, secular framework."

11 As quoted by Jean Morse-Chevrier, "Gare au pluralisme normatif" (*Le Devoir*, 4 June 2007), from an address by Leroux on 3 May 2007 to the Fédération des établissements de l'enseignement privé. The ERC philosophy is more commonly described, whether positively or pejoratively, as "secularism" or "relativistic secularism," but that description is too imprecise to be of much use. It does, however, appear in the manuals, where it is acknowledged as a world view in competition with religious world views such as that of Catholicism.

12 The Pluralism Project at Harvard University can be found at www.pluralism.org. The Eisenberg quotation is taken from a review of David Miller and Michael Walzer, eds, *Pluralism, Justice, and Equality* (Oxford: Oxford University Press, 1995), in *American Political Science Review* 90, no. 3 (1996): 636. Cf. the Proulx report's advocacy of "egalitarian neutrality" in Jean-Pierre Proulx, et al., *Religion in Secular Schools: A new perspective for Québec* (trans. of *Laïcité et religions: Perspective nouvelle pour l'école québécoise*, Ministère de l'Éducation, 1999), 79.

13 Leroux, "Ethics and Religious Culture," 17.

14 Peter Lauwers, "The Proulx Report and Educational Changes in Québec," 2 (a paper delivered in 1999 at the Centre for Cultural Renewal's Montebello symposium on Pluralism, Liberalism, Religion and the Law). Lauwers adds: "The Report is a brilliant piece of propaganda for its own policy prescription. It wraps itself in the cloak of human rights but it is really aimed at social homogenization."

15 Gavin D'Costa, "The Impossibility of a Pluralist View of Religions," *Religious Studies* 32, no. 2 (1996): 232. Exclusivism holds that only one religion or revelation is true. Inclusivism holds that, though one religion is definitively true, its truth may be found elsewhere in fragmentary forms. Pluralism holds "that all the major religions have true revelations in part, while no single revelation or religion can claim final and definitive truth." Thus in pluralism "all religions are viewed as more or less equally true" – or, we may add, false. But D'Costa (223ff.) argues that pluralism "must always logically be a form of exclusivism and that nothing called pluralism really exists." For the "transcendental agnosticism" found in pluralism also entails a set of truth claims that are as such exclusivist, and of course the same may be said of inclusivism. The typology is not merely faulty,

then, but "deceptive and misleading." Putting the word "normative" in front of "pluralism," as Leroux does, only highlights the exclusivist character of the enterprise.

16 Perhaps this is the place to observe that one should be careful not to equivocate with the word "pluralism." Pluralism in the sense of "increasing diversity" (a putative social phenomenon) and pluralism in the sense of "more open to diversity" (a supposedly unifying philosophy) are not the same thing, nor does the latter follow from the former as a self-evident good. Put "fragmentation," say, for "diversity" in these quoted phrases and the slipperiness of the language and logic becomes evident. The underlying confusion can be seen, e.g., in the opening paragraph of *Introduction to the Ethics and Religious Culture Program* (Québec Education Program: Secondary Education, Update May 2008).

17 See again Morse-Chevrier, "Gare au pluralisme normatif" (translation hers); cf. Douglas Farrow, "Rebuilding Babel in Québec City?" (*Catholic Insight*, March 2008): 23.

18 That is the preferred term in Québec, as this passage illustrates: "Democratic nations are displaying greater respect for diversity and are adopting methods of managing coexistence based on an ideal of intercultural harmonization. This ideal is permeating national cultures through an array of procedures and at different paces. Our investigation reveals that in Québec harmonization measures are now part of the day-to-day life of public institutions such as health establishments, schools and universities" (Gérard Bouchard and Charles Taylor, *Building the Future: A Time for Reconciliation* [Abridged Report, Commission de consultation sur les pratiques d'accommodement reliées aux différences culturelles, 2008], 23). What is at issue here is whether the "harmonization measures" that constitute the ERC program actually do respect diversity or whether, in rejecting runaway multiculturalism, they tend to a state-enforced monoculture.

19 When Leroux says that the program should "be placed safely away from political influence," what he means is: "from the sole requirements of the majority" ("Ethics and Religious Culture," 25). On Rousseau, see further chapter 9 of Douglas Farrow, ed., *Recognizing Religion in a Secular Society* (Montreal: McGill-Queen's University Press, 2004).

20 "Consultation on the Draft *Ethics and Religious Culture* Program" (Comité sur les affaires religieuses, Report submitted to the Minister of Education, Recreation and Sports, May 2007), 32 n. 22 (emphasis added). That said, the Comité is still trying to make clear what it means by "religious culture." In its Brief to the Minister of Education, Recreation and Sports of July 2007 it offers at p. 7 a rather garbled definition, the main

point of which seems to be that the program is "cultural" because it is not confessional. Among other things this begs the question as to what is meant when religions themselves are said either to be cultures or to contribute to culture.

21 There is ample evidence in the manuals not only of distortion but also of a bias that comes close to mockery, if not vilification. I have appended a couple of examples. [*Author's note*: An appendix to this report, not reproduced here, contained extracts from proposed manuals, the first three pages being from Daniel Goudgeon, *Éthique, Tradition et Modernité* (Éditions de l'École nouvelle, 2008) and the final four pages from Chantal Bertrand and Mélanie DuBois, *Dialogues: Éthique et Culture Religieuse* (Éditions La Pensée, 2008). To these were adjoined the following commentary: "Though the ERC curriculum may, according to M. Gougeon's introduction, leave the impression that good and evil have no objective existence, the manuals don't abandon good and evil altogether. Evil, it seems, in at least some of the manuals, is the oppressive Catholic past, while good is the liberated "secular" present. It is difficult to understand how the Ministry could approve such material, or for that matter how it could suppose that a curriculum that leaves students with the impression that good and evil are whatever we choose to make of them is a curriculum that will cultivate respect for human dignity and a more harmonious society. But to demand that Catholic schools themselves become the purveyors of this degrading material – in short, that they insult themselves, at another's bidding, and attack their own beliefs and norms – surely does not befit a civilized democracy or conform to the spirit of the Canadian Charter of Rights and Freedoms."]

22 *Gravissimum educationis* (Declaration on Christian Education, 1965), §1.

23 *Introduction to the Ethics and Religious Culture Program*, 2. The three aims of the Québec Education Program – "the construction of identity, the construction of world-view, and empowerment" – stand in a similar relation to a Catholic philosophy of education, and to Loyola's own mission statement. The latter indicates that the school aims to help its students "explore their religious experiences in an environment where Catholic doctrine and values are understood, cherished and fostered; form sound moral judgment and a firm will to act according to it; and develop a fraternal respect for people of differing creeds and cultures."

24 *Dignitatis humanae* §8 (Second Vatican Council, Declaration on Religious Liberty, 1965) is the *locus classicus*.

25 Viz., "carries out thorough reflection on ethical questions; demonstrates an informed understanding of the phenomenon of religion; engages in

dialogue with a view to contributing to community life" (Brief to the
Minister, July 2007, 5).

26 See *The Characteristics of Jesuit Education* (Rome: International
Commission on the Apostolate of Jesuit Education, 1986), §§23–25, and
cf. §33: "Students, teachers, and all members of the educational community are encouraged to build a solidarity with others that transcends race,
culture or religion. In a Jesuit school, good manners are expected; the
atmosphere is one in which all can live and work together in understanding and love, with respect for all men and women as children of God."

27 Preamble, *Introduction to the Ethics and Religious Culture Program*
(Update May 2008). What then are we to make of claims such as the following? "All indications are that we are not born human, but become
human. Humanity is a work in progress and not a mere fact, is a set of
values to be promoted, acquired and developed, values rooted in the dignity of the person, as recognized in the Charters and disclosed in the great
religious and secular philosophies of this world. The dignity referred to
here is 'acknowledged in others and in ourselves, rather than an object of
formal study, since human dignity is based on who we are and not on our
usefulness, accomplishments, skills, riches or talents.'" (Comité sur les
affaires religieuses, *Secular Schools in Québec: A necessary change in institutional culture* [Brief to the Minister, October 2006], 36, quoting *A New
Approach to Religious Education in School* [Brief to the Minister, 2004],
11f.) Examples of such programmatic – one might almost say dogmatic –
statements, replete with presuppositions and implications for religion and
ethics, are readily multiplied. At the other end of the spectrum, it is all too
easy to find such obviously rudderless statements as: "The Torah, the
Bible, the sweat lodge, the minaret, Puja, Christmas, the icon, the Buddhist
temple and certain street names referring to saints are all forms of religious expression" (*Introduction to the Ethics and Religious Culture
Program*, 36). One even finds rudderlessness *as* a dogma, or rather as an
anti-dogma questioning the objective existence of good and evil, inherent
dignity, etc.

28 See *Secular Schools in Québec*, 30ff. We have already rejected the naive
notion that "schools simply became neutral following the removal of all
provisions pertaining to the rights of Catholics and Protestants from the
Act," but in any case this can hardly apply to a Catholic school.

29 Cf. *Introduction to the Ethics and Religious Culture Program*, 12. What
some refer to as "the 'crisis of transmission' within modernity" – see *On
the Way to Life: Contemporary Culture and Theological Development as
a Framework for Catholic Education, Catechesis and Formation* (London:

Heythrop Institute for Religion, Ethics and Public Life, 2005), 28 – is linked to false understandings of secularity. (See further *On the Way*, 13ff.; cf. Farrow, *Recognizing Religion in a Secular Society*, chapters 6 and 9.) The authors of *On the Way* rightly note that "transmission requires not only successful discursive and conceptual structures but also social and institutional structures and traditions" (29).

30 See Anthony Bryk, Valerie Lee, and Peter Holland, *Catholic Schools and the Common Good* (Cambridge, MA: Harvard University Press, 1993), which demonstrates that Catholic schools have an exemplary record of bringing together students of diverse backgrounds (racially, culturally, economically, intellectually, etc.) *and* of enabling them to achieve a community of learning and a culture of respect that are the envy of most public school systems. (See further n. 58 below.)

31 Canon 795 (1983 CIC).

32 *The Catholic School* (Sacred Congregation for Catholic Education, Rome, 1977), §28f. (emphasis mine). See §§28–37 for a fuller understanding of how the pedagogy and the content of a Catholic education must be distinguished from that indicated in the 2008 Preamble and Introduction, equivalence in the matters indicated notwithstanding. There is a shared goal – "It must never be forgotten that the purpose of instruction at school is education, that is, the development of man from within, freeing him from that conditioning which would prevent him from becoming a fully integrated human being" (§29) – but a different understanding of how that goal is reached and of what is attained when it is reached: "If, like every other school, the Catholic school has as its aim the critical communication of human culture and the total formation of the individual, it works towards this goal guided by its Christian vision of reality 'through which our cultural heritage acquires its special place in the total vocational life of man'" (§36).

33 *Introduction to the Ethics and Religious Culture Program*, p. 13.

34 See further John Paul II, *Fides et ratio* (1998); cf. *The Characteristics of Jesuit Education*, §35: "In all classes, in the climate of the school and most especially in formal classes in religion, every attempt is made to present the possibility of a faith response to God as something truly human and not opposed to reason, as well as to develop those values which are able to resist the secularism of modern life." The Committee, however, summarily severs any connection between rational reflection on religion and faith-based responses; indeed, it posits "knowledge" and "confession" as contraries (cf. Brief to the Minister, July 2007, 4 n. 4, and p. 7). In her letter of 13 November 2008 to Fr Robert Brennan, the assistant deputy

minister, Line Gagné, is certainly right to see this as an important difference between the ERC program and what is done at Loyola in the study of
religions. But she is just as certainly wrong to suppose that this difference
constitutes a reason to demand that Loyola suspend its unitary approach
in favour of the Committee's dichotomous one. Nor does she take into
account the fact that the unitary approach applies, *mutatis mutandis*, to
all academic work at Loyola.

35 "Faith" is a word rarely found in ERC background literature. "Beliefs"
occurs not infrequently, usually grouped with "values, norms, convictions," etc. But it is almost as if the latter, being many and various, lie
wholly in the realm of the non-rational rather than the rational. One
sometimes gets the impression, in other words, that the goal of the ERC
program (the implementation of which "will facilitate the management of
religious diversity," as the July 2007 Brief puts it on p. 20) is to reduce a
dangerous Heraclitean flux of conflicting religious and moral commitments to something safe and less threatening, by insisting that it is all a
sort of game that can be played without injury so long as there are rational, level-headed referees who intervene the moment anyone's self-
constructed dignity is put at risk by an actual truth-claim. "The objective
is not to propose or impose moral rules" (2008 Preamble), or to study
philosophy or theology in any serious fashion, but only to learn how
to observe appreciatively, without discord, the never-ending play of
representations of the divine; that is, of the "authentic" self.

36 With Leroux, "Ethics and Religious Culture," 15, cf. *Characteristics of
Jesuit Education,* §§8f., 141, 145.

37 *Secular Schools in Québec,* 22 – a particularly confused passage, it has
to be said, against which compare *On the Way to Life,* 16f.; cf. also §1912
of the *Catechism of the Catholic Church* (Rome: Libreria Editrice
Vaticana, 1994).

38 *Introduction to the Ethics and Religious Culture Program,* which on p. 12
says: "Thus, to ensure against influencing students in developing their
point of view, teachers abstain from sharing theirs," and on p. 13:
"Teachers thus foster openness to diverse values, beliefs and cultures." For
evidence that the manuals themselves intend to influence students in developing a point of view, one might look, for example, at the discussion of
abortion in Bertrand and DuBois. Not only is Henry Morgentaler set
alongside the likes of Martin Luther King and Gandhi as an important
role model (*Dialogues,* 69), the potted history of the issue on 127f. is
clearly slanted towards the *prochoix* position, all the emphasis being
placed on the unsanitary conditions faced by some women (78,000

annually) during abortions and none at all on the decidedly unhealthy
conditions faced by every fetus (50 million annually) that finds itself the
object of this "operation." The same must be said of the summary of the
arguments of the respective sides, the whole being inexcusably tendentious. Whether a responsible ethics teacher in a Catholic school would be
more outraged by the moral incompetence or the procedural incompetence
is difficult to say; in any case, the bias is such that no Catholic teacher
could reasonably be expected to utilize this material without offering
clarifications that must amount to very pointed objections.

39 *The Catholic School*, §32; cf. *Characteristics of Jesuit Education*, §34:
"Since every program in the schools can be a means to discover God, all
teachers share a responsibility for the religious dimension of the school ...
Religious and spiritual formation is integral to Jesuit education; it is not
added to, or separate from the educational process."

40 The dialectic of *Dignitatis humanae* §8 is lacking in the ERC program.
Benjamin Berger's concluding observations in "Law's Religion: Rendering
Culture" (*Osgoode Hall Law Journal* 45 no. 2 [2007]: 277–314) also cast
light on the thinking behind the latter: "We protect autonomy because we
privilege the individual; equally, the individual is valued because he is the
source of choice, which is understood as the expression of freedom and
autonomy. From these intimately interrelated aspects of law's rendering of
religion, the jurisprudence leads us naturally to the third aspect of law's
understanding of religion – that religion is a private matter. Once religion
is centred on the individual and his or her personal choices and expressions of autonomy, the constitutional legal imagination is led to assign
religion to the realm of the private. The relationship works equally in the
opposite direction. Not an independently legitimate component of public
decision-making, religion falls on the private side of law's conceptual
divide. Once so designated, religion is bound not by reason, but by preference, is therefore a matter of choice and, as such, an expression of the
autonomous individual." But the Catholic Church, naturally, does not
regard religion in that way, just as it does not regard the person in
that way.

41 2008 Preamble. This may sound like an exercise in political liberalism, but
it is actually an exercise in the authoritarian "comprehensive liberalism"
that Rawls rightly resists in the sphere of education, as elsewhere; see
Political Liberalism, expanded edition (New York: Columbia University
Press, 2005), 199f.

42 Leroux, "Ethics and Religious Culture," 16.

43 See the entire section on Catholic education: canons 793–821.

44 "Presented by the Holy See to all persons, institutions, and authorities concerned with the mission of the family in today's world. October 22, 1983" (Rome: Pontifical Council for the Family).

45 Leo XIII, *Affari vos* (1897), §6. In *Rerum novarum* (1891) §14, Leo argues analogously respecting economic measures that those who set aside "the parent and introduc[e] the providence of the State, act against natural justice, and threaten the very existence of family life."

46 Marc Cardinal Ouellet, "Where is Québec going? On faith and secularism" (available at http://chiesa.espresso.repubblica.it/articolo/207117?eng=y, 8 October 2008; translated from *Vita e Pensiero*).

47 17 March 2008 (www.eveques.qc.ca).

48 October 2006, Executive Summary, §4. Article 41 was backed by the *International Covenant on Economic, Social and Cultural Rights* (1966), which in article 10.1 states that "the widest possible protection and assistance should be accorded to the family, which is the natural and fundamental group unit of society, particularly for its establishment and while it is responsible for the care and education of dependent children." Article 13.3 adds that signatories "undertake to have respect for the liberty of parents and, when applicable, legal guardians to choose for their children schools, other than those established by the public authorities, which conform to such minimum educational standards as may be laid down or approved by the State and to ensure the religious and moral education of their children in conformity with their own convictions."

49 Leroux, "Ethics and Religious Culture," 5. The Committee, however, puts forward rather tentatively its view that the ERC program, "in being non-confessional, respects the principle of freedom of conscience and religion" (July 2007 Brief, 4 n. 5). It is not explained how being non-confessional is a sufficient condition for the respect in question, or how imposing the non-confessional on confessional schools is in keeping with such respect.

50 The *Amselem* decision (2004 SCC 47) offers this attempt at a definition: "Defined broadly, religion typically involves a particular and comprehensive system of faith and worship. In essence, religion is about freely and deeply held personal convictions or beliefs connected to an individual's spiritual faith and integrally linked to one's self-definition and spiritual fulfillment, the practices of which allow individuals to foster a connection with the divine or with the subject or object of that spiritual faith." Its merits notwithstanding, this definition is problematic both because it prioritizes the subjective over the objective and because the term "spiritual," being undefined, imports vagueness on several levels. Catholicism, for its part, regards religion in the light of the first commandment, as "the duty

of offering God genuine worship," a duty that "concerns man both individually and socially" (*Catechism*, §2104). The *Catholic Encyclopedia* states that "religion, broadly speaking, means the voluntary subjection of oneself to God" (Charles Francis Aiken, "Religion," in vol. 12 [New York: Robert Appleton Company, 1911], www.newadvent.org/cathen/12738a.htm) but is careful to attend both to its subjective and its objective dimensions. That is because it does not share, as Justice Brown puts it (in a paper presented to the Canadian Institute for the Administration of Justice conference in Québec City on 24 September 2008), "the characterization of religion as a species of the modern value of autonomous choice" (David Brown, "The Court's Spectacles: some reflections on the relationship between law and religion in *Charter* analysis," 2).

51 Article 16, section 3, and article 26, section 3, respectively (cf. the Proulx report, p. 60). Richard Dawkins and Innaiah Nasiretti, for example, seem to regard all religious practice as violating the rights of children and to think that the state has a duty to protect children from the religious indoctrination their parents often provide for them. But children will always be indoctrinated somehow, for better or for worse; to this there is simply no alternative. The real question here is who, in the first instance, has the right to decide for children. If this right passes from parents to the state it does so in contravention of the *Universal Declaration of Human Rights* and as a body blow to a free and diverse society.

52 These words are drawn from Lucie Pépin's Senate speech on 25 November 1997 in defence of the amendment of section 93 of the Constitution Act, 1867 (*Hansard*, 1st Session, 36th Parliament, vol. 137, issue 21: www.parl.gc.ca/Content/Sen/Chamber/361/Debates/021db_1997-11-25-e.htm).

53 Richard John Neuhaus ("Turning the First Amendment on its Head," *First Things*, 26 September 2008) observes that the question of religious freedom is above all a question about "the access, indeed the full and unencumbered participation, of men and women, of citizens, who bring their opinions, sentiments, convictions, prejudices, visions, and communal traditions of moral discernment to bear on our public deliberation of how we ought to order our life together in this experiment that aspires toward representative democracy." When the state assumes excessive control over the process of communicating these traditions to young citizens it also exercises an improper control over public deliberation as such.

54 See H. Daniel-Rops, *The Church in an Age of Revolution, 1789–1870*, trans. John Warrington (London: J.M. Dent, 1965), 228ff., 354ff.

55 Both in Europe and in America attempts are being made to restrict religious freedom through laws or regulations in the sphere of education. To

some of these measures significant sanctions are attached, evoking memories of unhappier days under communist or fascist regimes. See, for example, the much discussed Konrad case in Germany, which saw the state – backed by the European Court of Human Rights (18 September 2006) – pit children's rights against parents' rights in order to justify the state's educational monopoly. This is the path taken by the Proulx report, which asks, on p. 77, "How can we reconcile parental choice with the fundamental interests of children, when the two differ?" and insists, on p. 82, "To the extent that children have fundamental interests independent of those of their parents, sufficiently to claim they too have rights, it therefore follows that the state is responsible for ensuring that appropriate institutions designed to allow the exercise of rights are created." The question "To whom do schools belong?" is thus transformed into the question, "To whom do the children belong?" (cf. Douglas Farrow, *Nation of Bastards: Essays on the End of Marriage* [Toronto: BPS Books, 2007], 63ff.). But in answer to that the Catholic will insist with Vatican II that "it is the parents who have given life to their children," and that parents have therefore "a primary and inalienable duty and right in regard to the education of their children" (*Gravissimum educationis* §5f.). The Proulx report, it may be added, reads like an upside-down version of *Gravissimum educationis*, subverting the latter's goods by reversing the relation between the family and the state. The Comité sur les affaires religieuses has acknowledged, however, as it should, that *parents* "have the prime responsibility for their children's education" (July 2007 Brief, 15).

56 "Reasonable Accommodation and Religious Liberty in Quebec": Cardinal Ouellet's submission to the Bouchard-Taylor Commission, 30 October 2007.

57 The letter of Assistant Deputy Minister Gagné (13 November 2008) confirms that the Ministry objects to the fact that the Catholic perspective is brought to bear, and that it intends to see that its own "very different" conception of the common good prevails. That Loyola should present the Ministry's view to its students is not enough; it must employ the Ministry's own approach. That Loyola's students should be capable of dialogue is not enough; they must engage in dialogue "in the sense contemplated" by the Committee and the Ministry.

58 Consider, for example, the findings of Martin West and Ludger Wößmann in "'Every Catholic Child in a Catholic School': Historical Resistance to State Schooling, Contemporary Private Competition, and Student Achievement across Countries" (CESifo Working Paper No. 2332, June 2008). This study, as *The Atlantic* (October 2008) notes, "finds that

international Catholic resistance to government-mandated schooling in the 19th century has resulted in higher student performance today – for Catholics and non-Catholics alike. The Catholic hierarchy historically encouraged the development of parochial schools to ensure the moral and religious training of Catholic children. As a result ... countries that had a higher percentage of Catholics in 1900 now have a greater overall number of private schools. Using an international student-assessment survey, and controlling for demographic factors, the authors calculated that countries with more private schools due to a 'larger historical Catholic share' in the population did substantially better on achievement tests in all three sub-jects measured – math, science, and reading – while spending significantly less money per student. The authors argue that Catholic 'opposition to state education in many contexts engendered private school competition that ultimately spurred student achievement.'" West and Wössmann's results can be added to those of Bryk et al. in *Catholic Schools and the Common Good*.

59 Article 18.

60 In an interview with *L'Osservatore Romano* (17 March 2008) Mary Ann Glendon points out that the important role of the Catholic Church in the formulation of the *Universal Declaration of Human Rights* is one that some prefer to forget, because it is their objective to disengage rights dis-course from the natural law tradition in which it is actually rooted. (See further, e.g., Glendon's *Traditions in Turmoil* [Washington: Catholic University of America Press, 2006] and Donald Dietrich's *Human Rights and the Catholic Tradition* [Piscataway, NJ: Transaction Publishers, 2007]; cf. John Witte, *The Reformation of Rights* [Cambridge: Cambridge University Press, 2007], xi.) Along with this disengagement and forgetful-ness, we may add, goes a certain animus against the Church that does not stop short, in some cases, of a willingness to suppress its voice by curtail-ing its rights and freedoms. While the courts cannot avoid adopting some point of view on the underlying issues (see again Justice Brown's "The Court's Spectacles"), neither can they with justice allow such forgetfulness or such animus to prevail.

61 As the *Catholic Times* reported in December, Professor Michel Despland went so far as to suggest in a recent McGill forum ("What is Religion?", 6–7 November 2008) that "the goal of public education is 'to release youth from the control of parents.'"

62 *Dignitatis humanae* §5. In full: "The family, since it is a society in its own original right, has the right freely to live its own domestic religious life under the guidance of parents. Parents, moreover, have the right to

determine, in accordance with their own religious beliefs, the kind of religious education that their children are to receive. Government, in consequence, must acknowledge the right of parents to make a genuinely free choice of schools and of other means of education, and the use of this freedom of choice is not to be made a reason for imposing unjust burdens on parents, whether directly or indirectly. Besides, the rights of parents are violated, if their children are forced to attend lessons or instructions which are not in agreement with their religious beliefs, or if a single system of education, from which all religious formation is excluded, is imposed upon all." Cf. the *Convention on the Rights of the Child* (UNGA Doc A/RES/44/25, 12 December 1989), article 29.2.

63 *The Catholic School,* §9.
64 The covenant (*supra*, n. 48) was ratified by Canada in 1976.

Index